For two of the greats Tim Robert Burry

JOURNEYS TO THE HEART OF CATHOLICISM

*Blackburn —
in the struggle
Ted Schmidt*

JOURNEYS TO THE HEART OF
CATHOLICISM

by Ted Schmidt

Seraphim Editions

The publisher gratefully acknowledges the financial assistance of the Canada Council for the Arts and the Ontario Arts Council.

The Canada Council   Le Conseil des Arts
for the Arts   du Canada

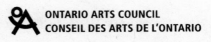

ONTARIO ARTS COUNCIL
CONSEIL DES ARTS DE L'ONTARIO

Library and Archives Canada Cataloguing in Publication

Schmidt, Ted, 1939-
    Journeys to the heart of Catholicism / by Ted Schmidt.

ISBN 978-0-9735487-9-2

    1. Catholic Church–History–1965-. 2. Catholic Church–Doctrines.
I. Title. II. Title: Catholicism.

BX1390.S337 2007   282.09'045   C2007-905689-X

Editor: George Down
Cover Photo: Julie McNeill
Author Photo: Jason Raposo
Cover Design and Typography: Julie McNeill, McNeill Design Arts

Published in 2007 by
Seraphim Editions
238 Emerald St. N.
Hamilton, ON
Canada L8L 5K8

Printed and bound in Canada

Remember not the things of the past,
the things of long ago consider not;
See I am doing something new.
Now it springs forth, do you not perceive it?
– Isaiah 43:18, 19

For our grandchildren
John and Douglas Mitchell
and Joseph Schmidt-George
in the hope that they perceive it,
this evergreen Newness which is always
renewing the face of the Earth
and for Hubert Richards, magnus magister,
who taught me where to look for it.

CONTENTS

Christmas

"Let Justice Roll Like Living Water"

CHRISTIANITY IN THE
JAWS OF CAPITALISM

Schools and churches are the last safe havens where the young can explore the sacred and hallowed grounds of their inner worlds without the incursion of the crass evangelism of business. In the last decade, we have seen an unbelievable assault on our senses with the virtual commodification of every space possible. For me, the breaking point was the use of the traditional "red rocket" (a.k.a. streetcars) as a locus of advertising for radio stations and shaving cream. We are talking about the whole streetcar as one ad!

For the young person, this hidden sensurround world engulfs them as natural and normal. Like carbon monoxide this visual toxin is so omnipresent that it is almost totally invisible. The inevitable march of advanced industrial capitalism has managed to colonize nearly every conceivable space of our urban worlds in its attempt to lower our thresholds of resistance to the products that we "must" have in order to lead meaningful lives. What would the great English poet William Wordsworth say today, if he complained in 1800 that "getting and spending we lay waste our powers?" Alas, humans seemingly can get used to anything.

One of the many joys of advancing age, however, should be the ability to evaluate the changes we see and cry foul or stop when we sense the alienation is deepening. "Change is inevitable," Lord Russell reminded us along with the caveat, "but progress is problematic." I was reminded of this when I reread an essay by the great cultural historian Jules Henry.

Writing in 1963, Mr. Henry related an incident which took place in a grade three class in downtown Toronto. The Kiernans had angrily withdrawn their daughter who was coming home singing jingles which she had learned in a new exciting hymnal called "The Educational ABC's of Industry." The melody, alas, is lost, but we do have the inspiring lyric: "G is for General Motors, M is for Milko, O is for Oxo," etc. The Kiernans, *père et mère*, suitably outraged, rescued their daughter from the apparent benefits of what Jules Henry called "pecuniary education."

Henry asked, in a mocking tone which would have escaped the true believers of the Mike Harris neo-conservative government of the late 1990s in Ontario, "What individual child is more important than the Gross National Product?" Henry went on to warn the reader: "Values like love, truth, the sacredness of high office, God, the Bible, motherhood, generosity, solicitude and compassion for others are the foundations of Western culture – and anything which weakens or distorts them shakes traditional life." The author went on to say that "pecuniary philosophy" also says that it embraces these values. Wait a minute, the wise Henry warns: "This is the embrace of a grizzly bear, for as it embraces the traditional values, pecuniary philosophy chokes them to death."

Thorstein Veblen and Simon Patten

In the early part of the last century Thorstein Veblen, America's most original economist, critically divined the deleterious effect that capitalist abundance was having on people. After World War One, the jazz age began its attack on self-control. This would be stalled in the Depression, but the super development of the post-World-War-II era, which would culminate in the new gilded age of excess and obscene remuneration for the captains of industry, was clear to Veblen. "The ancient Christian principles of humility, renunciation and abnegation had been virtually eliminated from the moral scene," he said. The great arch-critic who coined the expression "conspicuous consumption" saw that the new society was being shaped by brokers, investment bankers, real estate agents, and advertisers. To Veblen, their labour was unproductive. It consisted in "brokering" the wishes of others to "make money." These people, he said, "knew nothing about workmanship but everything about profit." They were turning the culture into one of "make believe." This "prevalence of salesmanship" was at cross-purposes with the common good. It only undermined the older traditions of "brotherly love."

Veblen's ideological opposite was Simon Patten, a Professor of Economics at the University of Pennsylvania from 1888-1917. Patten believed that denial and negation were at cross-purposes with progress. Traditional Christian values were the enemy of progress. Patten was among the true believers of the civilizing values of the market. It was the steady pursuit of private wealth and the expansion of market relations which led inexorably to peace and human betterment. For him, corporate capitalism was nothing but moral, creating more wealth. He actually believed that when people received more goods and services, the less they would desire! For Patten, the state and the school must help create the new order of the land of desire. Teachers had a key role in promoting this inherent (to him) biological need to have. It was not only a duty, but a moral law.

If we fast-forward our historical clock to the Kiernans' case of 1963, we see the natural progression of this "market" thinking. Forty years had transpired and the super capitalism of unbounded desire had advanced mightily in the postwar era. Most probably the hapless teacher saw little wrong with what she was doing. It was as old as the imperial Christianity that Columbus had brought to these shores 500 years before. The Kiernans, however, were correctly outraged. They operated with a different prism. In a similar fashion in 1999, many gutsy teachers were disturbed when some high school principals saw nothing wrong in offering up their students to Youth New Network's (YNN) daily broadcast which included commercial advertising. Schools as "sacred sites" immune from market evangelization seemed quaint to these so-called educators. Thankfully, teachers' unions, parent groups and media awareness organizations stopped this insensitive incursion into a protective space.

Market Mania of the 1990s?

By the mid 1990s market mania had almost bewitched the entire political landscape. Traditional Tories had morphed into right-wing conservatives, on fire with evangelical enthusiasm for the unfettered role of the market. One of the great traits of Catholicism has always been its insistence on the common good, and since the Depression its social teaching has always been wary of untrammeled capitalism. John Paul II in his 1991 encyclical *Centissimus annus* had reminded us that there is "a new limit on the market. There are collective and qualitative needs which cannot be satisfied by market mechanisms. There are important human needs which escape its logic. There are goods which by their very nature cannot and must not be bought or sold." (#40) Among those the pope named "natural and human environments." And so he warned that "these mechanisms carry the risk of idolatry of the market, an idolatry which ignores the existence of goods which by their nature are not and cannot be mere commodities."

Canadians have now finally had a chance to catch their breath after 30 years of unremitting market idolatry and the very embrace of those pecuniary values described by Henry and Veblen. All over the western world, people who should have known better uncritically embraced the market as the solution to our problems. The result has been a disaster for poor people, the environment and the suffering two-thirds world. On the one hand we have seen the total discrediting of big business as scandal after scandal erupted; Enron, Worldcom, Tyco, Arthur Andersen being but a few companies brought down by their overarching greed. The $8-trillion-dollar shareholder loss has demystified the corporate bosses who were treated like rock stars. The state-sponsored deregulation allowed these pirates not only to loot pension funds, but also to play footloose with their own economies and those of such places as Mexico and Indonesia.

In Canada's largest province, Ontario, formerly under traditional Tories who promoted gradual change and community input along with a commitment to the common good, the new neo-con Tories shredded safety nets, abandoned the poor, degraded the environment by slashing inspectors and, of course, gave huge tax breaks to the rich. After the neo-cons' two electoral triumphs the stunned populace finally made the link between tax cuts and bad water; tax cuts and corridor medicine; and tax cuts and exploding tuition fees and user fees.

What became increasingly obvious was that Christians themselves had been unable to correctly understand what was happening and vote accordingly. The pecuniary philosophy and financial success had slowly but surely entered the church sanctuary and suburban homes of too many believers. The blatant appeal to greed ("more money in your pocket") seduced many Christians into buying the false religion of tax cuts which put money into the hands of those who needed it the least. Tax cut mania had encouraged a culture of egoism over a culture of solidarity. These sops to the wealthy robbed many citizens of social services on which they depended, and in the end these tax cuts were simply a thinly disguised attack on the very poor with whom Jesus had identified Himself. The inevitable happened. The native Ontarians and many from the former Catholic immigrant population found themselves in the embrace of Mr. Henry's grizzly bear – with the results predicted 2,000 years ago by the Galilean – compassion, tenderness and a capacity for suffering dried up.

In time, the people woke from this bad dream, and Catholics especially began to re-understand the essentially communal nature of our faith. Along with many others, they did not like the bursting of our communal bonds. People were disgusted at the growing armies of the poor on the streets, the phenomenal rise of food banks (more than McDonald's outlets in Canada), and the shocking statistics on the poverty of children.

Ordinary working people, who saw their wages depressed worldwide as corporations busted unions, tried to keep up by working longer hours to pay the bills and stay balanced. All over the world wealth moved upward as corporations squeezed workers to work even longer hours. The United Nations noted a worldwide low-level depression with record numbers of sick days. Anxiety and depression mounted. People got cranky. The new Tories deflected their anger onto the poor and other groups who had to rely on social assistance. Divorce and breakups became epidemic and parents substituted cellphones for face-to-face parenting. The family became driven and scattered by these market forces. Split shifts and longer hours resulted in fewer family meals. The Canadian populace became more mobile, looking for work in the volatile labour market, with the result of further weakening of familial relationships.

This turbo-capitalism has been murder on families, murder on prayer lives and the time to reflect and take stock. The sacred symbols of Christianity often appear to have been overwhelmed by all of this. When there is little time to hear the sacred stories, to soak them in, we become driven and fearful. We often lose our best selves.

In the early 1920s Thorstein Veblen saw correctly what was happening. He intuitively understood what the modern economic system and the beginnings of market idolatry were doing to people; in particular how the character of desire was being distorted, how the market with its attendant massive advertising campaigns was turning us inward, loosening the bonds of solidarity among humans, disconnecting us from the poor and the marginalized, sundering us from our permanent roots and links to previous generations.

Conscientious parents like the Kiernans in 1963 intuitively knew and treasured the inherent dignity of their precious child. They did what was necessary to protect her in a school which should have known better. Today, over 40 years later, Christians need to be even more guarded that their faith is not overwhelmed by free market ideology and that their religious beliefs, symbols, and values are not becoming mere objects of consumption. This is the hard but necessary task which the Church must engage in today.

THE FLAG OR THE CROSS

Among the most extraordinary documents the Roman Catholic Church has ever proclaimed was *Lumen Gentium,* the dogmatic Constitution on the Church of November 21, 1964. It insisted, "The human race is but one family: Among all the nations of earth there is but one People of God, which takes its citizens from every race, making them citizens of a kingdom which is of a heavenly and not an earthly nature."

Not only are we "but one family," but it has "pleased God to make us holy and save us not merely as individuals but by making us into a single people."

Make no mistake about this: Catholicism privileges the collective, not the individual sailing off to salvation with no strings attached. We are, as Martin Luther King Jr. reminded us, "woven in an inextricable web of humanity."

I was reminded of this deep insight after the tsunami disaster in south Asia, on December 26, 2004. So great was the human suffering that the world was catapulted (the theological word would be "called" or "summoned") into action. Linked as never before by ligaments of interconnectivity, (largely television and computer), Canadians answered the call with compassionate action. Their response did not reflect "Canadian values," but deep human values. Once again we proved that we are hardwired for community.

Could this be a breakthrough for the human race? Only time will tell whether the ruthless capitalist assault which has been rolling like a needs-creating tsunami since the dawn of the television age, has been slowed down, much less reversed. Led by and championed by the dream merchants of the United States, this virulent soul-destroying capitalism – with few signs of restraint – has been eviscerating human communities like a runaway cancer. It has been corroding the very base of our existence, the bountiful and sacred womb of life, God's body, the earth itself.

If one were to point to a defining decade which legitimated this attack, it would be the 1980s and the never-to-be-forgotten cry of the fictional – but all too real – Gordon Gecko, the despicable antihero of the Oliver Stone movie *Wall Street*. "Greed is good," Gecko assured us as Ronald Reagan and Margaret Thatcher led the charge to pry open every last vestige of the public good and the global commons, and distribute it to their backers in the private sector.

Beginning in the 1950s, with the visual aid of television, a shift away from the family as the unit of consumption to the needs of the individual, accelerated. Ads initially targeted the single male. Now the pre-teens have become a lucrative market as consumers (hardly)-in-waiting. Self-indulgence could only be challenged by self-denial and deferred gratification. This necessary asceticism had long been part of the Christian credo as well as foundational to other religious traditions.

The Contradictions of Capitalism

Sociologist Daniel Bell in his writings warned us all that capitalism is torn by two radical contradictions: tradition and the hedonistic imperative to consume. Consumer capitalism and its chief exemplar, the United States, give wholesale permission to consume beyond all measure. And the irony is that the right wing never tires of its cultural critique of "too much permissiveness" while consistently genuflecting to every prompt of "the free market" which admits of no restraining orders. They scream "traditional values" – or as they have come to be called "family values" – all layered over with appeals to Christianity. They champion "community" but turn a blind eye to the very forces which erode community.

The United States is an amazing example of this as the rich retreat behind gated walls, and the country hires more security guards than police to safeguard their ill-gotten gains. The corporate leaders who make stunningly obscene salaries have no compunction about destroying local communities as their companies go offshore in search of greater profits. As well, they hide their wealth in tax havens, further eroding the capital available for rebuilding the community. The reason there are no full-scale riots in the US (merely world-leading social violence) is that the consumer culture has convinced the rest that their boat is about to come in either by lottery or by the rigged stock market. Americans are alone in their toleration and support of the growing gap between rich and poor. George W. Bush's $1 trillion tax cut which greatly favoured the wealthy is but one aspect of this assault on the marginalized.

An incredible drama is being played out these days when it comes to religion, traditionally the defender of the poor and, as the opening quote of *Lumen Gentium* stated, the great promoter of the global family and the unity of all peoples.

It is fascinating to watch the devolution of public religion in the United States. Why is it that in the most blatantly "religious" country in the World – where its president calls Jesus Christ his favourite philosopher – the US is the cheapest nation on earth when it comes to "loving thy neighbour?" One of the reasons, of course, has been the complicity of the "market Catholics" (America's largest faith group) who have risen out of immigrant groups and taken their places as worshipping acolytes in powerful American corporations. These predators have relentlessly promoted globalization and reaped the rewards. Economist Robert Reich explains that economic globalization has managed to separate the interests of the wealthy classes from a sense of national interest, and thus a sense of obligation to the poor in whom Jesus primarily locates himself. In this they have never been challenged by the inward-looking bishops.

It was not always this way. In 1945 the US gave 2 percent of its GNP to rebuild Europe with the Marshall Plan. Granted, this was more than simple altruism. America realized, like one of its great capitalist heroes, Henry Ford, that it's not enough to have a burgeoning economy. You need people to buy your products. Ford paid his workers twice the industrial wage and was considered insane by his competitors. Not so. He realized that the money would be recycled back into the economy – often to buy his Model T. The lesson was not lost on the US federal government. So Uncle Sam dispensed his largesse to Japan and Germany in the postwar era. Nevertheless, it was a generous gesture.

Pathetic Presidential Response

Let us consider the stunning performance of President Bush. On holiday in his Crawford, Texas ranch in December 2004, Bush first offered a measly $15 million for tsunami relief. Out of touch, as the super-rich usually are to human need, and unlike average Americans, the president totally missed the enormity of the moment and the need for radical solidarity. (His father lost the 1992 election to Bill Clinton after he walked into a supermarket for a photo-op and expressed amazement at the use of scanners at the checkout. The Bushes never seem to get to the Seven/Eleven.) Stung by critical opinion, and the thinly disguised verbal laser of Jan Egeland, the United Nations chief for humanitarian operations, who called the West's (read U.S.) response "stingy," he increased it to $30 million on December 28. Then, aware that he had misjudged the disaster, he upped the ante to $35 million. *The New York Times* was unimpressed. In a December 30 editorial, it said that the chintzy offering was "in keeping with the pitiful amount of the United States budget that we allocate for non-military foreign aid." Democratic Senator Patrick Leahy was more to the point when he said, "I went through the roof when I heard them bragging about $35 million dollars. We spend $35 million before breakfast in Iraq."

In relation to affluence, the United States lies at the bottom of the list of rich donor nations. It gave 0.15% of gross national income to official development assistance in 2003. By this measure, Norway at 0.92% was the most generous, with Denmark next at 0.84%.

Jeffrey Sachs, the well-known Columbia economist, commented, "… we actually do very little in comparison. The Asian disaster is a stark example of this for a lot of Americans. It challenges their perceptions of their own country." Just how badly out of touch with reality the insular US is can be seen in a poll taken by the Program on International Policy at the University of Maryland, a think-tank which studies American attitudes toward international topics. It found that the average American believes that the US spends 24 percent of its budget on assistance to developing countries! This is more than 29 times the actual figure. Presumably the 60 percent of Americans who believed Saddam was responsible for 9/11 were in this same polling group. Contrast the 2 percent that the US gave in 1945 with the miserly 0.14 percent it gives now.

As always it is the hypocrisy which is hard to take. Colin Powell said that Americans: "... care about the dignity of every individual and the worth of every individual." While it is true Americans are as generous as any people on earth, their government is not. As the saying goes, it has "interests" and not "values." Promoting corporate interests at home and abroad is the real policy. The best example of this is that the US gives one quarter of its foreign aid not to desperately poor nations, but to Israel, a highly developed nation. With no attempt at irony Powell went on, "I have been in war and I have been through a number of hurricanes, tornadoes and other relief operations, but I have never seen anything like this. The power of the wave to destroy bridges, factories, homes and everything in its path is amazing." The general knows of what he speaks. He was well aware of the power of the US military to destroy the same in Indochina – where he was complicit in the cover-up of the My Lai massacre. He certainly has seen similar man-made destruction in Baghdad and Fallujah – where casualties are not counted, remembered or mourned by many in the US. So much for the "dignity of every individual." Iraqis need not apply.

Lack of Prophetic Critique

Speaking as a Catholic who has spent much of his life energized by the vision of *Lumen Gentium,* I wonder why there was so little "official" institutional concern over the "man-made" American destruction of these Iraqi lives in this unnecessary and obscene conflict. The distinguished medical journal *The Lancet* revised the estimated number of Iraqi deaths to an astounding 655,000 as of October 2006. The absolute minimum in this statistically verifiable study was 350,000! On a pro rata basis this would translate into over six million deaths in the United States! Why was there no massive campaign to fast and repent in American Catholic parishes as this ungodly attack on the human family was unleashed? A well-known American theologian told me point-blank: "We just don't give a shit." These Iraqi fallen icons of God presumably are simply "collateral damage," the necessary price of a far-off war.

Why, too, the silence as foreign aid over the past 25 years has been slashed to unconscionable levels which deny the unity of the human family? Why the disengagement of the Church from the public square, save for pelvic issues?

I fear this is the price we have paid for a whole raft of bishops whose vision has been too small, whose concerns have been too narrow and whose leadership has been circumscribed by gender issues and hobbled by their pathetic performance in the sex scandals. The abysmal failure to protest national budgets which honour Mars, the god of war, and imperial misadventures, has been debilitating for American Catholic spiritual life. The poor at home and abroad have paid a heavy price for this silence.

American Catholics have hardly been immune from the bankrupt theology of "manifest destiny" and "American exceptionalism." Surely this was the gift of theologian Reinhold Niebuhr, who attempted to disabuse his fellow Americans of such arrogance. George W Bush's claim that he has been called by God needs to be challenged, as does the idea that any country is entirely righteous, alone beloved of God and not needing conversion. Americans, indoctrinated virtually at birth with exceptionalist nonsense and a misplaced reverence for the office of the president, too often have placed their fealty with power and privilege rather than with the poor. It has been almost 70 years since an American president (FDR) took his stand against "the malefactors of wealth" who were abusing the public interest. Roosevelt to his dying day endured the wrath of the propertied classes. Since then no president has led his people in shedding the self-righteous attitude which still bedevils the US.

American Christians need a higher loyalty than the office of the president. Too many American Catholics have in the name of "family values" voted for policies which have been nothing less than a frontal attack on the Gospels and the demands of biblical justice.

RELIGION AND POLITICS

In 1977, the then dynamic Conference of Canadian Catholic Bishops (CCCB) in *A Society to be Transformed* maintained, "Our country is still profoundly marked by the founders of liberal capitalism ... we carry forward many of the consequences of their lives, for their ideas have become our institutions." The bishops then went on to paint a negative portrait of "the (idolatrous) materialist aspirations, which now constitute an economic religion."

At the same time it can be logically argued that, as St. Paul suggests, life and death are always contending (2 Corinthians 4:10 ff). Therefore, also present in the sinews of the Christian people were the binding ligaments of concern and compassion, charity and rudimentary concern for one's neighbour. These virtues, forged by necessity and history as well as a deep religious inheritance of 18th and 19th century Canadians, whether they were Anglicans and Methodists in Upper Canada or Catholics in Lower Canada, have always been present. They have been woven into the mosaic, albeit sometimes denied by people with no religious affiliation.

Among Roman Catholics, a minority in the Canadian makeup and living out of a post-Reformation view of the church, the powerful currents of the social gospel went largely undeveloped. The great impact of this movement, evidenced in the writings of men like Walter Rauschenbusch, Henry Ward, the early Reinhold Niebuhr, Salem Bland and King Gordon in Canada, were largely ignored within Catholicism. The Vatican's deep concern over socialism, shaped by a deformed manifestation in the Soviet Union, was powerful enough to dissuade Catholics from embracing anything which used the words "social" or "solidarity." Operating out of a largely individualist framework, and still traumatized by the Modernist controversy, Catholics disregarded advances in the historical critical method, which had been gradually recovering the social horizon of the reign of God. Fearful of ecumenical contagion *(nulla salus extra ecclesiam),* the Church in large part proclaimed an individualist gospel.

The Protestant Social Gospel

Having said this, it is obvious that many of the best-educated Protestant clergy, shaken by World War One and then a Depression, had embraced the social gospel and the prophets' judgment on a fallen society. For men like J. S. Woodsworth, Bland, Gordon and a young Tommy Douglas, the ethics of Jesus Christ propelled them to demand changes in the structure of economic life. All, for example, supported the Winnipeg General Strike of 1919.

In January 2003, one of the sons of the social gospel, Winnipeg's Bill Blaikie, an ordained United Church minister, was runner-up in the race for the leadership of the New Democratic Party. In his acceptance speech, the new leader of the NDP, Jack Layton, who grew up in the same United Church, had no compunction about mentioning the social gospel. As well, every January we see our neighbours to the south celebrate a national holiday named after the foremost proponent of the social gospel, Martin Luther King Jr. So, if the bishops' statement of 1977 is correct that the ideas of capitalism have woven themselves into our lives, it is undoubtedly true that Canadians in many ways owe their fundamental collectivist orientation to those Christians whose faith helped fashion a Canadian narrative of which the concrete manifestations were social programs with a universality that bound us as family. It was, if you will, the legislated love of neighbour. Most are grateful for – even if unaware of – the struggle of a Baptist minister, Tommy Douglas, to institute Medicare in Saskatchewan in 1944.

Attack on the Collectivist Canadian Narrative

This Canadian narrative has been under furious monetarist assault for 30 years now. Under the advance of globalization and market idolatry, under the liberalization of trade barriers, exchange and capital controls, under the dismantling of the traditional *defensor populi*, the state, the idea that the community was sacred and the earth holy, has been sorely tested.

In 1977, the Bishops could write with no fear of contradiction, that "the single-minded pursuit of self-interest is presented as a value" and, quoting Pope Paul Vl from 1967, that "private ownership of the means of production is an absolute right that has no limits and carries no corresponding obligation." Since then there has been a staggering escalation of individual greed, most evidenced in the Savings and Loans scandal under Ronald Reagan and the stunning disclosures of Enron, WorldCom and others. Jesse Jackson's statement that any text without a context is a pretext rings true. To discuss religion and postmodernism without contextualizing the question within the new moment of accelerated globalization is to miss the mark.

We are all living in an axial period, the so called Third Revolution, a movement from mass labour (factories, manufacturing) of the post-WW II period to the elite labour of the information age, the latest stage of world capitalist development. Driven by the computer and an international labour force, spurred on by informatics and robotics, which facilitate rapid market exchanges, the world has moved at a dizzying pace. The end result is the "jobless recovery," the global driving down of wages and the emasculation of labour unions as wealth has flowed upwards in ever more obscene amounts.

Globalization and the Growing Gap

Globalization under neo-liberalism has accepted the tyranny of free market dogmas: thou shalt not tax, spend, intervene or temper. Despite the increased wealth of the few, Canada has seen a thirty-year high of child poverty, more food banks than McDonald's and increased fear among people caught in a social hurricane.

Since the mid-1970s, as neo-liberalism has swept the world, the new religion of the market has captivated western governments. This has been exacerbated by an advertising industry which has grown seven times as fast as the economy, fuelling an insatiable urge to buy and accumulate.

On the global stage Structural Adjustment Programmes (SAPs) led by the IMF and the World Bank have stripped social sectors in sub-Saharan Africa and Latin America, leaving these poor countries to pay up to five times more on debt-servicing to foreign banks than on health and education. The UN Development Report of 1997 reported that more than 100 developing countries "suffered disastrous failure in growth and more prolonged cuts in living standards than industrial countries through the Great Depression." There has been an unprecedented worldwide redistribution of wealth. In his book *High Noon: 20 Global Problems, 20 Years to Solve Them* (New York, Basic Books, 2002), J. F. Rischard noted, "Close to three billion people – half the world's population – live on less than $2.00 per day. More than 800 million suffer from hunger and malnutrition."

As corporations have assumed extraordinary power and as national governments have left the market unregulated, another apocalyptic horseman has appeared: ecological devastation. It has advanced with even greater speed. Global warming, threats to biodiversity, fisheries depletion, deforestation, water deficits and maritime pollution, are deep problems. Given these huge dangers and the reign of laissez-faire governments, there seems to be, in Rischard's words, "no pilot in the cockpit."

In Canada the National Anti-Poverty Organization (NAPO) took the unprecedented step of going to the United Nations to complain about the growing number of Canadians being denied basic rights. From 1992 to 2001, Canada had been anointed by the UN's human development surveys, as the best country to live in by quality of life standards. Despite this, UNESCO ripped into Canada's achievement. As Mahmoud Samir Ahmed, the Egyptian representative said, "You beat the deficit but at the expense of a high poverty rate."

A Democratic Deficit

All over the world, from Chiapas to Seattle to Quebec City and Genoa, we have seen the response to the dominance of capital. This is the rise of the civil society groups and non-governmental organizations (NGOs) resisting the corporate takeover and the transformation of citizens into consumers, resisting the conversion of public spaces into market opportunities. People have awakened to this movement – as continuing, rolling global protests after Seattle (November 1999) have shown. There is a greater understanding that NAFTA (North American Free Trade Agreement), MAI (Multilateral Agreement on Investment)and WTO (World Trade Organization) are bills of rights for corporations, that the state is constantly being usurped at a higher level, that land and labour have been subordinated to capital and that the economic order has been decoupled from the social order.

Beside the gross earth and gross social deficit of which Thomas Berry spoke, the developed world is witnessing a rising democracy deficit. All over the western world people have abandoned the ballot box in record numbers, the most shocking example being that of the United States, the self-promoting leader of the democratic world. Fifty percent of American citizens (100 million in the last election) did not bother to vote. Canada and Britain are descending on the same slippery slope as citizens widely sense that the power of the demos is in decline. A new futility has appeared which expresses itself in violence, lassitude and low-level depression everywhere. Under globalization workers are working longer hours, squeezed by corporations demanding more and more productivity. The American academic Juliet Schorr (*The Overworked American*) reports Americans working six weeks a year more than they did in 1971. The results have been dramatic: increased corporate profits, a worn-out work force, a growing depoliticized citizenry seeking escape in the dream factories of spectator sport and entertainment.

Individualism: A New Cultural Pandemic

Since the massive attack on the global commons by organized capital began, we have experienced what journalist Linda McQuaig has called "the cult of impotence." Governments with healthy budget surpluses cry poor, claiming they can't afford generous social programs or reduce unemployment.

The massive appeal to individualism in the advertisement bombardment (estimated at 1 million ads seen/heard by the time you are age seventeen) has had a devastating effect on faith communities over the past quarter-century. Most communities have not seriously analyzed the free market effect on faith lives.

The world capitalist development has produced the "growing gap" – a worldwide depression of wages for working people, more hours worked just to pay bills and stay even, less time to reflect and pray. It is an assault on the integrity of the family scattered and driven by these market forces – long hours, split shifts, deadly commutes.

This has created exhausted, depressed and angry suburbanites. They park their votes with cynical politicians (Ontario's Mike Harris and Alberta's Ralph Klein qualify here) who cleverly exploit the increasing alienation and the rising unanalyzed anger against convenient scapegoats.

As well, the increased mobility in today's volatile labour market weakens the relationships with those who have socialized us.

Devastating Effect on Faith Life

The powerful persuasive tools of mass marketing have managed to overwhelm the sacred symbols of Christianity, emptying them of their latent power to critique the dehumanizing trends in society which are shredding communities and coarsening our sensitivity to the fraying dignity of all people. Poet Anne Porter's line that "the Scatterer has overtaken us" rings so true. Evidence abounds in the astronomical divorce rate, and in exhausted parents abandoning children to the television as prime educator. Omnivorous and constant mass marketing encourages the young to adopt a prefab identity where material goods become visible symbols of inner worth. In general, we see a loosening of the bonds of the human community, a decrease in the solidarity we owe each other. We see consumerist values breaking our fellowship with the oppressed and increasing egoism. This is a global phenomenon.

Rampant individualism, relentlessly promoted by capitalism, has been attacking the sacred story, which is fundamentally a collective solidarity in the face of domination systems. As well, the relentless promotion of consumption and excess is decoupling us from the cosmic order of what Wendell Berry calls the "The Greater Economy." Rootless consumerism ends in commodification, a denial of the sacred human person and the holiness of the earth. All this has resulted in a flattening of transcendence, and as Abraham Heschel reminded us more than forty years ago, "We may forfeit the sense of the ineffable. To be alive is commonplace; the sense of radical amazement is gone; the world is familiar and familiarity does not breed exaltation or even appreciation." In the end what we have is Friedrich Nietzsche's "pitiable comfort" or Herbert Marcuse's *One Dimensional Man*.

The sweet seduction of consumer excess has sapped the vitality of prophetic biblical Christianity, leaving it with an institutional core but without what Heschel called "the power of defiance." Our institutions have been deeply penetrated by market idolatry. Unseen and unsmelt, much like carbon monoxide, it is brought into our homes after work. We bring it into our worshipping assemblies on Sundays as religious individualism, almost totally preventing any serious sharing with the suffering. Gibson Winter wrote about this privatization and deformation over 40 years ago in his classic *The Suburban Captivity of the Churches*.

Is it any wonder, given the relative acceleration of life and the frenetic pace of our world that the development of the global economy corresponds with both a rise in insecurity and a rising feeling of impotence, as McQuaig has stated? Impotence ultimately leads to exaggerated nationalism and violence. People who feel weak, without a stake in life, without power, have three avenues of release: apathy, violence and/or nationalism and religion.

A Crisis in the Narrative, Enter Postmodernism

Vaclav Havel, the philosopher and former President of Czechoslovakia, has maintained in several essays that there is indeed a crisis in the narratives of modernity. One of the hallmarks of postmodernism is the distrust of meta-narratives. Communism has disintegrated and deep fissures have been obvious in capitalism with the rapid rise of inequality around the world, the global shock waves devastating markets here and abroad, not to mention the financial scandals in the US. Political utopias as well as institutions have been seriously called into question. For many in the culture, apathy and privatized dreams have tried to fill the vacuum. Lawrence Friedman, a Stanford academic, has ably described our present cultural moment as master narratives implode. He refers to the horizontal society – no more priests, fathers, gods to listen to, no more agreed-upon values of the world religions like solidarity, compassion, sensitivity to the marginalized; now we have the authority of national tribes, identity groups and celebrities.

As churches empty, xenophobic nationalism with cruel messiahs like Slobodan Milosevic appear. Right-wing militias and vigilante groups reappear both here and in Europe. We see Montreal Canadien fanatics who used to be Roman Catholics, Liverpool soccer fans, or, as in Brazil, poor people gaining identity by wearing jerseys of their national team ... and of course, celebrities. The death of Princess Diana shook everybody with its extraordinary and bizarre ersatz deification. Oprah, Jordan, Madonna and other personalities fill a void. Magazines like *People,* and *Vanity Fair,* inter alia, fill us up with the lifestyles of the rich and famous. Even educators exalt the young for "pursuing their dreams" no matter how bizarre, immature or toxic they may be. God's dream, Moses', Jesus' or Mohammed's dream of a beloved community living a dignified life apparently is not sufficient.

Postmodernism and Religion

It is difficult for me to envisage, seeing the phenomenal power and ubiquity of the American hyper-individualist culture, how religion can gain political influence again. Given the new fragmented reality and the relentless evangelization by the dominant consumerist culture, the direct influence of faith communities is problematic. We have seen the terrible price to the commonwealth and social vision of Catholicism under Catholic prime ministers Mulroney, Chrétien, Turner and Martin, all supportive of a neo-liberal worldview. It is a credit to Martin that at least he periodically felt conflicted about it.

We have seen predictable and disturbing trends in world religions. There is little sign of a critical evaluation of scripture akin to the rise of historical biblical criticism in Judaism and Christianity. In general, within Islam so far there has been an inability to come to terms with modernity. As well, the deep pockets of poverty and marginalization have produced grave deformations in the universal aspects of Islamic teaching. Fundamentalism is still the general rule of thumb.

"Wingless fundamentalism" has also affected Christianity. The close-minded "identification of some feature of the Christian past" (the words of Pope Paul VI in *Evangelium Nuntiandi*) – wherein the gospel is equated with a notional acceptance of Jesus' Lordship with no social horizon – has parallels in the two-thirds world. There, growing immiseration created by globalization, has seen a rapid growth of Christianity suffused with mysticism, Puritanism, belief in prophecy, faith healing and dream visions. The increased mobility of migrant peoples uprooted and flocking to cities is creating a bizarre Christianity.

For Catholicism, terrified by these global trends, the answer has been centralization, certainly doomed to fail in the centripetal world of networking. The sheer speed and complexity of the modern world spells a death knell for top-down organizations. The aging leadership of the Roman Church has not responded to this reality, though several of its loving critics within suggest national synods may be an answer. To maintain stability within the whirling vortex of postmodern change, Catholicism as a social force has been sacrificed to a navel-gazing preoccupation with "Catholic identity." Rome has managed to squeeze the juice out of the redolent hope experienced at Vatican II with the church's dramatic turn to the world. There seemed to be a lamentable failure of nerve here, an insecurity that the faith was not up to the Enlightenment, that after Vatican II it could not walk with the secular nomads and unchurched prophets of hope on its own terms. The retreat to issues of Catholic identity and orthodox obsession has prevented Catholics from making prophetic contributions qua Catholics. Through his episcopal appointments and harassment of engaged theologians, a pope whose mantra was "be not afraid" created a timorous Church. The price for the universal church has been great. The warranted fear of social and cultural dissolution has been trumped by quietist dogmatism, therapeutic truncation of the gospel and widespread prophetic disengagement.

The Need for Catholicism's Deep Gifts

Catholicism with its rootedness, communitarian nature, commitment to rational and critical thought, and its social teaching still has a window of opportunity to engage a world in distress. The social teaching under John Paul II's long pontificate has at many levels continued the Church's long-term loyalty to the dignity of the human person and the common good. One can say with confidence that postmodern suspicion of any norm and its elevation of pluralism to absurd heights, its pragmatism and susceptibility to instrumental reason, its ennui and cynicism, its isolation and transitory relations and its secular horizon, absolutely needs a mature Catholicism and a historically engaged Christianity.

Christianity has the power with its symbols of radical discontent to criticize modernity and link it to its powerful memory and story. Life with God must propel Christians into the humanization of the world.

The papal encyclical *Evangelium Nuntiandi* in 1975, proclaimed one of the assured results of modern biblical scholarship, viz. that the root metaphor of Jesus, the reign of God is ultimate, that "Christ first proclaims a kingdom, so important that everything else becomes the rest ... this great gift of God which is liberation from everything that oppresses ..." Many people believe that "this hidden energy of the good news" is indeed operative largely outside the ecclesia to whom it was entrusted to live and proclaim. The *malkuth Yahweh* as proclaimed by the first-century Jesus is indeed the heart of the gospel. Moving beyond the Biblicist understanding (*the ipsissima verba Jesu*) leads us to the *ipsissima intentio* or to know Jesus in discipleship. The guiding hermeneutic, as Dorothea Solle suggests, will be authentic life for all. The horizon then moves beyond individual salvation to social salvation and the transformation of society. According to Jon Sobrino in *Spirituality of Liberation: Toward Political Holiness* (Maryknoll, N.Y. Orbis Books, 1988): "The ethic of the kingdom requires action directed toward structurally transforming society in the direction of the reign of God by doing justice to the poor and oppressed majorities, so that they obtain life and historical salvation."

Postmodernism seen negatively vitiates activism and substitutes apathy. It distrusts institutions and meta-narratives. The Church with its quaint notions of transcendence becomes de facto a non-player. Trivialized and sidelined by the modern secular mind, it is trotted out on state occasions to be used as a legitimating tool. For many, it escapes into an ahistorical and mystical ether, whose power is channelled into escapist realms. In this model, the Church will have no power to transform society.

However, we may look at postmodernism as purifying, as moving beyond isolation, apathy and alienation, as a constructive critique of modernity. There are signs that a real spiritual hunger is afoot, albeit in some instances misguided, directionless, and not properly anchored. The name New Age describes this false start. Nevertheless, it should not be dismissed as fatuous. The postmodern search appears to be open to the cosmological and the prophetic. Seattle, Quebec, Genoa and other mass moments, suffused with idealism, skeptical of corporate control and aware of deep injury to the earth, in my judgment are promising as authentic religious responses to the present time.

The Church in Exile

At the present time, these movements (ecofeminist in nature) alive yet inchoate in many parts of the world have no home in the churches, particularly in Roman Catholicism in its institutional form. It is in these cultural horizons where we see the Holy Spirit of Resistance. For the Church what we have is a crisis in sensibility, a failure to understand revelation as imagination. For a Church which sees itself as sacramental it is also a stunning failure, an unparalleled blindness. To watch the young protesters gassed and denounced and to retreat into a lifeless formalism is a betrayal of discipleship, an elevation of dogma over praxis. The risk-taking and earth-loyalty of these movements are impressive. They are also deeply communitarian.

That the Church is not there is obvious. Ecclesial life is still dominated by middle class morality. By engaging the society as a faithful partner with the secular nomads above, the Church may become a serious player and have some real influence, only by becoming itself, a countercultural community living the nonviolent values of the reign of God. At the present time, we are too compromised to do this. Walter Brueggemann and many others name this moment, one of Exile, a time of unfocussed wandering, disconnected from the rising global spirituality of cosmic love and loyalty.

The Church's failure to embrace the new spiritual moment of what might be called a covenant with the earth has left it autistic, without a language to engage the next generation. Yet this fundamental good news, accelerated by global sacramental and planetary vision of the Apollo space flights has spread like wildfire among secular nomads. Disgusted by corporate and governmental insensitivity to nature, millions of people have come home to the earth in a new spirituality ignored by the biblical religions, scorned as pagan and "New Age." These people, in my opinion, are the heralds of the future. They bear names like Greenpeace, Sierra Club, Friends of the Earth, etc. The phenomenal rise of NGOs is a contemporary manifestation of the Spirit.

Paul Ray, in the largest study of global attitudes, has described these people as "the cultural creatives," basically those people who have intuitively or otherwise embraced the new Creation story and are engaging to heal the soul sickness of the postmodern age. Many of the "cultural creatives" are religious and Christian. They have embraced the new holy moments of revelation (earth, feminism and liberation). They view this new moment as a growth of Christ consciousness (Romans 8).

Organized religion – anthropocentric, patriarchal and hierarchical for the most part – has retreated into marginated irrelevance. A bourgeois, domestic religion, "sick unto death with banality" (in the words of Johannes Metz), self-absorbed, obsessed with institutional survival, has no power to engage modern Christians. A religion sapped of its vitality by narcissistic consumerism, hobbled by instrumental reasoning and a mentality which merely imitates modernity, has little future. The present time, as Metz suggests, is one "of conflict between a bourgeois religion that cannot get beyond just taking care of its members and a messianic religion of discipleship."

The present moment is hugely instructive of this. The Christian President of the United States, who informed us that God told him to invade Iraq, has turned that country into a graveyard. The Christian church in the US has been immobile, caught between the civil religion of America and the dangerous biblical call to be peacemakers. In Canada, half a million pilgrims stood on Toronto's University Avenue to take part in the stations of the cross of World Youth Day (July 23, 2002). On January 15, 2003 15,000 people marched up the same avenue demanding peace. No bishops or parishes were present. Only the United Church encouraged participation. The largest Christian body in Canada (43%), the Roman Catholic Church – so energetic on the issue of gay marriage – remained virtually silent on this blasphemous attack which even the Vatican called "immoral, illegal and unjust." Where were the million Catholics of the Toronto archdiocese?

We appear to be victims of a terrible theology of transcendence which invites us to be spectators rather than participants in history. This can only be called an institutional exile, a refusal to embrace the life-giving cross of discipleship.

Metz has suggested that at this time of institutional disintegration, new life in the Church will come neither from great charismatic leaders nor from great prophets. "It will be much more a time of little ones steadfastly becoming subjects, a time of the little prophets."

I believe this is happening. The cultural creatives, tired and disgusted by puppet leaders who do not represent them or the interests of the globe, are increasingly finding themselves in an interconnected world. They have outgrown the old wineskins of their institutions, rejected the narrow fundamentalisms and trivial pursuits of their faith communities and are slowly getting their act together. Can it be that this is the Kingdom of God – the *basileia* – which Jesus talked about? I believe so.

THE CRY OF THE EARTH

The earth dries up and withers,
The world languishes and withers;
the heavens languish together with the earth.
The earth lies polluted
under its inhabitants;
for they have transgressed laws,
violated the statutes,
broken the everlasting covenant.
Isaiah 24:4, 5

O Lord, how manifold are your works!
In wisdom you have made them all;
the earth is full of your creatures ...
Ps. 104:24

The heavens are telling the glory of God;
and the firmament proclaims his handiwork ...
Ps. 19:1

Fundamentalism as we now know comes in many forms. With the rapid acceleration of globalization, the dizzying speed of change, along with the increasing natural disasters seemingly associated with global warming, people quite naturally seek assurances that the world is not out of control. One might add to these unsettling realities the growing prevalence of apocalyptic scenarios, often exacerbated by the dominant terrorist "narrative" promoted by the American White House. Are you with "us" or "them?"

Within the great world religion of Roman Catholicism some have responded with what one might call an "institutional fundamentalism." Culturally, a good symbol of this religious fear was the Mel Gibson film *The Passion of the Christ*. Thousands of traditional Catholics and evangelicals flocked to this blockbuster for some kind of ratification of their Christian faith. The Pope had a private viewing and reportedly approved. In this box office blockbuster, Jesus, "the innocent lamb," suffered and died for Adam's original sin. While the film shocked secular viewers with its fetishization of the suffering of Jesus, it struck a chord with Christians raised on a primitive understanding of the atonement.

The Catholic Catechism reassured believers that, "The Father handed his son over to sinners in order to reconcile us to Himself." This primitive blood sacrifice, this selfless self-donation is the act through which all people are saved. Jesus, as the Vatican consistently tells Catholics, "is the only saviour." Woe betide any theologian who moves beyond this elementary understanding of God and Jesus.

Gibson's gruesome bloodfest is typical of how irrelevant the telling of the Jesus story has become for most people today. To focus God's saving activity to one moment in the first century and expect it to say something to moderns is hopelessly limiting. There was nothing in this film which spoke about God's reign of peace and justice revealed by Jesus, nothing about this "Incomparable Mystery", this Cosmic Christ, this Blessed Wisdom which had been active in creating the stars and was manifest in Jesus. There is nothing in this Gibson god which energizes us, co-creates with us, makes us get out of bed to help remake a broken world. This is not Paul's God who "is not far from each one of us. For 'in Him we live and move and have our being'" (Acts 17:27, 28). As Anglican theologian Carter Heyward remarks, "We ought not participate in a social or religious order constructed on the blood sacrifice of anyone for the common good. Nor should we worship a God who legitimates it."

By lionizing past formulations and raising them to iconic status beyond criticism, fundamentalism – both biblical and theological – often misses the fresh out-breaking of God in our times. In theology as in life, a rearview mirror is necessary, but a rear-view mirror alone (be it dogmatic, scriptural or creedal) will literally cause you to crash as you miss the lifegiving promptings of the ever-new God arriving on the horizon. In the end this is a failure of faith, an inability to appropriate a healthy doctrine of the Holy Spirit. While correctly distrusting fads, literalists too often miss new moments of clarity, old truths which suddenly are seen with new eyes. Such is the grace we may call "creation spirituality."

Forty years ago Christians understood little about the revelatory impact of creation. Certainly from a cursory glance at the theological output of that time, the environment was barely mentioned. Catholics sadly shared in this silence. One searches in vain for any mention of the environment in the liberating documents of Vatican II (1962-1965). So obsessed was the Church at that time with humanity's place in salvation history that its purview was decidedly, and almost solely, anthropocentric. The emphasis was on human flourishing. The natural world and all living things waited silently for the recognition and care with which the Creator had sustained and permeated nature. Section 12 of *Gaudium et Spes* (1965) appears typical: "According to the almost unanimous opinion of believers and unbelievers alike, all things on earth should be related to man as their center and crown." Yet it was this same Council which readied us to listen to "the signs of the times," the presence of God in the world, perhaps a presence so obvious we may have overlooked it.

It was in 1967, shortly after the revolutionary Council, that a much-respected professor of medieval history at UCLA, Lynn White Jr. (d.1987), launched a laser beam at a somnolent theological academy. White's area of expertise was the relationship of technology to human society in the medieval period. Writing in the journal *Science,* he stated the obvious – viz. that the Industrial Revolution was a quantum leap in humanity's interaction with the natural environment. But White's essay "The

Historical Roots of Our Ecologic Crisis" went much farther. For him Christianity bore "a great burden of guilt" for the crisis.

"We are superior to nature, contemptuous of it, willing to use it for our slightest whim," he wrote. "Our present science and our present technology are so tinctured with orthodox Christian arrogance toward nature that no solution for our ecological crisis can be expected from them alone. Since the roots of our trouble are so largely religious, the remedy must also be essentially religious, whether we call it that or not." White made some extravagant statements such as: "God planned all of this [creation] explicitly for man's benefit and rule: no item in the physical creation had any purpose save to serve man's purposes." White never explained how he knew the mind of God nor did everybody share his dark conclusion that "we shall continue to have a worsening ecologic crisis until we reject the Christian axiom that nature has no reason for existence save to serve man."

Many theologians pointed out that this rich vein of creation thought goes back to the Psalmist, Paul, and the mystics – all have seen God as the divine milieu, deeply immanent and part of the creation. This is called "panentheism" or literally "everything in God". This theological current is an ecological way of thinking about God. Is it new? Not really. We may call it a recovered truth.

Creation-Centred Theologies

The oldest "creation-centred" theologies go back to First Nations on several continents – the Aborigines in Australia, Native North Americans, and the Celtic peoples of Great Britain all have their roots here. Their holy books are the trees, the bluffs, the sky and the water. Their relatives are the finned ones and the winged ones. Their great cathedrals are not shopping malls with controlled temperature and faux waterfalls. Their worship is centred on the universe, its origins etc. Their sermons often privilege earth/human rather than human/human language and metaphors. It is with this in mind that Thomas Berry has often said that we need to put our Bibles away for fifteen years and read the book of nature. Another mystic, Thomas Aquinas, said something similar.

An extraordinarily fruitful period of creation mysticism flourished from the twelfth to the fifteenth centuries. Hildegarde of Bingen (d.1179) stated that "there is no creature that does not have a radiance." For her, every creature had a spiritual life. Her inspired insights precede the 20th century growing awareness that all beings partake of the divine. So maintained Aquinas (d.1274). Our great nature mystic Francis of Assisi (d.1226) embraced this vision. In his *Canticle of the Sun,* the poor man of Assisi understood all creation – earth, air, water, moon, plants, etc. as "brothers and sisters," partaking in God and, in effect, "sacramental," reflective of the self-donation of God. Thousands of sacraments then explode around us, inviting us to a deep reverence for life, a theology more centred on creation rather than fallenness and redemption.

The Dominican friar Meister Eckhart (d.1327), condemned in his lifetime for his mystical intuitions, taught theology at Cologne and Paris. For him, "God sits around all day giving birth" and it was the Divine who poured God's essence into all creatures. Eckhart asked, "What good is it to me if Mary gave birth to the Son of God fourteen hundred years ago and I do not also give birth to the son of God in my time and in my culture?" Other mystics one can easily include in this list are Julian of Norwich (d. circa 1416) and Mechtild of Magdeburg (d.1280), a laywoman who studied under the Dominicans and created a spiritual classic entitled the *The Flowing Light of the Godhead.*

These nature mystics and cosmologists were constantly in trouble with the institutional hierarchy, yet their work survived. In 1600 Giordano Bruno was burned at the stake and in 1616 Galileo Galilei's work was condemned. The "new" cosmology went underground. In the seventeenth century René Descartes (d.1650) laid the philosophical foundations for a more mechanistic understanding of reality. Descartes focused on the mind of the individual; creation for him was soulless, without life or any animating principle. The numinous and ineffable were in full retreat. Francis Bacon (d.1626) and Isaac Newton (d.1727) led the scientific ways of tapping energies to control nature and new technologies were developed to pry open secrets of the earth. The Industrial Age commenced and accelerated. The mystical vision of a divine creation faded and nature's wonders quickly became commodities to be sold and traded. In Berry's felicitous phrase, wonderworld was replaced by wasteworld. This of course did not happen without lamentation and sorrow. As always it would be the artists who resisted. William Wordsworth (1798) is typical of one such voice:

The world is too much with us; late and soon,
Getting and spending, we lay waste our powers;
Little we see in Nature that is ours;
We have given our hearts away, a sordid boon!
This Sea that bares her bosom to the moon,
The winds that will be howling at all hours,
And are up-gathered now like sleeping flowers,
For this, for everything, we are out of tune;
It moves us not.

William Blake (d.1827) followed Wordsworth in his rejection of untrammeled progress. He railed about the "dark Satanic mills" cropping up all over England, obscuring the divine. In turn, and as the assault on nature quickened, came Victorians like Elizabeth Barrett Browning (d.1861) and Jesuit poet Gerard Manley Hopkins (d.1899), both of whom discerned God's Holy Spirit reflected in nature.

The rape of the world continued with little protest from the churches, so enmeshed were they in the promise of the technological age and the wealth it was producing. The twentieth century, bewitched by technical prowess and instrumental reasoning, launched a ferocious and unprecedented assault on the natural environment. Air, water and soil were despoiled in ways that defy description – all under the banner of progress. Max Weber (d.1920) the brilliant German sociologist of religion, coined the expression "the disenchantment of the world" to describe the state of things. For him we had become "spiritually anorexic" and "specialists without spirit." Productivity soared as did man-made cancers, diseases of all stripes, along with the environmental degradation mentioned above.

Theologians, Geologians and Ecofeminists Arrive

In retrospect, we all owe a debt to Lynn White Jr., who in his latter years joked that he might be considered the godfather of ecological theology. Hundreds of articles and books have appeared since the professor's provocative shot across the bow. His article appeared in several places in the popular press and, along with Rachel Carson's seminal book *The Silent Earth* (1962), it has brought forth much creative thinking. Ecotheologians took on White's too-simple condemnation of the Judeo-Christian heritage, pointing out that the Bible, in too many places to mention, fosters not only a stewardship of creation but an embrace of the Cosmic Christ (John's prologue, Colossians, Romans etc). Biblical scholars quickly pointed out several strands of scripture supported Berry's cosmological vision (see opening quotes).

In 1969, the extraordinary Apollo spacewalk beamed back to earth the luminous and breathtaking shots of "the big blue marble," our planet in all its radiance. This stunned the human community and the words of British astronomer and cosmologist Fred Hoyle (d.2001) soon became true: "Once a photograph of the earth taken from the outside is available a new idea as powerful as any in history will be let loose." Earth Day was first celebrated in 1970 and proved a powerful stimulus to the global community. The first real shoots of green consciousness began to appear.

Theologians, many of them female and maybe closer to the earth, began to theologize about the simple fact that the earth, not the Bible, is our fundamental meeting place with God. The aforementioned Thomas Berry, the brilliant 92-year-old Passionist priest who for decades has been in the vanguard of this movement and who styles himself a "geologian," puts this newfound emphasis succinctly. "The earth is primary, the human secondary." Berry wishes to refocus theology away from "the personal saviour orientation" of the last two thousand years to a much broader horizon of God's intimacy with the earth which has been there since the Big Bang fourteen billion years ago. For Berry this "personal saviour orientation" leads simply to an "interpersonal devotionalism" which basically dispenses with the earth. For Berry and fellow ecotheologians, salvation is a cosmic matter, not simply personal. It is only language like this which has any remote possibility of connecting with modern Christians and fellow earthlings. The idea that somehow the world is redeemed by a personal saviour who is handed over to a transcendent God to buy back our salvation has no purchasing power for us today. Mel Gibson is fighting a losing battle. As well, to keep reciting the Nicene and Apostles' Creeds bereft of any references to creation will continue alienating all of us.

All our faith traditions are struggling for a new framework and a new language to speak ultimate truths. Scientists and cosmologists have led the way forward in this exciting evolutionary journey. Berry has attempted to place the science in the context of a sacred story. This he calls the New Story. The potential to unite all humans, fellow earthlings is exciting and awe-inspiring. It is now obvious that the old symbol system which served us well for centuries can no longer hold our new understanding of the universe. The old wineskins have simply become porous, dried up and are cracking under the strain. New wineskins are dramatically needed. The church, and in particular the Catholic Church with its highly centralized Roman theology, seems incapable now of breaking out of the fall/redemption model so beloved by Gibson and indeed the Roman bureaucracy. The Vatican documents resemble the preacher who, unable to convince his audience, wrote down in his notes, "At this point, shout louder." Examples are many but the following will have to suffice here. In *Dominus Iesus* (2000) this statement:

> "As an innocent lamb he merited life for us by his blood which he freely shed. In him God reconciled us to himself and to one another freeing us from the bondage of the devil and of sin."

and from the Catholic Catechism, Adam and Eve are real people:

> "390 The account of the fall in Genesis 3 uses figurative language, but affirms a primeval event, a deed that took

place *at the beginning of the history of man*. Revelation
gives us the certainty of faith that the whole of human
history is marked by the original fault freely committed
by our first parents."

Sally McFague has given the ecumenical ecological community new
ways to look at God – as friend, lover, mother and embodied in the world as
God's body. These metaphors are particularly apt for us today since they are
creation-centred rather than redemption-centred. They are focused on the
incarnational presence of God in nature. McFague states the obvious: how
utterly holistic this analogy when compared to, say, God as king or judge or
lord. Monarchical models like these connote distance, power, hierarchy and
patriarchy. They are out of tune with our age. They say nothing to the non-
human, sensate world. "God's body" (and remember it is metaphor) con-
notes intimacy, closeness, care, nurturance and sustenance. Though not
reduced solely to the Body (pantheism) God is absolutely present. This
body may be poorly cared for, unattended and suffering, vulnerable to be
sure. Here the metaphor hints at the suffering love of Jesus on the cross.
This is a God at risk, in the evolutionary process but again, not reduced to
it. One major plus for this model would be that it suggests that God loves
fleshy bodies – surely an antidote to the anti-sexual and negative "anti-
body" teaching too long associated with a male celibate Church.

Another plus might be the acceptance of evil in our world. The body is
ravaged, in pain. Sin then is to ignore the body, to walk on by the pain, to
refuse responsibility for caring for it. This speaks to our sense of sacrament; the divine is present in the world. Most of all, this model resonates
with our contemporaries. There is a language here that communicates
powerfully to fellow earthlings in ways which are much more dramatic
and cogent than what Michael Morwood calls the "elsewhere" God. It links
us in a compelling way with the earth.

All theologies in the end are metaphors, which serve in enabling us to
understand the relationship of God to the world. None can exhaust God
but it should be obvious that the distant transcendent monarchical and

patriarchal God has seen its day as a metaphor capable of energizing contemporary believers. Theologians like McFague, Thomas Berry, John B. Cobb, Matthew Fox, Rosemary Radford Reuther and others are tapping into a rich vein here. A massive paradigm shift is afoot, although being fought tooth and nail by fundamentalists in all major religions. Readers of this essay might wish to familiarize themselves with those writers' liberating thoughts.

The universe, our world then is "in God" though God is not reduced to the world. But what we have seen and understood only latterly is that with the coming of the postwar Industrial Age, God's body was being ravaged, scarred and torn apart. Forests began disappearing along with topsoil; species vanished, water became polluted and ozone depleted. In the last few decades we noticed that weather patterns have been disrupted with the incidence of destructive storms, hurricanes and tidal waves increasing. Mother Earth literally was dying while mothers' milk became polluted. Children with puffers are a common sight in our elementary schools. Radiation experts like Rosalie Bertell consistently have warned us of the damage to children in neurodevelopmental disorders, increasing congenital abnormalities and an increase in certain childhood cancers.

Our Aboriginal peoples who kept this wisdom alive are barely surviving. The "free enterprise" turbo-capitalism has left a world in ruins. The market mania of ever-expanding Gross National Product has created a Gross Earth Deficit. Up until the past few years virtually no one could challenge the economic fundamentalism, the founding myth of capitalism. The Dow trumped the Tao and the venture capitalists and robber barons that brought us WorldCom, Enron and corporate megalomania became the saints of the modern world. The largest Canadian newspaper, the *Toronto Star,* contains two "Wheels" sections glorifying fossil fuel depletion. There is no Ecology section in the paper.

And then something happened. The Great Turning began. This phrase of Buddhist scholar Joanna Macy well describes the global awareness that a *kairos* was upon us. In a relatively short span humanity seemed to shake itself from its trance, rise from its autism. All over the world people began to name the shadow side of modernity described above. A spiritual revolution began which linked human beings to each other, to the earth community and to the cosmos.

As the Bard said, "… the readiness is all." It seemed that the human community was finally ready to hear the cry of the earth. For years the eco-prophets had been drowned out by the humming of the technological world, submerged by the arrogance of the neo-conservative moment which had trumpeted corporate power, patriarchal control and the economics of empire. Finally the damage done to every part of creation became abundantly clear to all and the Holy Spirit of Resistance broke the global trance. No longer could global warning be denied with any seriousness. A former US vice-president, Al Gore, in 2006 produced a film called *An Inconvenient Truth* which was literally shown all over the world to great acclaim. A DVD was produced in November 2006 and is in constant use in schools. Governments at every level started to move, though predictably the Canadian government under neo-con Stephen Harper lagged behind others. Harper previously had described the Kyoto Accord, which limits greenhouse gas emissions, as "essentially a socialist scheme to suck money out of Canadians." He then uttered a dire warning that such a priority was too expensive.

The Catholic Church and the Ecological Moment

In this final section I would like to deal with the role of the church in this new postmodern moment. In brief, one might quote the oft-heard remark that the church always arrives a little bit late and a little bit out of breath. And this certainly is true about the issue of the environment. In some ways this is understandable. A huge structure like the Catholic Church moves slowly. Yet historically we know that she has always had an ability to move. Her great theologians have always served her well in adapting to new historical moments. Gregory Baum well expresses this in *Amazing Church.* "As the Church enters a new ethical horizon it rereads the scriptures and rethinks its teaching in a process that involves debates on all levels of the Catholic community and eventually leads to modification of the official position." Baum quite rightly also points out that the present Church structure and hierarchical leadership today lags behind the faithful in responding to today's ethical horizons. He posits three areas. First, the Church's authoritarian centralism, secondly the equality of men and women, and thirdly the meaning of sexuality.

In my judgment we might also add the failure to understand and embrace the cry of the earth as an authentic "sign of the time." This is particularly strange in that sacramentality is at the heart of the Catholic enterprise. All of reality is sacred, created by God, sustained by a loving presence. The invisible God touches us through creation. We baptize with water. We commune through bread and wine. We sanctify with oils. And in the Incarnation we believe that God puts flesh on divinity. As the poet Yeats graphically phrased it, "God has pitched His tent in this place of excrement. We are on holy ground."

So why hasn't the Church been in the leadership of the environmental movement? Why has out-and-out resistance been so great? Why the demonization of over one hundred theologians who wish to place Jesus and the Bible in the new Universe story? Why has environmental degradation been coterminous with Christianity, particularly in North America?

First let me deal with Thomas Berry's reflections here. It is obvious from this essay that I hold Berry in the highest regard as a theologian or "ecologian" as he prefers to be called. *Time* magazine rightly has placed him among the top one hundred thinkers of the 20th century.

Berry believes we have been in the stacks way too long. We have lost the second book of God, nature and the cosmos. Living under polluted skies we no longer see the stars. The divine presence in all of history was always perceived in the natural order but the Church obsessed with the transcendent "elsewhere" God, forgot the immanent God reflected in nature. This amnesia began after the great Black Death ravaged Europe in 1347 and continued through the Enlightenment's embrace of instrumental reasoning. Only the mystics and the poets remained faithful to the goodness of creation which Aquinas had insisted on. In a similar vein, a Platonic focus on another world, our heavenly destiny mitigated against taking this world seriously.

Although Vatican II produced a "signs of the times" theology, one which suggested there was yet more truth to break forth, the increasingly defensive leadership of the Church was reticent to cede any powers of discernment to the broad membership of the baptized, the *sensus fidelium*. In particular it chafed at ecofeminists who suggested that the oppression of women and the oppression of the earth were interconnected and it might take feminine wisdom to solve the issue. The earth like the feminine is noted for fecundity and nourishment rather than dominance and power. The sacred feminine of this new "Magdalene moment" (a term used by Jane Schaberg and Richard Wightman Fox), a special time when the earth and the feminine have reappeared with a holy insistence, seems too much for the patriarchal leadership of the Church under the John Paul II/Ratzinger restoration. These necessary "green" voices have been augmented by the rising tide of the highly-educated baptized laity who have also been marginalized as a crucial component of the Church's teaching office. Catholic theology states that the Spirit has been given to the whole Church, not simply the clerical caste.

Rome finally caught on in 1988 in the papal encyclical *Solicitudo Rei Socialis.* In 1990 Pope John Paul II really turned up the jets and issued a document for World Peace Day entirely on the environment. "Christians," the pontiff proclaimed, "realize that their responsibility within creation and their duty towards nature and the Creator are an essential part of their faith." The pope, however, in the following years never seemed to move beyond a philosophical understanding of human centredness. The Catholic Catechism improves a bit but there seems no overriding urgency to address the growing catastrophe. Certainly not as much emphasis as there has been on "pelvic orthodoxy."

As we look back in history from this 2007 perspective one wonders if we can ever account for our unprecedented human destruction. It certainly ranks with the great crimes of human history. Yet guilt will not do much for us at this point, the fact that this all happened on Christianity's watch. We must move on, trusting in God's mercy and the Spirit's presence.

In the past number of years in Canada we have watched with admiration some of the pastoral programs the Anglican and United Churches have developed for their congregations. Invariably when I ask in public addresses about the response of the largest denomination in Canada, the Roman Catholic Church, to the greatest crisis we have ever collectively seen I get blank stares. Few recall any homily and certainly little pastoral planning on the issue. There have been letters to the government on same sex, but no parish actions on the environment. Yes, there have been statements to sign the Kyoto Accord and individual parishes may have taken on some projects, but generally there has been abysmal clerical leadership. We have paid a steep price for the episcopal appointments of John Paul II in this regard.

Many progressive Catholics have left the church in anger over the institutional Church's misplaced priorities. Many have found their way into secular groups who have been actively defending creation – such as Greenpeace, Friends of the Earth and the Sierra Club. As I was writing this I heard a priest at mass talk about the Serra Club (a group promoting male celibates for the priesthood). I chuckled at the thought that each parish might have a Serra Club but not a Sierra Club! As if the fundamental priestly vocation of all of us today is not to help save the earth. Prophets, however, are among us – men like the atheist David Suzuki and the amazing Thomas Berry. Let me close with the latter.

Berry maintains we have now moved from the Cenezoic to the Ecozoic age. A *kairos* is at hand, a mystique of the earth has grasped us. We have realized that the earth is a one-time endowment. If we lose it, it is all over. The earth, as he never tires saying, is primary, we humans are secondary. Economics needs to be rethought with the earth at the centre. This is beginning to happen in huge corporations, states and provinces and in private homes. George Bush and Stephen Harper may be out of it but millions do get it. Evangelicals previously tied in to fall/redemption models are getting greener by the day. The apocalyptic endtimers are rapidly losing voice; the earth is gaining one. Medicine, technology and education are finally beginning to reinvent themselves. The Universe story in all its staggering wonder and beauty is gaining adherents. For Berry, women have had to endure the four patriarchal establishments which have brought the world to the brink of extinction: ancient empires, the clerical establishment, the nation state and the corporation. Ecofeminism and a focus on the gifts of nurturance which we associate with women and the earth are the only way forward. Men must learn this. The Church must learn this.

Berry the Catholic ecologian suggests that a new exodus is at hand but it involves the species-self and the entire planet leaving an old world behind. For sure we are in the beginning stages and the resistance will still be great. Possibly this is "the new thing" (Isaiah 43) which is happening at this juncture in history. God has spoken to us through the universe. The role of religion today, then, is to join the holy nomads, the secular saints and prophets like Berry who are leading the way. We are finally making an option for the earth and with the earth we are moving into God's new future. In his exile in Babylon Isaiah's role was to spread hope that the living God had not abandoned them.

His words (43:18-19) seemingly are addressing the entire Church today.

Do not remember the former things
or consider the things of old.
I am about to do a new thing;
now it springs forth: do you not perceive it?

KINGDOM AND COMMUNION CATHOLICS

It has often been said that only by constant vigilance can the gains of history be safeguarded. The forces of reaction are omnipresent and timidity is always an option. So it is and has been with the history of the Catholic Church. The extraordinary efflorescence of the Church with its new birth in the halcyon days of the 1960s has been stalemated at its highest institutional levels. The pontificate of John Paul II, as time goes by, has proven to be the inevitable historical response to the revolutionary impulses of the Second Vatican Council. "The greatest change in thinking in the history of the Church" was the analysis of the late great bishop of Durban South Africa, Denis Hurley. In many ways it was naïve to expect that such a revolution would proceed with no bumps in the road.

It was naïve to think that power, no matter what the institution, is ever willfully ceded. It was naïve to believe that a Church which redefined itself as the "People of God," with all its inclusiveness of baptism, would not be resisted by a clerical culture – secretive, exclusive, patriarchal and hierarchical. Nevertheless the global clerical sex scandals, and the awareness that all over the Catholic world celibacy was simply not being observed, has ended lay deference and the unearned status of the clergy. For a creative minority of clergy the change has been welcomed as necessary and salubrious, but to the institution it has not been without a struggle. The tendency (as in any institution) as we saw so clearly in the sex abuse scandals was to protect the club (the institution) at all costs, even to the point of denying core values that the club was mandated to preach – the protection of the *anawim,* the voiceless ones, those with no power.

The Post-Conciliar Church Evangelizes Culture

As the powerful Spirit roiled through the Church in the 1960s and 1970s, lay people flocked to theologates, graduate schools and summer institutes, becoming more and more theologically sophisticated and ready to put into practice the collegial vision of the Council. Many parishes hummed with activity with a wide variety of ministries. Pastors welcomed the "co-responsibility" the Council promoted. When one reads the progressive social documents of national episcopacies of these decades one is struck by the prophetic attempt of the Roman Church to evangelize the culture, to attempt to purify it of its xenophobic tendencies, its structural addictions to war-making, racism, and economic marginalization. This was a time of immense pride and ferment in the Church as it moved beyond an individualist paradigm to a socio-cultural critique of society at large. Catholics awoke to the fact that sin was more than individual transgression and was often defined by apathy, silence, and complicity. The liturgy asked forgiveness for not only the things we did, but also the things we failed to do. Sin was more often willful blindness than active malevolence.

As Catholics became more attuned to scripture and were encouraged to let go of crude fundamental approaches to God's word, it was inevitable that new understandings of Jesus and his world would develop. The Council had liberated the Catholic world to a deeper understanding of literary forms and their use by biblical authors. It also forced us to get away from abstractions, and in the challenge of the atheist Albert Camus, "to confront the bloodstained face of history." The Council Fathers, many of whom saw first-hand the horrors of World War II, grasped the radical failure of a Christianity based on the pillars of a worn-out Thomistic philosophy. There was an immediate need to make Christianity real and existential, a God walk more than a God talk.

Catholicism had managed somehow to separate the head and the Body. Sixty million people, 37 million of them civilians, were killed in the heart of Christian Europe. Baptized Catholics put children in the ovens of Auschwitz. A Catholic chaplain blessed the dropping of the A-bomb on Japan. Huge numbers of Catholics thinking they were serving Christ were duped into supporting anti-gospel ideologies – like Nazism, fascism, and the mass murder of non-combatants killed by firebombing of civilian areas. Catholics were now ready to confront "social sin."

Gaudium et Spes, the great document of the Church in the Modern World, addressed this in many passages. "Sacred Scripture teaches us that love of God cannot be separated from love of neighbour" (#24). No more separating God from humanity. "The new social order must be founded on truth, built by justice and animated by love" (#26). Now the Church was demanding that we move beyond the individualist paradigm. Hess the commandant of Auschwitz, a Catholic, loved his children. He forgot what the Council demanded. "In our times a special obligation binds us to make ourselves the neighbour of absolutely every person"(#27). Social justice now became a rallying cry as "the human family now comprises a single world community" (#33).

The Church was not naïve about the price to be paid, because it already had been paid by Jesus "who taught us by example that we too must shoulder that cross which the world and the flesh inflict on those who search after peace and justice"(#38).

A decade after the Council, the marvellous Pope Paul VI wrote quite possibly the greatest encyclical of the twentieth century, certainly of his own pontificate. He reminded us in *Evangelium Nuntiandi* (On Proclaiming the Good News, December 8, 1975): "Christ first proclaims a kingdom, the kingdom of God; and this is so important, by comparison everything else becomes 'the rest' which is 'given in addition'. Only the kingdom is absolute ... and it makes everything else relative ..." And that includes the Pope, sacraments, the Bible, priesthood and even the Church. Only God's reign of peace and justice is ultimate.

Vatican II saw the coming of the new-world Church leaving behind the old Eurocentric model. The bishops of Africa, Latin America and Asia were speaking a new word to a rapidly shrinking world. Philosophical argumentation withered next to the monumental suffering of the poor. A new universalism embracing the whole human family was emerging. The technological and communications revolution brought this all home to our living rooms. Ignorance was no longer an excuse for inaction. The civil rights movement, the shocking merciless bombing and killing of over a million civilians in Vietnam were right in our face demanding a response. The emergence of 60 new nations was marking the end of imperial and colonial adventurism. Catholics were galvanized by all of this as the wind and the fire of the Spirit summoned us to deeper involvement in the world.

The Role of Pope Paul Vl

Paul Vl in insisting on Jesus' central proclamation of God's reign in history was merely pointing out what the Church Fathers (sic) had said a decade earlier in *Gaudium et Spes.* "The spiritual agitation and the changing conditions of life are part of a broader and deeper revolution." This wasn't simply the 1960s. This was the Holy One, the Divine Disturber inviting us to "scrutinize the signs of the times and of interpreting them in light of the Gospel"(#4). Pope John XXIII named the cry of women, of the poor of the earth as a divine summons. The sanctuary needed to embrace the street; the broken bread on the altar needed to be seen in the broken bodies of every society – or else there was no authentic communion.

In a famous address at the Council, Paul VI insisted on this spirituality of the Samaritan, where "behind the face of everyman ... we must recognize the face of Christ, and the heavenly Father." When this happens, then "our humanism becomes Christianity." There is no better answer to those who accuse activists as simply doing "social work." Within six years of this statement, the bishops of the world reminded all Catholics that social justice was not simply an option for Catholics but "a constitutive dimension of the Gospel."

Pope Paul went searching for bishops to put the kingdom into practice – and where better than in the United States. He sent an amazing Belgian named Jean Jadot to get the right men who would become authentic Catholic leaders.

Robert Blair Kaiser writes, "Jadot took his instructions from Pope Paul VI, who saw an evolving role for his nuncios after Vatican II – not to be the Pope's eyes and ears, but his heart … Nuncios should travel, Paul VI said, not so much as the representatives of Rome to secular governments, or even as legates between Rome and the world's bishops. They should 'show the Pope's concern for the poor, the forgotten, the ignored.'"

It was Jadot who from 1973 to 1980 appointed "kingdom" men who were in synch with the Council's reformist tendencies. For example: Richmond's Walter Sullivan, Milwaukee's Rembert Weakland, Saginaw's Ken Untener, Roger Mahony (who marched with Cesar Chavez), and Rochester's Bishop Matthew Clark. There was also Seattle's Raymond Hunthausen (who challenged America's first-strike nuclear policies), San Antonio Archbishop Patrick Flores, former Newark Archbishop Peter Gerety and Texan Leroy Matthiesen (who challenged the production of nuclear weapons in his diocese). The much-loved Joseph Bernadin became a bishop of a major see under Jadot too. As soon as John Paul II became Pope, Jadot was summoned back to Rome and immediately the "Pope's men," cautious, conservative, chancery types were imposed on dioceses. These were "company men" certainly loyal to the Church, but men who had never engaged in the social struggle like those mentioned above.

One such papal appointee was Cardinal Edward Egan (now the Cardinal Archbishop of New York) who was a Vatican insider with no experience as a parish priest. Egan became notorious for his remark that bishops and the Church hierarchy could not be held responsible for paedophiliac crimes against minors, because priests were private contractors rather than employees! What was Egan's summary of the Jadot bishops? "He hurt the Church in the United States by picking the very worst bishops. This is because John Paul II had changed the criteria. It was part of his plan to bring a runaway, post-Conciliar Church back to its senses."

Cardinal Egan (and too many like him) certainly fit the description of Notre Dame theologian Richard McBrien who wrote in *The New York Times* of the John Paul II bishops: "These bishops tend to be uncritically loyal to the Pope and his curial associates, rigidly authoritarian and solitary in the exercise of pastoral leadership and reliably safe in their theological views ... Since 1980, with the exception of the Archdiocese of Chicago ... every major appointee has been more hard-line than his immediate predecessor."

In Canada in the post-Conciliar years Jesuit Bill Ryan and layman Tony Clarke, working for the Canadian Catholic Conference of Bishops (CCCB), marshalled the Church with an extraordinary litany of impressive statements, which focused on the Church's commitment to the broader society and the common good. In particular the 1976 statement *From Words to Action* stands out as a model invitation for Catholics to be heralds of justice. Bishops like Remi De Roo, Bernard Hubert, and Hull's Adolphe Proulx stood out as true progressives committed to the reign of God.

This all stopped during the last pontificate. It was ironic that John Paul II had a marvellous understanding of the Church's social mission, and had been active in his native Poland, yet he micromanaged episcopal appointments in a way that hobbled the Church. Few of his appointments raised up men with any record of social engagement.

Kingdom Catholics and Church/Communion Catholics

These new appointments were "Church" Catholics not "Kingdom" Catholics, supposedly fixated on "Catholic identity." Under these men the Church has ceased being a major player in the Great Spirit movements of our time, preferring to focus on internal "Catholic" issues. In particular their failure to challenge Rome on the female question has done serious damage to Church credibility. As male vocations to priesthood diminished all over the world, the Church adamantly refused to consider ordaining married men and women. The reasons given were so embarrassing, so intellectually unworthy of refutation that it has done serious damage to the Church's great intellectual tradition. Suffice it to say, it has virtually nothing to do with God's reign and everything to do with a genuine fear to change. Baptism inaugurates a kingdom of equals – yet patriarchy, hierarchy and clericalism continue to deform the Body.

The former Master of the Dominican Order and a self-described 1960s radical, Timothy Radcliffe, attempted to deal with this in a talk he gave in California in 2006. Radcliffe rightfully expressed sadness at the polarization in the Church and chose to describe the division thusly: There are Kingdom Catholics and Communion Catholics.

The Kingdoms see themselves as the pilgrim people on the way to the kingdom. Influenced by great theologians like Karl Rahner and Edward Schilebeeckx – and latterly Gustavo Gutiérrez – they are open to the world, and see the Spirit outside the institution working for freedom and justice.

The Communions – who came after the Council – see the need to rebuild the inner life of the Church. They are associated with Hans Urs Von Balthasar and Joseph Ratzinger. They are wary of modernity and stress the cross. Radcliffe admits this is a caricature (developed more fully in his book) yet not a bad starting point. Try to see their positions, he asks. Fair enough. Both groups are suffering "root shock," their identities threatened and undermined. The Communions in particular saw their comfortable Catholic world crumbling, sliding into a Church with no rules, no discipline, and no deep beliefs.

Here Fr. Radcliffe fails to convince. One can relate to the disequilibrium felt after the Council. For many it was too new, too fast. Beyond a doubt this is true, but to imply that "Kingdom" Catholics have no fundamental beliefs is a gross distortion verging on a calumny. The issues that exercise Kingdom Catholics are seldom dogmatic and mainly involve issues of church governance (parish control, lay leadership) and discipline (celibacy, female ordination) all of which could be changed, as Pope John XXIII said, by a stroke of a pen.

The Cross

As for Communion Catholics focusing on the Cross, I see no evidence at all of this. The Cross is the price paid for following Jesus, for becoming serious disciples. It is a freely chosen act to live out the reign of God in a world which inevitably will resist as it did the prophets and Jesus. I see little evidence of this in the Communion camp. There seems to be an obsession with "orthodoxy" here, an unwillingness to even grant that dogmas grow and develop with time. The attack on the brilliant theologians of the last 30 years, men like Roger Haight, Edward Schillebeeckx, Jacques Dupuis and Charles Curran – with nothing ever proved – has cast a McCarthy-like pall over the authentic role of theologians. But what about "orthopraxy," the authentic following of Jesus in history?

Communion Catholics too often do not "swim in the current with others" (as Rahner would put it) but are content "to stand on the river bank of eternity" ready to die for a conclusion, yet not for a cause. There seems a distinct unwillingness to join those religious nomads, many unbaptized and unchurched, who are challenging the enemies of life. There seems little understanding that dogmas neither inspire nor animate; real movements and holy martyrs do. It is often said of the Catholic Church that if it is not leading the parade, it's not in it. However, as history shows, the Spirit blows where it wills (John 3:8), and there's a howling gale outside too many chancery offices.

How utterly appalling to see some of those well-heeled Communion spokesmen cozy up to the Bush regime in Washington supported by wealthy think tanks and reactionary foundations. Where is the Cross in all of this? If the kingdom relativizes everything else, then America is not Lord, nor the Republican Party (nor the Democrats for that matter). By publicly supporting the Bush agenda the Communion spokesmen are not only making war on the global poor and the environment, but on the domestic poor as well. As Richard Rohr has said so bluntly: "Our religious doctrines have been allowed to become the smokescreen for our real doctrine: Our privileged position. Christ is too often a cover for our *de facto* allegiance to Caesar."

Timothy Radcliffe is a fine churchman with much of value to say, and it is certainly important to engage in ongoing dialogue (and "conversation" as he prefers) with all segments of the Church. But in my judgment he is off the mark in equating kingdom and communion. The Cross is the question as the Communions suggest, but it is not to be found in Church statements or dogmas, as important as they are. Catholic identity as well is important, but there is no identity which bypasses the *anawim:* Those left behind in a vicious turbo-capitalist world where three billion live on less than two dollars per day. There is no identity which does not radically side with God's Body, the earth slowly being rendered uninhabitable. Jesus lived and died for God's dream, not for the power and respectability of the Church. A Church which refuses to serve the reign is creating an idol to which few will be attracted. An old Church saying goes, "*Ubi ecclesia, ibi Christus.*" (Where the Church is, there also Christ.) But if the Church is not anchored in the poor and the reign of justice and peace, Christ will be elsewhere – which is why we pray, "Thy kingdom come, Thy will be done on earth."

ROCK-SOLID AND STEADFAST

We confront the Catholic Church, other Christian bodies and the synagogues of America with their silence and cowardice in the face of our country's crimes. We are convinced that the religious bureaucracy in this country is racist, is an accomplice in this war and is hostile to the poor.
Philip Berrigan at Catonsville – May 17, 1968

I die with the conviction, held since 1968 and Catonsville, that nuclear weapons are the scourge of the earth; to mine for them, manufacture them, deploy them, use them, is a curse against God, the human family, and the Earth itself.
Philip Berrigan's last statement – December 6, 2002

We arrived bleary-eyed and broken-hearted after a 16-hour bus ride from Toronto: three mourners ready to walk the last mile on December 9, 2002 with our recently-deceased brother, Philip Berrigan. The news had travelled fast via phone and e-mail from the great man's community, Jonah House, located in the poor West End of Baltimore. Dwyer Sullivan and Lorne Howcroft, longtime friends in the peace movement, were my travelling companions.

We gathered in the below-zero weather on the edge of a graveyard where Jonah House is located. The plan was to process over to St. Peter Claver Church, a little over a mile away. Immediately, we were warmed by the instant camaraderie of so many fellow travellers – peace and justice advocates, Catholic Worker folks, young families surrounded by omnipresent banners – the constant talismans of any peace gathering, chanting: "Organize a national strike," "Disarmament is the only way to avert war," "Love your enemies" (Jesus), "Kill your enemies" (Uncle Sam), "Swords into ploughshares." Many people were festooned with "No-war-in-Iraq" buttons.

One of the first persons I spotted was the eminent 80-year-old American historian Howard Zinn (*A People's History of the United States*). I immediately approached him and told him how much I had valued his work over the years. A TV reporter followed me and told the bemused Zinn, "I was told by somebody that you were worth talking to."

I struck up a conversation with Al, who had flown in from Chicago that day. He told me he had been a member of the peace movement from 1960. Similar, animated conversations bubbled up around us as they usually do among folks who knew that they did not have to explain themselves. It was obvious why we were all here. No words were necessary. You felt the deep love and the respect for the man one paper called "the most radical peace-maker of the 20th century."

Solemnity and Reverence

The procession was about to begin and the 300 mourners were enjoined to follow with "solemnity and reverence." This was a crowd where no such admonition was necessary. The blue Ford pickup carrying Phil's casket led the way with his smiling daughters, Frida (28) and Katie (21), and his son Jerry (27), sitting beside their dad's varnished wooden casket. A huge, kilted bagpiper struck up "Amazing Grace," and the last mile began. In the front were Phil's beloved wife, Elizabeth McAlister, and his brothers, Dan and Jerry. Moving up North Bentalou Street, we turned right on Presstman Street and, immediately, I was struck by the poverty of the area and the black demographic. There were rows of boarded-up houses, some demolished, others crying for reclamation. Indeed, Habitat for Humanity was on the job next to *Ms. Thang's Wings and Fries and Neighbourhood Cut-Rate Liquors* and the *Odyssey Lounge*, which had "the coldest beer in town – 40 ounces for $1.40." We passed *PJ's Auto Repair* as the members of the New England Peace Pagoda drummed and chanted.

A powerful, Latin American touch was added when the names of deceased martyrs were invoked, followed by the assurance that they were, indeed, presente. Oscar Romero – Presente. Ita Ford – Presente. Stephen Biko – Presente. Francis of Assisi – Presente. Clare of Assisi – Presente. Thomas Merton – Presente. The moving litany of the peacemaking, justice-championing names was intoned: Chico Mendes, Marcus Garvey, Dorothy Day, Victor Jara, Jean Donovan, A.J. Muste, Henri Nouwen, Dorothy Kazel, Dick McSorley, Bill Stringfellow and Fannie Lou Hamer. Talk about your communion of saints. I half expected, given Phil's tenure in an all-black, segregated school in New Orleans (1956-63) and his great commitment to civil rights, to hear those great funeral dirges, "Flee as a Bird" and "Didn't He Ramble." It didn't matter. I heard Louis Armstrong playing them inside my head.

Several marchers had been in the civil rights movement and those wonderful refrains were heard once again: "We're marching forward and never turning back" and "Step by step the longest march" and "Since love is born of heaven and earth, how can I keep from singing?" If we needed any proof of the Pentagon's obscene budget and that Afro-Americans are still struggling in the Land of Plenty, we saw it all along Presstman Street; and just before we made it to St. Peter Claver Church, we passed the smouldering ruins of a house recently burned to the ground.

St. Peter Claver Church

St. Peter Claver Church, a heroic, inner-city parish dedicated to African-American ministry, was well prepared to send off her faithful son. It was from here that Phil, as a 45-year-old Josephite priest, had driven the parish car to participate in the famous burning of the draft cards on May 17, 1968 in Catonsville, Maryland. Banners had been hung reminding us that "It is wrong to bomb and kill in Iraq or anywhere;" "Break the chains of war, choose non-violence;" "They shall beat their swords into ploughshares."

John Dear S.J., Phil's co-felon and a main celebrant, invited us all to turn to "the God of peace and to thank this God of peace for welcoming

Phil Berrigan into the new life of Christ." The Mass of the Resurrection resonated deeply with me, as I am sure it did with all. Eucharist makes so much sense when those who gather have been about breaking their own lives open as bread for the world and hope for the marginalized. Traditional hymns like "O Come, O Come, Emmanuel" fill us, once again, with the Advent realization that we have tasted the sweet reign of God and that we yearn ever so much for its fuller coming. This was a liturgy where tradition came alive instead of hanging like a dead letter.

After a portion of Tobit, "who walked in the ways of truth and the righteousness all the days of my life," Psalm 115, a fitting rejection of idols, was read: "... the work of human hands ... and those who make them are like them; so are all who trust in them." In effect, the lordship of the bomb was rejected and the lordship of the sovereign Lord was affirmed: "Not to us, O God, but to your name give glory."

An excerpt from an interview with Phil was used as the second reading. In part, it said: "We all have to take responsibility for the bomb. The bomb is destroying us, morally, psychologically, emotionally and humanly. This responsibility will create the new human, the new creation and the just social order that the Scriptures speak about.

"Non-violence in the best sense is a strict and definitive social justice. God is perhaps most present to us through the enemy, through the war-makers who make nuclear hostages out of us; through the politicians who lie to us; through the generals who supposedly protect us, yet, in reality, protect only the rich; and so on. They're our true enemies and we have to love them and to work for their conversion. All of that comes out of the heading of non-violence.

"Living out the resurrection today means turning away from the violence of our lives and taking responsibility for the violence of the state. We resurrect to the extent that we take responsibility for the victims of the state."

Dan Berrigan's Homily

In a strong, clear voice, Elizabeth McAlister, Phil's stalwart wife, read the resurrection story of Lazarus (John 11:1-44), and Dan Berrigan reflected on it in his usual, potent, poetic way. Before his brief homily, he read a short poem about Phil carrying the Scripture as contraband into jails as the doors were slammed behind him. Dan likened the community around Phil to that around Lazarus. Both were "held by tears and obscure hope."

In John's Gospel, "Jesus prayed to a God who appeared as St. Elsewhere." Quoting Thomas Merton, Dan acknowledged that "there was no palliative to disgrace the near-despair by which we make our way." Dan also described the rapidity of his brother's decline: "The near cleansing of death was terrifying. What did we hope for? Were we chasing moonbeams? No, we were not cheated. Jesus came to us as he often does in disguise, in the amazing friends and family who rallied and gave us strength." Quoting Revelations 6:9-10, Dan reiterated the words of the souls who asked how long (before deliverance). They were told to "rest a little longer." The elder Berrigan drew knowing laughs from those assembled when he likened this to Phil's "patience and his impatience. He learned patience from the slammed bars of jails, the cold hands of judges and a complicit church," reflected Dan. "But was he ever impatient! I remember the trial in 1972, the stacked cards and the Catholic judge who hated Vatican II and the protesting priests ... but, in the end, he was a mastermind of grace and human sweetness."

In contrast to Dan's gentle hymn to his brother, Brendan Walsh of the Viva House Community, who went back 35 years with Phil, caught the "rock-solid, steadfast Berrigan; the street-savvy brother to the suffering servant. The man was one intense and honest brother who understood the mystical body better than anyone we knew, who felt in his bones what we were doing to the poor, the dismissed, those robbed in ditches all across this planet, and as Stokely Carmichael said, 'one of the few white people who knew the truth of racism in this country.' He gave 11 years of his life locked up tight, and he never complained; he never wavered. He knew that the system had to be resisted always and everywhere. He dared to call Cheney, Rumsfeld what they were – terrorists. To you, Phil, *Deo gratias,*" Walsh concluded.

Afterwards, in the hall, I asked the noted Catholic writer Gary Wills to sum up Phil, to which he replied: "Blessed are the peacemakers." Dick Cusack, father of the acting Cusacks, Phil's college roommate of four years at Holy Cross in Boston, Mass., thought for a moment and said: "He taught us how to live and, in the end, how to die. So many of those grads at Holy Cross thought he was crazy."

The 15-hour bus ride back to Toronto gave me ample time to think about Phil and the many settings in which I had shared his company: the different venues in Toronto, Baltimore, King of Prussia, a prison in Pennsylvania where he broke a fast to spend time with us, retreats, our home. I think Dan and Brendan caught his tough sweetness perfectly. When I was on retreat with Phil, Liz and Dan in September of 2002, Phil was hobbling with a walker after a hip replacement, and we walked outside for a chat. He could hardly finish a joke – he was laughing so hard between drags of a cigarette. "So, really, how are you?" I asked. His answer was quintessential Phil: "Just about well enough to take on this f---ing empire again," he exclaimed.

As the bus moved through the winter darkness of Wilkes-Barre, Scranton and Binghamton, I concluded that my life had been enriched, questioned and challenged by one of the most authentic disciples of the 20th century; a fierce follower of the Galilean agitator, one whose life fused politics and spirituality, mysticism and action. In a phrase, integrated holiness.

Phil Berrigan – Presente!

GENTLE AND TENACIOUS

The former primate of the Canadian Anglican Church was one of the most remarkable bishops of the twentieth century.

Canada has lost a great spiritual leader. Ted Scott's role in the struggle against apartheid helped change the course of history in South Africa.
Nelson Mandela

The untimely and sudden death of Archbishop Edward "Ted" Scott on June 21, 2004 brought to a close one of the most extraordinarily authentic church lives in living memory. Killed in an automobile crash at age eighty-five, near Parry Sound, Ontario, the former Anglican primate of Canada (1971-1986) was one of those rare people who managed to combine, in one singular life, the personal and the prophetic. As another bishop, Nobel laureate Desmond Tutu, described him in his eulogy, "Ted was confrontational, but not aggressive, he was gentle and tenacious ..."

A son of the manse himself – his father Tom was an Anglican priest – Scott seems to have inherited his passion for justice from his father, described by biographer Hugh McCullum as "a thorn in the side of many fellow clergy, a man who challenged systems, both political and ecclesiastical."

Ted Scott was born in Edmonton on April 30, 1919. A Depression baby, raised in the dust bowls of Saskatchewan, Scott's personalist philosophy and social concern were indelibly stamped on his mind in those formative years. "There was strong mutual concern and support. It gave me a sense of what community and relationships were all about. Everything hinged on the reactions and concerns of people." (McCullum, p. 36).

Because of his father's failing health, the Scotts, now numbering four children, moved to a friendlier climate – Ladner, B.C in the Fraser River Delta. In 1937, at the age of 18, Scott enrolled at the University of British Columbia. Unsure of future directions, he dove into university life and found a bevy of like-minded activists in the dynamic Student Christian Movement. It was here that Scott was able to combine his desire for social service and social action, learning to analyze the structural causes of injustice and the obvious failure of the capitalist system during the Depression.

Rejected on medical grounds from the armed services, Scott entered the ministry and theological studies. This choice he described as "less of a vocation to the priesthood than trying to live out the nature of the Christian community, rather than focusing on the obvious deficiencies of the institutional church." Ordained in 1943, Scott became priest-in-charge of St. Peter's, Seal Cove. At his side was his new wife Isabel Brannan, whom he had married in 1942. It was also at this time he became acutely aware of entrenched racism in Canada when thousands of Japanese-Canadians were interned and their homes and businesses were snatched from them.

From 1945 to 1965, the Scott family grew to four children as Ted threw himself into parish work in Winnipeg. Friend Elizabeth Driscoll recalled those days with what would become a familiar refrain about her driven friend: "… going to bat for broke students, single mothers, disabled people, divorced women when divorce was out – he never failed the little people."

Ted Scott was named bishop of the Kootenays in 1966 and moved to Kelowna, B.C. He and his family revelled in their new life in the Okanagan Valley. Indefatigable as always, the future primate spent 100 days a year on the road developing shared ministries with the United Church and advancing ecumenism with other Christians.

It was in the Kootenays that Scott developed his episcopal style, which endeared him to all the people and yet became the bane of the institution. With him, people came first and institutions last. Because he was universally loved and respected for his simple, unaffected ways, the Anglican Communion would come to tolerate his often chaotic administrative style in the following fifteen years (1971-1986) during which he served as the tenth primate of the Canadian Anglican Church.

Scott Read the 1960s Well

Ted Scott came to the job at a tumultuous time. The spirit of the 60s, which both animated the church and challenged it to become transformative rather than an adjunct of the establishment, needed thoughtful interpretation.

In 1965 the Anglican Church, well aware that its days as the smug "Tory party at prayer" were coming to an end, hired *Maclean's* writer Pierre Berton to analyze it. Berton's book, *The Comfortable Pew,* caused a sensation. The church had abdicated its moral leadership in society, the noted iconoclast wrote. In such critical times it had retreated behind the walls of institutionalism, sat silent in an era of brinkmanship when the peace movement needed its voice, and, when racial justice was demanded, the church was found gazing inward. It had failed to demand ethics in commerce, an area in which many Anglicans were prominent. As well, its sexual morality needed updating. It was Ted Scott's genius to ride this whirlwind and move the church into the broader struggle. In this, a golden age of church activism, he was often joined by fellow travellers on the kingdom road, people like Roman Catholic bishop Remi De Roo and United Church moderators Lois Wilson and Clarke Macdonald.

Always close to Canada's First Nations, Scott supported them in treaty disputes including the northern pipeline. He decried global poverty, opposed cruise missile testing, and advanced the cause of women's ordination. His leadership gifts were acknowledged as well by the Church universal. From 1975 to 1983 he was named moderator of the World Council of Churches, where he threw himself into such issues as bank divestment in South Africa and the scandal of the global arms trade.

When his tenure as primate was ending, Scott took on "the greatest challenge of my life" as a member of the Eminent Persons Group, a Commonwealth initiative to help end apartheid in South Africa. "We owe him an immense debt of gratitude," South African Archbishop Desmond Tutu proclaimed at Scott's memorial service.

Scott's so-called retirement years focused on pastoral relationships with many on the margins – the disabled, the depressed, gays and lesbians, as well as ordinary people for whom he was a constant source of strength. It was no big deal for him. As he told McCullum: "My concern for these people comes from my political position. I was always concerned for people on the margins, people impacted by the aging process."

A Bishop for the Margins

One named by McCullum who was absolutely devastated by Scott's sudden death was the "Bishop of Cabbagetown," Ken Caveney, a well-known urban activist whose moniker had been given by the street people and prostitutes he had befriended. For 30 years in the midst of Scott's busy life, the bishop always had time for the often-volatile Caveney. The latter, orphaned at 15 and jailed soon after, would pepper his language with assorted vulgarisms. Once, about 15 years ago, after we had shared lunch with Ted, I told Ken he had a helluva nerve carrying on in a loud voice in a cafe within spitting distance of Anglican headquarters.

Accustomed to Caveney's rough-and-tumble manner as well as his salty language, I was nevertheless staggered by the following episode:

We no sooner had sat down than Kenny asked Scott for some advice.
"What's the problem, Ken?"
"Well, Ted, I often go into Catholic schools and rap with the kids. And last week one of them asked me about the Virgin Birth."
"And what did you tell him, Ken?"
"I told him it was simple – just like it says in the Bible, the angel came down and balled Mary."
Scott never blinked. Simultaneously catching my eye and with a twinkle in his own, he said to Caveney, "Well, Ken, that's one way to express it." He then proceeded to lay out a more acceptable interpretation of this Christian

mystery. That was typical of Scott. No feigned ecclesiastical outrage, no temper tantrum at Caveney's lack of decorum. Just a simple direct reply. Scotty wasn't one to reinvent the human. Like the Master he so faithfully emulated, he took everyone where they were on their life journey and went from there.

In the summer of 2004, as I listened to Ken Caveney pour out grief over the loss of his beloved friend, my wife reminded me of the above occasion. I said, "If there was any doubt that Ted Scott is a saint, I just received irrefutable proof."

Caveney recalled an incident that sums up the beautiful witness of Ted Scott. Ken often frequented a greasy spoon, a haven for prostitutes and drug dealers, near his downtown apartment. There in the heart of Toronto's tenderloin, Caveney, the "street bishop" was known to all the local rounders of the demimonde. As he walked in with Scott on one of their frequent outings, one of the prostitutes hailed him.

"Hi Bishop, how ya doin?"

"Fine, sweetie, how are you?"

"Not bad. Say, who's that good-looking guy with you?" (meaning Ted Scott who was, as usual, in civvies).

Without missing a beat Ted walked over and said, "Hi, I'm Ted Scott."

This was quintessential Scott, the measure of the man, one whose deep compassion and solidarity pervaded all his relationships. In one slight body the personal and political were married. Solidarity was his middle name.

Ted Scott breathed authenticity. His eschewing of ecclesiastical pomp and episcopal posturing made the Anglican Church more credible and the Christian Church a little more real.

Scott understood at a deep level that religious leadership had little to do with archaic honorific titles and a whole new set of vestments. He would have chuckled at the Vatican insistence that somehow priests are "ontolog-ically" different. He intuitively understood that the Christian gospel is only made real to the extent that those who proclaim it themselves honour without exception the divine seed we all bear. His life of downward mobility shone out like a beacon at a time when church leadership had just about vanished into the trivial and the irrelevant.

Catholic bishops will find no greater model to emulate today than the life of Edward "Ted" Scott. I personally yearn for the day when the mitres, the croziers and episcopal rings are replaced by the outstretched hand, the warm smile, and the words Ted Scott used throughout his life. "Hi, I'm Ted."

JOHN PAUL II:
GLOBAL WITNESS AND CHURCH REACTIONARY

I was never afraid to appoint bishops who disagreed with me.
Leo XIII, on being asked why his papacy was so successful

Admittedly, the church as a human institution is continually in need of purification and renewal; the Second Vatican Council acknowledged this with courageous candor.
John Paul II, "Memory and Identity," 2005

In writing about Pope John Paul II two years after his death, we are now in a position to make a more sober analysis of his life and his papacy. The hysteria surrounding the death of the first modern superstar pope has abated. Those well-planted "spontaneous" funeral chants (*"Subito santo"*) and the mass-produced placards demanding instant canonization are now silent. They were the products of clerical reactionaries probably of the neo-catechumenate movement or of Opus Dei members.

A distinction must be made between John Paul II's role *ad extra,* outside of the church, and his role *ad intra* within the body of Roman Catholicism. Let us begin with deep admiration for the shining example of humanity who bestrode his times like a religious superstar, a marathon evangelist who traveled the world breaking new ground among world religions, championing human rights and raising the voices of the poor and the weak. With his ruggedly handsome looks, his youthful vigour and his obvious compassion and concern for those on the margins, he spent himself on behalf of the gospel. This was a man of outstanding intellect and simple tastes who was unafraid to enter a profound dialogue with most earthlings about what constituted the human. What a witness.

Coming into prominence at a time of a deep religious vacuum spawned and exacerbated by the excesses of an amoral turbo-capitalism, John Paul II used the advance in telecommunications to reach out to those left behind and forgotten by the reigning ideology of market idolatry. Though he pooh-poohed his role in the in the death of Communism, his gospel personalism posed an attractive alternative to the grey oppression behind Iron Curtain countries. Bearing an intense spirituality refined in the fire of resistance to the dehumanizing onslaught of Nazism and the totalitarian ravages of Stalinism, he became the foremost defender of the transcendent value of the human person on the human stage. From the womb to death row, he preached the sanctity of human life.

One of the pope's greatest achievements was fostering a seismic shift in Catholic attitudes to the barbarism of capital punishment. In the name and sacred memory of his Lord whose life was brutally extinguished by state violence in the garbage dump of Jerusalem, he began a new dialogue on this odious practice. It was virtually proscribed in the new Catholic Catechism. As well, and to the chagrin of free market Republican Catholics, he was as unsparing in his criticism of the consumer values of the West as he was of the oppressive side of communism.

A victim of war himself, he prophetically denounced Gulf Wars One and Two, and predicted war "would leave behind a trail of resentment and hatred." The recent revelations (*The Lancet*, October 2006) of the staggering number of dead Iraqis recall the pope's admonition in May 1991. Writing at the end of his encyclical *Centissimus Annus*, he exclaimed, "War never again. Never again war which destroys the lives of innocent people, teaches how to kill, throws into upheaval even the lives of those who do the killing." All this before Abu Ghraib and other revelations of American barbarity. How right he was.

Consistent in his dignified personal witness, he carried his final infirmities with grace and immense courage. The world correctly mourns a moral giant of our times. He will remain a compelling universal symbol of engaged holiness. If official sanctity and canonization is your thing, Karol Wojtyla surely would be an ideal candidate.

And yet, while it is painful for us to say this, his papacy remains a huge disappointment. The troubling prediction of an outstanding English bishop remains as true today as it did the day he uttered it on Karol Wojtyla's elevation to the papacy on Oct. 16, 1978. "I know this man and it is not good news for the church."

While others were cheering that a non-Italian had been elected, this bishop understood too well that a man forged in a church frozen in time, a church which for historical reasons brooked no dissent, was distrustful of democracy and was structured as an authoritarian monolith – patriarchal, hierarchical and clerical – could hardly carry out the reform agenda of Vatican II.

Internal Aggiornamento Stopped Dead

Catholics had every right to think that the *aggiornamento* called for by Pope John XXIII would continue. The church that Vatican II proclaimed was to be *semper reformanda,* always in a state of renewing itself. That such a church would proceed incrementally was understood. In 1990, Bishop Alexander Carter expressed his frustration to *Catholic New Times* saying he could not believe how slow we as a church were in addressing the growing problem of priestless parishes. Carter had pushed hard ordaining married men in native communities, then moving on from there. As a young priest in Rome, Alexander Carter had been privy to Pius XI's final public address in 1939, where the pontiff shocked all by saying that "The church, the mystical body of Christ, has become a monstrosity. The head is very large, but the body is shrunken. You young priests must rebuild the church and mobilize the lay people." Vatican II had begun the necessary change by its designation of the church as the people of God. With the huge growth of educated lay people and the massive defection of priests largely for reasons of celibacy, it was natural that the church would begin to democratize in order to utilize the abundant gifts of its members. Besides that, a more collegial approach among bishops and dioceses would be the norm.

Synods would be activated to flesh out this new exciting communion. Authority would be shared in new ways. This never happened. Clericalism still bedevils the church.

A new pall descended over the church. Collegiality was stripped of its meaning. Dialogue turned into monologue. A listening pope failed to materialize. Authority was centralized. Bishops – theologically pastoral leaders on their own – became servants, not brothers. Poor local leaders, recognized for their docility, and who owed their advancement to their absolute uniformity of opinion on women priests and celibacy, were imposed on dioceses. As a result, according to Archbishop John Quinn the former president of the US Bishops Conference, widespread dissatisfaction was felt all over the Catholic world. "Even a modicum of consultation has disappeared." A few powerful gatekeepers in the US, Cardinals Law (Boston) and O'Connor (New York), vetted most of the appointments, making sure that all new bishops were rigid on women's ordination and birth control. Fr. Richard McBrien, the distinguished theologian from Notre Dame, phrased the festering situation well. "Their constituency is the constituency of one – the pope. The people do not come first. The bishops feel it is their job to represent Rome to the people rather than representing the people to Rome." Cardinal Bernadin Gantin, who had headed up the Curia's Congregation for Bishops, was equally scathing in his evaluation. He stated that he was shocked at "the arrivism and careerism" of too many bishops. As well, many episcopal conferences and synods watched in smouldering anger as conclusions to their deliberations were written beforehand by the Curia.

European Revolt

Eleven years into his centralized papacy the dam burst. In January 1989, 170 German-speaking theology professors from four countries publicly criticized the pope. The Cologne Declaration attacked John Paul for his opposition to artificial birth control and his use of authority, particularly his choice of conservative bishops. The signers, who included theological giants Hans Kung, Edward Schilebeeckx, Bernard Haring, Norbert

Greinacher, and Franz Bockle, reminded the pope that "the procedure of nomination is not some private choice of the pope." The latter had over-turned long-standing tradition in Germany of local churches to be involved in choosing bishops. John Paul II infuriated many by unilaterally appointing arch-conservative bishop Joachim Meisner as Archbishop of Munich. The latter has successfully winnowed the church of Munich since then. It is estimated that 250,000 Catholics have left the church because of his rigid tenure.

The statement went on to rue the new "Roman centralism" and the "questionable forms of control" which were shutting down the right of free and open discussion. Shortly after the Declaration's publication, 23 Spanish theologians added their names. In June, 63 Italian theologians fol-lowed suit with their "open letter to Christians." It contained much of the same criticism.

The new JPII bishops executed orders from 'Rome Incorporated,' appear-ing like branch plant managers of a lifeless corporation, hardly suffused with the spirit of Jesus. Many papal impositions proved to be disasters. When the most respected European Cardinal Franz König of Vienna stepped down in 1985, he was publicly humiliated by the choice of an obscure Benedictine, Hans Hermann Gröer, who was in charge of a Marian shrine at the time. A hopeless authoritarian, he alienated most of Austria's priests and was forced to resign in 1995 when it became known that he had molested monks under his charge. Again König was insulted when his choice Helmut Krätzl was bypassed by another Vatican loyalist, Christolph Schönborn. Many wonder-fully pastoral bishops were deeply hurt and humiliated by this brutal clamp-down. Cardinal Bernadin, the much loved Chicago cardinal, just before his death, was crushed by an embarrassing public humiliation by Cardinals Law, (Boston), Hickey (Washington), Bevilacqua (Philadelphia) and Maida (Detroit) as he attempted to launch his Common Ground Initiative. Bernadin, great pastor that he was, had become increasingly alarmed at the huge gap between bishops and lay people. His initiative called for wide-ranging and frank discussions on a host of problems – the role of women, the sexual teachings of the church, co-responsibility of lay and cleric for the church. Bernadin made it clear that "no group has a monopoly on the truth." Then came the gentle cardinal's mugging by his fellow bishops. Three months later Bernadin was dead of pancreatic cancer and his Common Ground Project barely limps on. In Ontario, one of the kindest Canadian bishop-pastors was hauled to Rome just before retirement and treated like an errant child. A smouldering stasis has resulted since then, exacerbated by the fact that the very bishops who moved around paedophile priests are still in office, apparently unaccountable for their shocking dereliction of duty.

The sex scandal which erupted in Boston in 2002 was perceived by Catholics as a dismal failure of leadership from men who misplaced their fundamental loyalties. By being blindly faithful to the institution and never knowing a parent's bottomless love for their children, these men forgot what the institution is there for: the care, protection and flourishing of the weakest in society. The greatest scandal since the Reformation occurred on John Paul II's watch. Supine bishops who failed to challenge the celibacy requirement for priesthood were forced to keep serial paedophiles on the job, shuffling them from parish to parish to keep the institution humming. This was John Paul II's terrible Achilles heel – naming dull, ambitious clerics more known for their ability for taking marching orders than creatively engaging the people of God in a more collegial ministry.

As Richard McBrien so succinctly stated above, "the constituency of one" had almost become like a monarch. Not a few papal critics reached back to the nineteenth century to quote Cardinal Newman's description of a lengthy papacy: "It is an anomaly and bears no good fruit; he becomes a god and no one contradicts him, does not know the facts and does cruel things without meaning to."

Treatment of Theologians

Second perhaps to the poor calibre of bishops named by John Paul II was his shocking treatment of theologians. Using Cardinal (now pope) Ratzinger as his "bad cop," over one hundred bishops were silenced. It is hard to reconcile John Paul II's kindly expressions of affection with this aspect of the papacy. The global champion of human rights denied them in his church. Very good theologians exploring the 'Divine Mystery' were cast out of Catholic institutions, and many fled the same Catholic universities, bringing moral theology almost to a dead stop. Although John Paul II often said he supported the role of theologians, he allowed his enforcer, Cardinal Ratzinger, to brutally suppress the necessary "new theological investigations" which Vatican II called for – questions which were coming from "science, history and philosophy." Theologians "among all the faithful" had been encouraged "to seek for more suitable ways of communicating doctrine." These people were guaranteed "a lawful freedom of inquiry and thought and the freedom to express their minds humbly and courageously."

Public humiliation and examples were made of giants in their respective fields – Leonardo Boff was made to swallow the hemlock for his role in the exciting liberation theology, Hans Kung in the area of doctrine, Charles Curran and Bernard Häring in the area of moral theology and Edward Schilebeeckx in Christology. Häring, the Redemptorist priest whose *Law of Christ* in 1954 changed the course of the Church's moral theology, sadly lamented after his harassment by the Holy Office that he "would rather stand once again before a court of war of Hitler" than the Holy office itself.

In 1989, the same year as the Cologne Declaration, Archbishop John May of St. Louis, president of the National Conference of Catholic Bishops, strongly defended theologians in a speech before the Catholic Theological Society:

"There are too many sweeping accusations leveled at the theological soundness and creedal fidelity of the theologians," he said. "There are too many vague but insistent attacks, telling bishops that the theologians will supplant them in their teaching office or ignore their pastoral guidance or lead the people of God into antagonism, division and virtual schism."

The US Catholic bishops, living in a rigorous democracy, wrote at this time (1990) that "scholarly competence can be shown when theologians ask searching and serious questions as they seek to discern and communicate the abiding truth of Christ. The constructive critical quality of theological scholarship does not compromise its fidelity to the church and its magisterium, but indicates the disciplined reflection characteristic of genuine scholarly investigation."

In June of 1990, the Catholic Theological Society of America (CTSA) with Canadian Basilian Walter Principe as its president, affirmed "the right of theologians to freedom of research, their right to raise questions, their right to re-examine the meaning of dogmas, and even more to explore the import of past authoritative statements by the magisterium, and finally the right within a faithful unprejudiced presentation of the official teaching to disagree publicly with that teaching under certain circumstances."

The statement "Do not Extinguish the Spirit" was critical of the growing chill within the church and the increasing denigration of theologians who were now seen as "dissenters," rather than loyalists who had a different opinion. Principe addressed the Vatican criticism about "harm being done to the faithful by theologians." He countered with the harm being done by "the Vatican issuing of documents without prior discussion and consultation with bishops and theologians, their inhibiting legitimate discussion by premature decisions on complicated questions, their condemnation or silencing of theologians and their presentation of reformable teaching almost as if they were matters of faith." Do not extinguish the Spirit was concerned about excessive Roman centralization that diminishes the role of local bishops and which impugned the authority of bishops' conferences.

We must contrast this extraordinary clampdown on the intellectual freedom of theologians with the confidence of the post-Vatican-II pope, Paul VI. Paul understood that an intellectual Pentecost had descended on the church and that there would be some false starts among the exuberance. It was both natural and inevitable. Yet he also believed that these theologians were sincere scholars who would self-correct each other within the established methodology of peer review. He did not silence or humiliate one theologian. He refused to "extinguish the spirit."

This was seen by Pope John Paul II (whose papal mantra ironically was, "Be Not Afraid") as "weakness" and by the papal watchdog Ratzinger as chaos. There has always been speculation as to whether John Paul II knew what was going on in the Holy Office. In an interview that Cardinal Paulo Arns gave a Brazilian newspaper in 2005, the much respected senior prelate, himself humiliated when his huge diocese was chopped up to diminish his influence, related the following incident.

Always on cordial terms with John Paul II, Arns arrived in Rome in 1998 to hand in his resignation. Chatting away in German, John Paul said to him, "Paulo I have this letter for you to sign." It had been prepared by the Curia and all Arns had to do was sign it. Arns began to read the three-page memorandum written in Portuguese to the pope. It was highly critical of the Brazilian archbishop. After the third paragraph, the pope exploded. "I am not going to sign this, Paulo. I never said these things about you." He then threw the letter on the floor.

Though it was well known that John Paul II was not the most hands-on administrator as popes go, it begs the question as to where the pope stopped and the Curia took over. Nevertheless, it was on the pope's watch that these shameless McCarthy-like purges took place.

A New Humility

Surely this intelligent man was aware of the widespread dissatisfaction of his restorationist policies and the "creeping infallibilism" of his papacy, his desperate attempts to halt discussion on topics (like clerical celibacy) dear to him but not shared by many of the baptized. That this absolute conviction of the Church's possession of THE truth has become even more heightened under the present pope goes without saying. This is why it was so refreshing (and reportedly so disturbing) when John Paul set out in the year 2000 to beg forgiveness for the Church's many historical failings. This stunning act of contrition entitled *Memory and Reconciliation* was extraordinarily moving and long overdue.

In these humble gestures Pope John Paul II acknowledged the servant nature of the Church, its checkered history and its blind spots which every institution, mired in the ambiguity of history and its own sinfulness, must own. In Jerusalem, John Paul II formally expressed the Church's deep sadness for centuries of Jewish persecution. Though stopping short of an apology for the institution, he pointedly mentioned "displays of anti-Semitism directed against the Jews by Christians ... there are no words to deplore the terrible tragedy of the Shoah." Two weeks before, the pope stunned the curial cardinals when he launched into the contemporary failings of the Church. Among those failings he mentioned "sins against the dignity of women ... too often humiliated and marginalized ... no more discrimination, exclusion, ... *mai piu,* never again." According to writer Luigi Accatoli, the pope apologized ninety-four times for past transgressions.

Although Catholic theology reiterates that reconciliation is good for the soul and a requisite for a mature spiritual life, the pope's apologies were not appreciated by the Curia and the present pope. The subtext of John Paul II's frequent confessions is the subtle hint that there may indeed be defects in his own tenure as pope. This has apparently disturbed the more conservative elements in Catholicism who yearn for perfect papal clarity after the "wishy-washy" tenure of Paul VI. Possibly, given the loving criticism of so many of his contemporaries who love the Church no less than the pontiff, John Paul II has prudently paused. With these many gestures of humility he has ratified the obvious: we are not a "perfect society" but a church of sinners, human stumblers in need of divine help. There is always more truth to come. Vittorio Messori, the veteran Vatican watcher and friend of Pope Benedict XVI, stated the obvious concern of papal infallibilists: "If we can say that past popes have erred, how can we be certain this pope isn't erring?" The answer is we can't. We can all breathe more easily.

Proof that this strong-willed pope has a deep sensitivity to this issue is his 1995 encyclical *Ut Unum Sint* (That all may be One, 1995). Based on the line (17:21) in John's gospel, the pope stated that he was convinced that, "I have a particular responsibility in acknowledging the ecumenical aspirations of the majority of the Christian Communities and in heeding the request made of me to find a way of exercising the primacy which, while in no way renouncing what is essential to its mission, is nonetheless open to a new situation." He went on to say that "this is an immense task we can not refuse" so he invited future theologians and church people to get to the task of discerning the will of Christ in this area.

This holds much promise particularly for Catholics. The collegiality promised by Vatican II has been stalled. The autocratic structure, more monarchical than democratic, must become a central reform project of the next pope. Authority needs to be restored where it truly resides, in the whole church where the Spirit lives and breathes. The Catholic Church, an ongoing work in progress, will move ahead, convinced that other spring times are possible and new graces will be given. This is our history, our ongoing pilgrimage.

We give thanks for Karol Wojtyla, his abundant gifts and his loyal service to the church and the world. He "fought the good fight, finished the race and kept the faith" (2 Timothy 4:7).

BENEDICT XVI:
JOSEPH RATZINGER, AN APPRAISAL

Religion will not gain its old power until it can face change in the same spirit as does science. Its principles may be eternal, but the expression of those principles requires continual development.
Alfred North Whitehead

You also are sheep belonging to Christ, you bear the Lord's mark in the sacrament which you have received, but you are wandering and perishing. Let us not, therefore, incur your displeasure because we bring back the wandering and seek the perishing; for it is better for us to obey the will of the Lord, who charges us to compel you to return to His fold, than to yield consent to the will of the wandering sheep, so as to leave you to perish. Say not, therefore, what I hear that you are constantly saying, "I wish thus to wander; I wish thus to perish;" for it is better that we should so far as is in our power absolutely refuse to allow you to wander and perish.
Augustine, a bishop of the Catholic Church, to Donatus, a Presbyter of the Donatist Party, Sends Greeting. Letter 173 (A.D. 416)

Joseph Cardinal Ratzinger, the Dean of the College of Cardinals, Prefect of the Congregation of the Faith (CDF), President of the Pontifical Biblical Commission and of the International Theological Commission, succeeded Pope John Paul II as the new pope on April 19, 2005. The rapid confirmation of Ratzinger surprised many people, but in retrospect it should not have. One hundred and fifteen of the 117 cardinals chose the former pope's right-hand man. There was to be no "fat pope to follow a lean one" this time.

What does this mean for the Roman Catholic Church?

In the short run, it appears to be a lamentable failure of nerve for the church, a paralyzing inability to address its many festering problems. Acting more as a sclerotic institution than a dynamic *communio*, having opted to stay the course of the centralized John Paul II pontificate, she continues on the lamentable path of the restoration of the *status quo ante,* the rejected minority position of the Second Vatican Council.

In the long run many are convinced that this cannot last, that the inevitable last-ditch stand which always follows any radical historical restructuring will give way to the necessary reforms. The "great grace of the twentieth century" (John Paul II) will once again bear fruit. Presently this is not the case and the clerical leadership of the Church has refused to heed the "signs of the times," those graced moments in the culture which illuminate the human condition and force Christian believers to say 'Yes' to the emergence of a fuller expression of God's revelation. Over one hundred years ago the official teaching of the Church rejected civil rights and religious liberty. Prior to that the papacy had endorsed slavery and usury. Gradually, as Gregory Baum, Canada's noted theologian reminds us, as the Church moves from "one ethical horizon to another," there is a discontinuity in her teaching. She learns and she changes. Few doubt that, for example, the present adamantine teaching on homosexuals and celibacy will stand the test of time or the soft winds of the Holy Spirit.

Baum, in his valuable little book *Amazing Church,* puts the present Ratzinger moment (without overtly naming him) in perspective for us.

It is quite true that popes and bishops who offer an inspiring interpretation of Catholicism do not make a great effort to put their teaching into practice. Nor do they halt the currents in the Church that betray universal solidarity. Still the official texts are there.

Baum, as a *peritus* at the Second Vatican Council, has never flagged in his enthusiasm for the great document, *Gaudium et Spes,* which stated, "The joys and the hopes, the griefs and anxieties of the people of this age, especially those who are poor or in any way afflicted, these too are the joys and hopes, the griefs and the anxieties of the followers of Christ."

The Church is a learner as well as a teacher. Aligning itself, as Jesus did, with societies' victims, it understands the dark side of the world, but, in entering into a deep solidarity with the victims, profound graces bring forth new insights and holy energy which allows it to renew itself and change.

It is the contention of this essay that the present pope has set his face against the "signs of the times" – in particular those signs regarding the role of women, contraception, human sexuality, church governance and justice. For many Catholics, it will be the last straw. The optics of the conclave with aging celibate men dressed in medieval costumes parading into the Sistine Chapel spoke volumes to the modern mind, particularly to half the human race not represented.

Let us look at Joseph Ratzinger, Benedict XVI, and while drawing conclusions let us be open to the new which has always surprised us. It is our hope that this still may happen, but a realistic glance inhibits our enthusiasm.

Ratzinger's Early Life is a Clue

Joseph Ratzinger was born in a small provincial town in Bavaria, Germany. His father Joseph, the town policeman, was fifty years old at his birth. According to his famous son in his book *Milestones,* the father was a harsh law-and-order cop, a man "of excessive strictness." The young Joseph, an extremely sensitive child, hopeless at sports, found his refuge in the ordered life of liturgy and the beauty of Mozart's music. With the rise of Hitler, and the beginning of the war, he entered the minor seminary at the age of twelve, immersing himself in his studies and the liturgy. This came to a halt in 1941 when he was drafted into the Hitler Youth and, in 1944, at the age of seventeen, the army. He never saw active service, as the war ended in April 1945. In November he entered the diocesan seminary.

As biographer David Gibson (*The Rise of Benedict,* Harper San Francisco) notes, Ratzinger has always been defensive about his family's role in the Nazi era. While describing his father as a staunch foe of the Nazis, he made no public protest. That was left to others like the local pastor, the fiery Josef Stelzle, arrested for his prophetic rejection of the new "Aryan Christ" who denied that Jesus was "the child of Jews." Stelzle was expelled from Träunstein but survived the war. He is never mentioned by Ratzinger. Nor does Ratzinger mention, according to literary critic Carlin Romano (quoted by Gibson), the slave labour camp 12 kilometres from Träunstein – much less the notorious sign which hung in the town square: "Do not buy from the Jew. He sells you, farmers, out of house and home." No mention of Kristilnacht when Jewish homes were attacked in Träunstein. While positively ecstatic about his family and Bavaria in general, the future pope filters out the ugly side of those years. Gibson concludes (and this would become a pattern), "The Nazi experience ... reinforced in him a kind of distancing, a pattern of removing himself from unpleasantness, isolating the pure ideal – of the faith, the church, the family, the nation – from the inevitable corruptions of the world."

Joseph Ratzinger's now famous theme of the rejection of the "culture of relativism" seems to find its own rationalization in the incorruptible citadel of truth, Catholicism. This would be his constant lodestar, his unerring compass. Only the pure form of faith, defined by him, can stand against the world and the Father of Lies, Satan.

The writer John Allen Jr., generally a church loyalist, was harsher than Gibson in discussing Ratzinger's fanatical purging of Catholic intellectuals in his role as Papal enforcer: "Having seen fascism in action Ratzinger today believes that the best antidote to political totalitarianism is ecclesiastical totalitarianism."

The key to Ratzinger is to be found in his early life, his willing escape from life's harshness, his retreat into very often Platonic realms of pure abstraction. What we will see is a life almost totally lived within the intellectual cocoon of the Roman Catholic Church, the only real bulwark against the realm of Untruth. To this young Joseph Ratzinger would devote his life, but as we will see it is a life virtually devoid of human experience and, as we know, there is a terrible price to be paid for inventing the human.

Bernard Häring: An Interesting Contrast

During the time that the innocent schoolboy Ratzinger was making his way back to the shelter of his family's arms and the security of the Roman Church, a giant of Catholic morality was trudging across Europe, a medic/chaplain who was much loved (and saved) by Poles and Russians, the putative enemy of the Third Reich. Bernard Häring (b.1912), fifteen years older than Ratzinger, came to opposite conclusions about theology, moral reasoning and church reform. Though it is beyond the purview of this essay, Fr. Häring aptly sums up the differences:

"What most influenced my thinking about moral theology was the mindset and criminal obedience of Christians to Hitler, a madman and a tyrant. This led me to the conviction that the character of a Christian must not be formed one-sidedly by a leitmotif of obedience but rather by a discerning responsibility, a capacity to respond courageously to new values and new needs and a readiness to take the risk." (*Free and Faithful in Christ*, 1978)

Häring later was appalled at the "creeping infallibilism" of the John Paul II pontificate, an almost hysterical attempt to define non-infallible teachings as dogma. Like so many others, Häring became a marked man for his loving criticism of the Church. He watched in disgust as Joseph Ratzinger, chief guard dog of the Holy Office, purged theologian after theologian from Catholic faculties.

Ratzinger from 1950 -1970

Joseph Ratzinger was ordained in 1951 and spent a troublesome year as a parish priest. The everyday lives of ordinary Germans, particularly in the hurly-burly post-war years, were simply not his cup of tea. It was the academy which would be his future. The rest of his life would be spent cosseted behind the safe and secure walls of tenured professorships, with a brief unsatisfying time as archbishop of Munich. Then there was his life in the Curia, all the time served by his unmarried sister Maria, who died in 1991. Such a life, albeit in the service to the Church, runs a terrible risk of unreality, almost a divorce from the daily struggles of ordinary people. Here there is a great potential to reinvent the human. There often appears in the life of Joseph Ratzinger an ethereal abstract quality.

Ratzinger's formidable gifts of erudition and general knowledge, combined with a stylistic elegance, brought him to the attention of Josef Frings, the Cardinal Archbishop of Cologne. The latter took the 35-year-old Ratzinger with him to Rome in 1962 as his theological advisor at the Second Vatican Council. There the young German seemed to catch the spirit of the Reformers, backing positions he would later disavow – such as collegiality, the use of the college of bishops as collaborators in the Petrine ministry and the use of synods ("a permanent council in miniature") or mini-Councils which would help the Church hear the grassroots. At this time he said that the Pope had a "moral obligation to consult the voice of the Church universal." To read the early Ratzinger is literally to be astonished at his later volte-face. Few today would guess the present pope as the author of the following:

"The servility of the sycophant – false prophets – as they were branded by the true Old Testament prophets, those who shy from and shun every collision, who prize above all their calm complacency is not true obedience. What the church needs are not adulators of the status quo, but men whose humility and obedience are not less than their passion for the truth." – 1962

"Conscience is the supreme and ultimate tribunal, even beyond the official church, and it must be obeyed." – 1966

In that year of revolution 1968, Professor Ratzinger was one of 1,360 Catholic theologians who signed a statement that called for open proceedings against any theologian suspected of nonconformity with Rome. The accused should have a bill of rights, a right to counsel, to representation among those scrutinizing his work, to judgment on the whole of his work, taken in proper context – in other words, due process. All of these rights would later vanish in the secretive shadows of the Holy Office when Ratzinger took on the office of what many styled as "The Grand Inquisitor."

One would be most interested if after 25 years of the hounding of theologians the pope would still adhere to the words he supported in 1968, that: "Any form of inquisition, however subtle, not only harms the development of a sound theology, it also causes irreparable damage to the credibility of the church as a community in the modern world."

Many posit 1968 as the year that Ratzinger began to change. It was the time of worldwide student revolts which were being played out in "the summer of love," a name the bookish professor would never recognize. He would not be the first reactionary unable to separate the authentic wheat from the transient chaff. Suffice to say, the excesses of the zeitgeist really stuck in the craw of the cerebral professor, then teaching at Tübingen. Instead of seeing the excesses for what they were, a temporary exuberance which would run its course in due time, Ratzinger's aesthetic senses were deeply assaulted and insulted. Most professors could shake this off, but he never did. As one of his former students said to Ratzinger biographer John Allen Jr. (*The Rise of Benedict XVI*, Doubleday): "Suddenly Ratzinger saw these new ideas were connected to violence and a destruction of the order of what came before. He was simply no longer able to bear it." Colleague Hans Kung remarked about this unpleasant time, "For a timid personality it was horrifying." Ratzinger's shocking comment on this time, which casts a negative judgment on other theologians, was this: "Anyone who wanted to remain a progressive in this context had to give up his integrity."

The "timid professor" left Tübingen for the more quiet campus of Regensberg. Each summer through the 70s Ratzinger taught a course at the Gustav Siewerth Academie, a very right-wing seminar closely tied to apocalyptic Marian prophecies. In 1976 he was elected to the archbishopric of Munich where he stayed for four years. All reports maintain that he never clicked at all with the clergy. It was also in Munich that Ratzinger displayed the intolerance for creative theologians which he would take into the "The meaning of prophecy is the protest against the self-righteousness of the institutions. God throughout history has not been on the side of the institutions but on that of the suffering and the persecuted."

Munich, Metz and Rahner

Johann Baptist Metz was and is one of those "progressive" theologians whom no one in theological circles believed had "lost his integrity." Developing a branch of theology called political theology which insisted that Christians must engage in justice, Metz, a former colleague and friend of Ratzinger, was acknowledged as one of Germany's great theologians. The first choice of the senate of the University of Munich to replace a retiring professor, Metz saw his hopes dashed when Archbishop Ratzinger quashed the appointment. This set off a firestorm in Germany, and in an uncharacteristic public outburst Germany's greatest theologian and a giant of Vatican II, Karl Rahner, publicly blasted Ratzinger in a newspaper article:

"You had no reason for rejecting Metz. You yourself had previously offered him an identical position at Wartzburg. What grounds do you have to justify your reversal now? Is the real reason Metz's political theology? This violation of a century-old tradition in the manner of appointing professors makes a farce out of your responsibility to protect academic freedom."

Rahner was outraged over the ecclesiastical power play which would become a signature of Ratzinger in the Congregation for the Doctrine of the Faith (CDF, the former Holy Office): a condemnation with no formal hearing.

Rahner stated the obvious: "The average Christian often has the bitter impression that his faith-inspired loyalty to the church is abused. And yet, he knows that he is powerless before the law. In society in such a case one can legitimately revolt against misused power. But not so for the believing Christian. We can truly say that that sensitivity to basic human rights must still develop within the church."

When Ratzinger was summoned to Rome to be the chief enforcer of dogmatic purity in the Holy Office he would continue his merciless assault on theologians. Rather than relying on peer review and trusting the legitimate role of theologians to gradually advance new responses to changing horizons, Ratzinger disciplined over one hundred theologians under the new pontificate. In the evaluation of many, Catholic theology came to a standstill and what Rahner calls a new "ice age" had begun. Ratzinger in 1981 was summoned to the CDF as John Paul II's "bad cop."

Paul Collins, a leading priest intellectual in Australia, resigned his priesthood in 2001 as a protest against the radical narrowing of Catholic thought. For him the once-tolerant acceptance of "schools of thought" and an attention to the "signs of the times" promoted by Vatican II, has been replaced by a rigid sectarianism and by an inability "to understand, as does the historian, the 'stuff' of history, the people and processes, the unpredictability and serendipity. Their tendency is to 'absolutize,' to turn history into ideology." This is similar to the comment of Charles Curran, the much loved Catholic moralist who also had his licence to teach in a Catholic setting revoked. "The problem is that Cardinal Ratzinger has identified the truth with what the magisterium has taught at a given moment. The Holy Office cannot have a copyright on what it means to be a Catholic."

Vatican II was exceptionally forceful on reading the "signs of the times" and interpreting them in the light of the gospel. It was this very openness to the world that traumatized Ratzinger. For him the world was fallen and the Catholic Church had succumbed to the naïve optimism of the 60s. This is a false understanding of the so-called naïve optimism.

Ganz Schwarz

For many in Germany Ratzinger is simply *ganz schwarz* – way too black and pessimistic. As a matter of fact he would certainly fit into the category of doomsayers which Pope John XXIII mentioned in his early remarks on the Council in September 1962:

"In the daily exercise of our pastoral office, we sometimes have to listen, much to our regret, to voices of persons who, though burning with zeal, are not endowed with too much sense of discretion or measure. In these modern times they can see nothing but prevarication and ruin. They say that our era, in comparison with past eras, is getting worse, and they behave as though they had learned nothing from history, which is, nonetheless, the teacher of life. They behave as though at the time of former Councils everything was a full triumph for the Christian idea and life and for proper religious liberty.

"We feel we must disagree with those prophets of gloom, who are always forecasting disaster, as though the end of the world were at hand.

"In the present order of things, Divine Providence is leading us to a new order of human relations which, by men's own efforts and even beyond their very expectations, are directed toward the fulfillment of God's superior and inscrutable designs. And everything, even human differences, leads to the greater good of the Church."

The pope who followed John, Paul VI, shared much of John's positive Thomism. He too was convinced that: "The Gospel is light, it is newness, it is energy, it is rebirth, it is salvation."(1964)

Ratzinger has always admitted that he is "a decided Augustinian." His academic work was focused on the brilliant Church Father (d.430 CE) who wrote in the declining years of the Roman Empire. Augustine was deeply pessimistic about human nature. Rather than focusing on humanity's goodness and seeing in creation (which included our ability to reason and our free will) a beneficent God, Augustine saw the world as fundamentally flawed and the material world as evil. Perhaps Ratzinger, given his coming of age in the ruins of World War II, saw the world as absolutely alienated from God. A case can certainly be made for at least understanding this orientation, but Bernard Häring came to a more positive conclusion. For Ratzinger, like Augustine, error almost has no rights, and like the great Church Father he might have to *cogere intrare* (compel them to come in, see opening quote). John XXIII rejected this heavy-handed approach – the same one that Ratzinger adopted with so many church theologians. Listen further to John's remarks from 1962:

"The truth of the Lord will remain forever. We see, in fact, as one age succeeds another, that the opinions of men follow one another and exclude each other. And often errors vanish as quickly as they arise, like fog before the sun. The Church has always opposed these errors. Frequently she has condemned them with the greatest severity. Nowadays, however, the Spouse of Christ prefers to make use of the medicine of mercy rather than that of severity."

Ratzinger, seemingly with complete equanimity, displayed little mercy in his medicine chest as he proscribed theologian after theologian in his ruthless attempt to remake the Church in his own narrow image. Many found their health broken and their reputations in tatters as they attempted to follow John XXIII's advice to recast ancient doctrines into contemporary thought.

"The substance of the ancient doctrine of the deposit of faith is one thing, and the way in which it is presented is another. And it is the latter that must be taken into great consideration with patience if necessary, everything being measured in the forms and proportions of a magisterium which is predominantly pastoral in character."

"Signs of the Times"

Joseph Ratzinger is in need of a more balanced view of the "signs of the times" – always to be judged in light of the gospel. The zeitgeist of any age brings forth the good and the bad, the transient and the eternal. For the Church not to acknowledge the constant working of the Holy Spirit would be theological suicide and a recipe for static irrelevance in the modern age. A case in example would be the gift of feminism to the Church. The great pastoral pope, John XXIII, flagged this in his 1963 encyclical *Pacem in Terris.*

"Women are gaining an increasing awareness of their natural dignity. Far from being content with a purely passive role or allowing themselves to be regarded as a kind of instrument, they are demanding both in domestic and in public life the rights and duties which belong to them as human persons."

It is quite obvious that The Church has yet to integrate this valuable insight into its teaching and its structures. Progressive theologians point to the adamantine refusal of Rome to acknowledge this as an "authentic sign of the time" which needs a like response from the Church. Lay people increasingly sophisticated, theologically aware and in deeper relationships with women, acknowledge this and approve of it in huge numbers on every continent. For Benedictine nun Joan Chittister, the "rising tide of women's claims to fullness of humanity are now clear in every part of the world" and men like Joseph Ratzinger who insist on demonizing this movement as "radical feminism" will be dismissed "for lack of insight, academic understanding and relevance."

Forty-four years after John XXIII pointed to the changing understanding of role of women as a potential sign of the time women still are not integrated with full rights into every level of the Church. Was this the breath of the Holy Spirit or another excess of the 60s zeitgeist? Bernard Häring, while not answering the question in his 1976 response to Vatican's charges against him, said this: "The signs of the times according to both the Second Vatican Council and the Vatican's own preparation to the 1974 synod stated that the signs of the times are to be considered a locus ... evangelization must pay attention to how God reveals His (sic) will through the signs of the times, God's ongoing self revelation in salvation history."

Häring, one of the giants of the Vatican II era, went on to state that all of this must be judged next to "Christ the decisive and final word which the Father speaks to humanity ... No knowledge of history will ever be able to surpass Christ ... The unfolding of the history of the world and the Church through the millennia can and should contribute to an awakening of the knowledge of Christ through its works and its progress in history. Christ does not become greater ... but our knowledge of the plan of salvation ... does become more complete and close to life in our heart through the working of the spirit in the history of the Church ... Therefore we must listen to the Word."

This is precisely the point. The "good cop" John Paul II was notorious for not listening to the world. In one famous instance in Germany when he was respectfully addressed by a young woman about the Church's failure to address women's rights, he prayed his rosary. Ratzinger is hardly better, so convinced is he that only the Catholic Church is in full possession of God's truth interpreted solely by the Magisterium. All other churches are "gravely deficient" as he stated in his (or JP II's) *Dominus Iesus* (2000). This was rejected out of hand by another giant of Vatican II, Cardinal Franz König. "The other Christian Churches are certainly not gravely deficient in the modern meaning of that term ... those horrible words sound offensive and crude." God as the inexhaustible Mystery can never be the exclusive property of one religion. In this sense Indian theologian Samuel Rayan, writing in a 1993 issue of *Concilium: International Journal for Theology,* has it right: "All religions are God's gift to his people imperfect in themselves ... the differences are as important as what in common they make for wealth and richness."

Papal Fundamentalism

One sometimes wonders about Ratzinger's staggering confidence about truth. It appears that for him the Spirit seems to be in the sole con-trol of the Petrine office rather than in the entire Church. This view owes more to the defensive "infallibilist" view of Vatican I where during an extraordinarily insecure period in the Church's history she chose to pro-tect the largely uneducated faithful from any error or whiff of ambiguity. The hierarchical Church with the pope as its infallible voice once and for all defined the objective truth. Since that time, aided by a revolution in the human sciences and a corresponding humility in the Church, such a crass understanding has fallen by the wayside – dialogue, revision, deep conver-sation and serious attempts to hear the Spirit's promptings in the lives of the baptized and indeed in all of creation have become the norm. This new modesty regarding "the incomprehensible Mystery" (Rahner) is at the core of Catholic belief today. Ambiguity and paradox, more often the approach of the Christian mystics and eastern religions, is the only way forward. The threat of such pluralism strikes Ratzinger with terror. It should not. We will always "see through a glass darkly" as Paul phrases it. After all we have four gospels, many schools of theology, endless images of Jesus.

It is tragic to watch the march of papal fundamentalism.

One wonders how Ratzinger can define as he has (*Ad tuendam fidem,* 1998) such open-ended issues as contraception, women priests and married clergy as basically infallible pronouncements. And then watch as he hammers anyone who dares dissent. Paul Collins, the Australian theologian, said this about Ratzinger (NCR. April 11, 1999) a year before he resigned from the priesthood:

"It would be great if we had a church where one could simply dismiss what inquisitors like Ratzinger say and do, but that's not Catholicism today. Too many real people are being hurt by his power plays, and somebody has to speak on their behalf. If our commitment to the marginalized means anything, it has to apply to the marginalized inside the church. That means challenging the likes of Ratzinger when they refuse to ordain women or when they silence theologians or in other ways try to squelch the gospel."

For Collins and other critics of Ratzinger it is his absolute failure to be open to the world and the Spirit working there which defines him. World War II seems to have proved definitively that "the world" had nothing to say. It was only the Catholic Church who prevailed against Hitler. In David Gibson's *The Rule of Benedict,* Ratzinger is quoted as saying:

"Despite many human failings the Church was the alternative to the destructive ideology of the brown rulers; in the inferno that had swallowed up the powerful, she had stood firm with a force coming to her from eternity."

This of course would be news to most historians ... and to Bernard Häring.

So terrified is Benedict XVI of any new truth emanating from the world that he virtually rules out any hope of newness. The much vaunted "Catholic identity" the present Roman bureaucracy trumpets can only be defined by Rome and it will use the most reprehensible, unChristlike actions to ensure this. Anybody who does not totally assent to the Roman line will be ignored, banished, humiliated by the proconsuls (bishops) who have been set in place to ensure this univocal diktat. A favourite tactic in the "provinces" is not even to respond to requests for meetings or personal letters. The strategy, as hard as it is to believe, is to cull the Church to the precious "little flock" who will be deemed the authentic Catholics. It is to weep at such stupidity.

The Little Flock

In interviews which go back decades Ratzinger reiterates that the future of the Church will be smaller, maybe "a mustard seed," where it will exist in small seemingly insignificant groups. These groups, of course, will be utterly loyal to anything which comes out of Rome. A necessary culling will be the order of the day, say like the 300,000 Catholics driven out by the archbishop of Cologne, Meissner. "Chaff and wheat must be separated," Ratzinger said to journalist Peter Seewald. While few expect Benedict XVI to mount a massive proscription of 'dissident' Catholics, the probability is that the docile bishops promoted in the past 25 years will, by their increasingly irrelevant navel gazing and authoritarian centralization, drive progressives out.

The "little flock" concept seems a polar opposite to James Joyce's definition of Catholicism as "Here comes everybody" and Jesus' very own injunction to ignore the 99 and go seeking the lost one. In a brilliant small book written after Vatican II, Karl Rahner had this to say about "the little flock:"

"When we speak of ourselves today as the beginning of a 'little flock,' we first remove a misunderstanding. 'Little flock' does not mean a ghetto or a sect, since these are defined by a mentality: a mentality which the church can afford in the future even less than today. A sectarian or ghetto mentality is propagated among us – not under this label, but under the pretext that we are becoming Christ's little flock which has to profess the folly of faith and of the cross. Any deviation must be fought with the utmost severity in the name of true faith and authentic Christianity.

"If we talk of the 'little flock' in order to defend our cosy traditionalism and stale pseudo-orthodoxy, in fear of the mentality of modern society; if we tacitly consent to the departure of restless, questioning people from the church so that we can return to our repose and orderly life, and everything becomes as it was before, we are propagating, not the attitude proper to

Christ's little flock, but a petty sectarian mentality. This is dangerous because it shows up, not under its true name but in an appeal to orthodoxy, church-loyalty and strict, Rome-dictated morality."

The "cosy traditionalism and stale orthodoxy" are thin gruel for a pilgrim Church marching through history. This narrow view of the Church is alienating too many of the Catholic faithful who long for something like John XXIII's magnanimous and invitational "medicine of mercy." We need a pope, not of the little flock but the big tent. Ratzinger, *"ganz schwarz,"* with his abstract, ethereal theology hardly ever filtered through life, has simply shown up at the wrong time.

There are other popes Benedict might emulate at this time. In 1964 Pope Paul VI wrote a brilliant encyclical on dialogue. His main points are still worth taking very seriously:

"The dialogue of salvation did not physically force anyone to accept it; it was a tremendous appeal of love which, although placing a vast responsibility on those toward whom it was directed, nevertheless left them free to respond to it or to reject it.

"But it seems to us that the relationship of the Church to the world, without precluding other legitimate forms of expression, can be represented better in a dialogue,

"79. This type of relationship indicates a proposal of courteous esteem, of understanding and of goodness on the part of the one who inaugurates the dialogue; it excludes the a priori condemnation, the offensive and time-worn polemic and emptiness of useless conversation. If this approach does not aim at effecting the immediate conversion of the interlocutor, inasmuch as it respects both his dignity and his freedom, nevertheless it does aim at helping him, and tries to dispose him for a fuller sharing of sentiments and convictions."

"81. The dialogue is, then, a method of accomplishing the apostolic mission. It is an example of the art of spiritual communication. Its characteristics are the following:

"(1) Clearness above all; the dialogue supposes and demands comprehensibility. It is an outpouring of thought; it is an invitation to the exercise of the highest powers which man possesses. This very claim would be enough to classify the dialogue among the best manifestations of human activity and culture.

"(2) A second characteristic of the dialogue is its meekness, the virtue which Christ sets before us to be learned from Him: "Learn of me, because I am meek and humble of heart."[Matthew 11:29] The dialogue is not proud, it is not bitter, it is not offensive. Its authority is intrinsic to the truth it explains, to the charity it communicates, to the example it proposes; it is not a command, it is not an imposition. It is peaceful; it avoids violent methods; it is patient; it is generous."

"85. Many, indeed, are the forms that the dialogue of salvation can take. It adapts itself to the needs of a concrete situation, it chooses the appropriate means, it does not bind itself to ineffectual theories and does not cling to hard and fast forms when these have lost their power to speak to men and move them.

"And before speaking, it is necessary to listen, not only to a man's voice, but to his heart. A man must first be understood; and, where he merits it, agreed with. In the very act of trying to make ourselves pastors, fathers and teachers of men, we must make ourselves their brothers. The spirit of dialogue is friendship and, even more, is service. All this we must remember and strive to put into practice according to the example and commandment that Christ left to Us."

It is difficult to see much of this dialogue in Joseph Ratzinger.

Leo XIII (1878-1903) could be a second teacher to the present pope. He acknowledged that his pontificate was successful because: "I was never afraid to appoint as bishop somebody who disagreed with me." There is something extremely disquieting about Ratzinger's clinical evisceration of so many creative theologians who disagree with him. Do we really think these men do not love the Church as he does? Does not the fact that so many had their reputations trashed, their health endangered bother this Mozart-loving prelate? Do we really believe that the God of Mystery can be so limited to the univocal voice of brother Ratzinger? Many of us share the respected theologian from Chicago Fr. David Tracy's view that "Cardinal

Ratzinger seems to be conducting a campaign to impose a particular the-ology upon the universal Church and upon all theologians. It won't work."

No it won't work, because in the words of another great churchman of years ago, J.B. Phillips, "Your God is too small." The God of Life, the God of History and that God's Holy Spirit who "blows where it wills" (John 3:8) is no captive of the Catholic Church. That Spirit is working through univer-sal justice movements and the humanization of the world. These are the "signs of the times" which the Church needs to attend to, one less Catholic and more catholic, another pilgrim for justice and agent for God's reign.

We do not need a little flock "purified of anthropological, sociological or horizontal accents" but a Church like its Jewish founder, who emptied himself for God and God's project. This is the only Church which makes any sense and one Joseph Ratzinger believed in when he said in 1962: "The meaning of prophecy is the protest against the self-righteousness of the institutions. God throughout history has not been on the side of the insti-tutions but on that of the suffering and the persecuted."

CELIBACY:
HARDLY A
NEW TESTAMENT VALUE

Beginning in the mid-1980s Catholics were again and again scandalized by the growing phenomenon of priest paedophilia. This tsunami of abuse reached epic proportions in the first years of the new millennium. Much of the revelations crystallized in the Boston area around three notorious abuser priests – James Porter, John Geoghan and Paul Shanley. The thorough reporting of these heinous crimes in a largely Catholic area resulted in a Pulitzer Prize for *The Boston Globe* and the disgrace and fall of the powerful Boston Cardinal, Bernard Law.

In like manner, the Philadelphia diocese imploded in September 2005, with the long-awaited release of a grand jury's exhaustive report. As in Boston, the staggering results have permanently impaired the reputation of a papal loyalist, in this case Cardinal Anthony Bevilacqua. The findings of the investigation show how "dozens of priests sexually abused hundreds of children" and "were excused and enabled" by the Archdiocese of Philadelphia and its leaders, Bevilacqua and his predecessor John Krol.

As this catastrophe was unfolding, probably the worst ecclesial disaster since the Reformation, the faithful were also jolted by the phenomenal abrogation of duty by a new breed of bishop, whose primary loyalty was seen to be the protection of the institution rather than the well being of defenceless children and the heartbreak of families. Priest Donald Cozzens in his book *Sacred Silence* (Liturgical Press, 2002) reckons that the scandal has directly touched one hundred thousand victims and – with family factored in – about one million people. Add to this the disgust and dismay of parishioners and you have a full-blown crisis. The fiscal implications, while pale in comparison to the pastoral, nevertheless are considerable. In the US alone it is estimated that about $1 billion has been drained from Church coffers. The only positive side of this has been the increased demands of lay people in dismantling archaic clerical structures which have isolated the ordained from those in the pews.

The somnolent laity, too long codependent and enablers of patriarchal and clerical control of the people of God, quickly organized themselves in the US and demanded serious change in the way the Church operates. The paedophilia/bishop leadership crisis had inevitably led to some serious analysis of deep structural problems, namely that because of the depleted ranks of male celibate priests (one half of the world's parishes do not have a resident priest), many misfits who should have been fired were kept on the job. To alleviate the crisis, the American bishops, weakened by obsessive loyalty to Roman policies and cowed by an authoritarian pope, were loathe to raise the obvious conclusion that celibacy was not working. Long ago, the laity had recognized the "elephant in the sacristy" and were not afraid to name it. Except for the courageous few, why did the majority of the episcopate fall silent? Why had they forgotten that a bishop is not a servant but a brother? Why had they become mere stenographers for the Bishop of Rome? Tragically, as a whole they embodied the wishes of Pius XI who famously said, *"Io non voglio collaboratori ma esecutori."* ("I do not want collaborators but those who will execute my orders.")

It seems the bishops were terrified of even addressing the issue, as it would look like disloyalty to the pope and would call into question the fact that 80 percent of those who were abused were male adolescents. This admission would highlight the fact that large numbers of Catholic clergy are homosexual. Though gays are no more predisposed to molest than straights, and homosexuality is not the cause of the abuse, there are simply a very high number of gays in the priesthood. While one should not prescind from this that homosexuality is the cause of paedophilia (the abuse of young male adolescents), to even question the cornerstone of Church organization would lead God knows where. Possibly to a change in the celibacy requirements for priesthood? Possibly to a recognition that the Holy Spirit of God might be signaling (gasp!) that it is time for the radical equality of leadership roles at every level of the Church? Might this not be the inclusion which the Gospel demands today?

Raising this thorny issue despite its obvious cogency would be an episcopal career ender. Only the secure bishops had done so in the past. In 1985, the great cardinal of Brazil, Paulo Evaristo Arns, had earnestly delivered a letter from the Brazilian episcopacy imploring the pope to relax the celibacy requirements. The pope rudely tore the letter up in front of the embarrassed cardinal. Similarly, John Paul II pounded the table when Canadian Bishop Remi De Roo said that he thought the Church was sacrificing the Eucharist on the altar of celibacy. Many also recall the pope sitting in cold fury in 1979 as Sr. Theresa Kane suggested ministry should also be open to women. Now of course, such common sense requests are seen by papal sycophants as "disloyalty."

The attempts of so many committed Church people to drag the Church into the 21st Century should be contrasted with the irrational and cruel harshness of the episcopal class toward dissent or even suggestions that celibacy, ministry, and sexual ethics need to be dramatically rethought. Witness the episcopal pillorying of priest Ed Cachia of the Peterborough Diocese in Ontario. In response to a reporter's question about women being ordained, Fr. Cachia had the actual gall to welcome them and suggest it might open a dialogue in the broader Church.

The Fear of Paul VI

The modern-day aversion to raising the issue can be traced to Pope Paul VI's intervention in the midst, not only of the Second Vatican Council, but also at the height of the 1960s – that decade of sexual liberation. On June 12, 1965, the French paper *Le Monde* published a leaked draft of a speech by a Brazilian bishop by the name of Koop. Desperately short of clergy, the good bishop asked the council to permit married priests to augment the diminishing number in his diocese. Koop's heartfelt plea would be later repeated by dozens of realistic bishops around the

Catholic world. Canada's own Alex Carter, the late bishop of North Bay, made a similar plea at the synod of 1971. Ever the realist, Carter was looking for help among the indigenous peoples of his diocese where celibacy simply was not accepted. In conversation with me over a decade ago, the affable Carter chuckled at the shock his request evinced from the Italian and Spanish hierarchies: "They almost crapped." (Yes, we used to have bishops like that.) Similarly, our bishops of the north have repeatedly been turned down by an intransigent Vatican.

Paul VI, aware that the request by Koop was about to hit the conciliar floor, pre-empted the world's bishops by refusing to allow even a discussion of the issue. Gary Wills in his book *Papal Sin: Structures of Deceit* (Doubleday 2000) quotes the Vatican peritus, Fr. Rene Laurentin, who wrote an article in *Le Figaro* at that time. The scholarly priest, the author of over one hundred books, basically said that the reason that the Vatican would not consider the end of celibacy was that any concession here would force the Church to deal with the thousands of priests who had mistresses all over the Catholic world. The Church at its highest echelons knew then that any serious discussion of this boiling issue would lead most thinking people to second curial Cardinal Franjo Seper's honest admission (1971), "I have no confidence that celibacy is working." Two years after the pope's refusal to air the question, he wrote an encyclical on the topic, supposedly to end the discussion.

This papal letter makes for tortuous reading. Much of Paul's reasoning hinges on the Matthean line (19:12) about "eunuchs for the kingdom of heaven." Many scholars find this line problematic as a saying of Jesus (it is only found in Matthew). Taken in context the passage emphasizes the values of marriage and children. Although it is impossible to flesh this out here, we can safely say that the eunuch metaphor has nothing to do with lifelong celibacy and probably nothing to do with celibacy itself. There simply is no interest in the Gospels about celibacy. As well, as several scholars have pointed out, the concept of voluntary renunciation of marriage is virtually unheard of in Judaism. While Pope Paul, a deeply sensitive churchman, certainly believed that celibacy was a "jewel," his use of the New Testament to prove his point seems less than forthright.

Only three places refer to celibacy in the New Testament. Paul cites but does not quote two of them. In 1 Timothy 3:2 it states, "A bishop must be irreproachable, the husband of only one wife," and virtually the same in Titus. What is shocking is the evangelist Paul's remark, "Do we not have the right to take a Christian wife like the rest of the apostles?" (1 Corinthians 9:5). Though Paul says he has not made use of this right (v.15), the truth is the disciples and apostles were not celibate (eunuchs for the reign), nor were priests celibate – for eleven hundred years.

The proclamation of the Gospel and true discipleship has nothing to do with celibacy, and the embarrassing lengths to which the Church has gone in insisting on this mandatory discipline has done little for the people of God. In the end it has starved the people of Eucharist, increased the exodus of heterosexual priests who left to marry, and left behind a predominantly gay priesthood, many of whom serve the Church with zeal and dignity. Yet now it appears they too are becoming the scapegoat for the paedophilia crisis.

CELIBACY:
A HISTORICAL FAILURE
WITH TOO HIGH A PRICE

Ecclesiastical celibacy is not a dogma. The scriptures do not impose it.
It is even easy to effect the change. I take up a pen, I sign a decree,
and the next day, priests who wish to may get married.
John XXIII

Studies have consistently shown that the main reason for a dearth of candidates in the Roman Catholic priesthood is the celibacy requirement. The great Pope John XXIII stated he could end it with a stroke of his pen. The time was not ripe for the sainted pope, but it assuredly is today.

Nobody questions that effective ministry need be coupled with celibacy. Our Orthodox and Uniate relatives as well as our Protestant and Jewish cousins seem to get along quite well without it. Granted marriage by itself does not confer effective leadership on a community either, but why this adamantine refusal to countenance a relaxation of a medieval demand? One reason of course was the ferocious personal commitment to the discipline by the late Pope John Paul II. There can be no doubt that Karol Wojtyla lived his celibacy in an heroic manner, yet the personal predilection and iron discipline of a pope should never override the wisdom and wishes and demonstrable needs of the whole Church. The simple fact is the insistence on celibacy has had grave consequences for the credibility of the Church.

Quite simply, celibacy does not work and has not worked, and the pretence that all is well is badly damaging the credibility of the Roman

Church. The explosive sex abuse scandal has once again focused people's attention on this "precious jewel," as Paul VI termed it. And while celibacy cannot be deemed the reason for such widespread sex abuse, there can be no doubt the unresolved and unsuccessful integration of sexuality is a major cause.

In the past (from 1139 CE onward), celibacy was merely the price that many paid for priesthood. For many it was a necessary burden which came with the territory. Many seemingly succeeded largely because of the extraordinary seamlessness of the Catholic culture – the great respect with which priests were held, their status unquestioned in the community along with the many unearned perks they received as "men of the cloth." The iron discipline and hierarchical nature of the Church was a given, as was the overall culture conservatism of repressed sexuality. The legalist author-itarianism structure was tacitly accepted by Catholics who found them-selves in a largely Protestant culture. All this changed with the 1960s. The Second Vatican Council, described by English historian Eamon Duffy as "the most revolutionary Christian event since the Reformation," pro-claimed that holiness was endemic to every state in life. Celibates had no great claim to virtue or holiness. Marriage now was championed as much for its mutuality as its procreational function. Celibates began to feel alone and unsure of themselves. The mass exodus of priests began, the over-whelming percentage so that they could marry.

Celibacy always had been a burden, but had been propped up by the Catholic culture. It is commonly accepted that the most talented men left the priesthood, leaving many of the remnant angry, confused, and bitter. They had to work along with the genuinely fine priests who had made their peace with the hard discipline. With the cultural props disappearing, and with a more holistic view of sexuality appearing, celibacy's casualties became more obvious. The higher rate of alcoholism in the priesthood was revealed. One did not have to be Freud to observe the deleterious effects of celibacy – the "dried prunes" of crotchety pastors, their often-stunted emotional lives along with their loss of affectivity and capacity for laugh-ter. Too many were obviously suffering a low-level depression. Michael

Crosby quotes fellow Capuchin Martin Pables' reference to "low-level hostility" among some clergy. "They are not angry people; they are quietly and passively resentful. They resent the burdens of celibacy, the ineptness of religious leadership, the confusion of theology and the ingratitude of the faithful."

Crosby also points to process addictions among clergy – gambling, shopping, working, and exercise. The most severe, of course, is the power addictions which surfaced in the sex abuse scandals. While this is not the subject of our exploration here, it is necessary to point out the obvious problems which celibacy has brought. In my previous essay I referred to the huge examples of concubinage existing in Africa and Latin America, not to mention that, given the mass exodus of healthy heterosexuals and the obvious homosocial environment of the clerical life, we now have a predominantly gay priesthood. While this should not be seen as condemnatory of homosexuals, serious questions certainly need to be asked about such high percentages.

Why Celibacy in the First Place?

As we know the Church came out of Judaism as a reform movement led by Jesus, a liberal Pharisee. In the Jewish world, celibacy, the voluntary renunciation of marriage, is an utterly foreign concept. This is so obvious that we need not discuss it. "Be fruitful and multiply" was a duty, particularly in a world where longevity was not known.

Judaism, however, like many movements of antiquity was radically affected by the dualism of Greek culture. From Pythagoras (6th century BCE) to Plato (d. 347 BCE), the body is suspect while the soul is elevated and noble. We know Plato had a huge influence on Christianity with its distrust of matter and the body. We shall see this in the writings of the Church fathers later.

Historian Joseph Swain tells us that "a wave of asceticism swept over the whole Greek world in the first century BCE." Philosophical schools like the Epicureans and Stoics promulgated celibacy. Stoicism, the greatest school of ancient philosophy, had its most profound impact from 300 BCE to 250 CE. Stoicism naturally lauded celibacy over marriage. A true Stoic like Seneca (d. 65 CE) could write that one "resists the assault of passions and does not allow himself to be swept into the marital act." Pliny the Elder (d. 79 CE) praised the elephant for mating only every two years! All over the Mediterranean pagan priests observed purity laws, denying themselves sexual intercourse before the sacred ablutions were performed. The Vestal Virgins were honoured in Rome and the largest mystery cult of that time, that of Mithras, championed the unmarried state.

Uta Ranke-Heinemann writes that "the negative assessment of sexual pleasure in the two centuries after Christ was further strengthened by the invasion of pessimism ... which came out of the east ... and would prove to be the most dangerous competition for Christianity. This we know as Gnosticism." The latter movement greatly exacerbated the distrust of the senses and the hatred of the body which so infected the new religion. The only worthy part of the human is the spark of light from another world, the soul. The body was "the grave you carry around with you." A further departure from God's good creation you could not find – and Gnosticism's denigration of corporality had a deadly effect. Marcion, a Christian Gnostic leader (c. 140 CE) identified sex with evil matter. For Marcion, Jesus could not have been born through the sex act and probably floated down from heaven. He himself was celibate and demanded the same of his followers. Though he had a large impact on the early Church, Marcion's extreme sexual asceticism got him bounced from the Church of Rome in 144 CE. In the desert area of Syria the Encratites held sway and they, too, deeply influenced the early Church. For them marriage was "polluted and a foul way of life."

Although the Church rejected the most extreme of these teachings, there is no doubt that she was radically influenced by them. The year 150 CE is chosen by historian Peter Brown as a Rubicon in this area. By then the powerful life-affirming and positive influence of Judaism had begun to wane, and the dualism and pessimism of the Hellenic world became dominant within Christianity, especially in the areas of marriage and sexuality.

Looking back we see nothing in the apostolic community which wedded celibacy to the essentials of Christianity. The earliest witness, Paul, says he received nothing from the Lord on this matter. The canonical Gospels do not raise the issue. The first apostles and leaders were all married. We know nothing of Jesus' marital state and the fact that nothing is said in the gospels about his traditional single state probably indicates that he more than likely was married. The writers assuredly would have commented on an itinerant Jewish rabbi who was unmarried. The Gospels are simply disinterested in biography. Other than the fact that we know Jesus had brothers (Mark 6:3) we know little of his biographical details. The Gospels are simply not that type of literature. They are proclamations, sermon fragments, testimonies of His lordship. There is so little material about his life that there is much we simply cannot know. What we have in traditional spiritual writing is well recognized today as sentimental conjecture with no historical basis. The eminent Notre Dame theologian Richard McBrien phrases it well: "Is it possible he was married? Yes … and without any compromise of the church's historic faith in him as truly God and truly, truly human." That the Church had a vested interest in proclaiming his single celibate status is beyond question. Infected by the Gnostic pessimism described above and the denigration of the body, the early Church fathers (and most especially the giant Augustine) elevated celibacy over the married state.

Virgin Birth

As Christianity moved into the Hellenic world hobbled by the pagan asceticism above, and as the Hebraic unity of flesh and spirit was broken apart by this new anti-body sentiment, sexual abstinence was elevated to new heights.

As early as 310 CE, the Council of Elvira (Spain) was the first Church council to attempt to separate the sacred from the sexual and establish a clerical elite. Prominent of course in this whole area has been the use of the Virgin Birth story as a welcome support to the superiority of the single state and the degrading of sex. The story, unknown to Paul and to Mark, was interpolated into the Christian scriptures at a late date. The early Church theologian Justin Martyr simply understood the myth as parallel to other Mediterranean stories about superstars like Plato, Alexander and Augustus who, it was said, were sired by gods copulating with women. The story is about Jesus, not Mary – his uniqueness, his singularity and deep origin in God. Nobody in the first century would have taken it as history. Yet the beautiful myth of "God's paternity" often seen in Hebrew Scriptures (Isaiah 43:6-7, Hosea 1:10) was literalized. The poetry that new life was "fathered" in Mary by God's spirit has been rendered dead by fundamentalism. Even the genius Aquinas, a man of his time, had fallen prey to this anti-sex bias. In response to Jerome's nemesis Helvidius (c. 380 CE), who dared to suggest that Joseph had sex with Mary after the birth of Jesus, Aquinas huffed, "This error is an insult to the Holy Ghost whose shrine was the virginal womb wherein he had formed the flesh of Christ: wherefore it was unbecoming that it should be desecrated by intercourse with man." (Summa lll.28.3)

Here we see something which should not shock us. Aquinas, the greatest doctor of the Church, breathed in quite naturally the noxious fumes of the Church's anti-body history. Today this need not trouble us. But to insist on celibacy and an all-male celibate priesthood is to ignore the persistent promptings of the Holy Spirit.

Augustinian Legacy

Augustine, the towering Church father of the fourth century, seemed consumed by his supposed sexual depravity (though not his abandoning of his concubine) and handed on to posterity his sexual pessimism, his linking of sin and sex. It was Augustine who gave the name *pudenda* to our genitals. The Latin translation means "to be ashamed."

For Augustine, the Virgin Birth myth proved to be a perfect canister to safeguard Jesus' absolutely pure birth. No human contact. No sexual arousal as Jesus was conceived. Behold the only human not to pass on "the original sin" of Adam. It is impossible to estimate the staggering effect this negative teaching has had on generations of Christians. Lost to history are the writings of Augustine's antagonist Julian, the son of a bishop and married to a bishop's daughter. Julian rejected Augustine's negative view of sexual desire and original sin. For him, sexual desire within marriage furthered the divine plan and was only abused in extramarital affairs. Sadly, Augustine's defective thinking won the day, and as Richard Sipe has written, "Sexual pleasure = women = evil." The championing of celibacy can be traced in large part to Augustine. The unbalanced ecclesiastical thinking, this preoccupation with sex throughout the centuries, is a negative gift from the man from Hippo, North Africa. It has nothing to do with Jesus.

Augustine's contemporary, St. Jerome (d. circa 420 CE), the greatest biblical scholar of antiquity, had a profound effect on the linking of celibacy with priesthood. The towering scholar of priestly celibacy Henry Lea states, "No doctor of the church did more than St. Jerome to impose the rule of celibacy on its members, yet even he admits that at the beginning there was no absolute injunction to that effect." Jerome, like Origen, castrated himself as he went about extolling virginity as superior to marriage. So galling was the fact that the apostles were married that Jerome even changed the translation of wife to "female servant." In a fit of celibate fervour, he maintained that all the great biblical heroes were single.

Jovinian (d. 406 CE), a monk from Milan, had the effrontery to challenge the whole Church, including the pope, on the topic of celibacy. Jovinian redefined the word prophet with the simple declaration that marriage was as virtuous as virginity. This set the whole clerical establishment against him. He was vilified and chased from town to town with his many adherents. The "monster who spreads poison" Jovinian was cornered, tortured, and excommunicated. The same dynamic continues today. Now exile in the Catholic Church is internal, as dissenting theologians are kept from challenging non-infallible teachings like celibacy, and only those who swear never to raise this issue – and that of female ordination – are raised to the bishopric.

Pope Innocent I (401-17), the pontiff of both Augustine and Jerome, had a novel idea which if implemented would have allowed the Church to come to grips with celibacy. One lapse of chastity and one was out of the priesthood. As simple as that. Celibacy equals chastity. This was never enforced and never became law, for the simple reason that the long experience of the Church has shown how absolutely unworkable celibacy is. As the recent sex scandals have proven, the hierarchical leaders have tolerated every lapse, no matter how grave, for the simple reason that the Church could not function otherwise.

This is not new. It has been the consistent experience at every level of priesthood – from the papacy to the curia to the parish. At the highest levels of ecclesial decision-making the obvious truth that biology is difficult to circumvent is acknowledged. Unless celibacy is freely chosen, explored in depth in seminaries instead of evaded, unless it is painstakingly and gradually implemented, serious repercussions necessarily will ensue. The history of failed imposition is there for all to see. Elizabeth Abbot in her *A History of Celibacy* states, "In Africa clerical celibacy is practiced mainly in the breach ... and in Latin America there is a teeming morass of under-serviced Catholics and surreptitiously uncelibate priests ... a majority of Brazilian priests are uncelibate, perhaps 60-70 percent ... in the Philippines a small majority of priests live with women."

Popes were Sons of Priests

Many popes were sons of priests and bishops. For example: Boniface (418-22), Gelasius (492-496), Agapitus (535-536), Silverius (536-7), Theodore (642-649), all before we get to that epoch of dissolution, the Renaissance. Historians estimate the number of married popes at around 40, and four have been canonized as saints. "No historian," Hans Kung writes in *The Catholic Church: A Short History,* "will ever discover how many children these holy fathers fathered, living in monstrous luxury, unbridled sensuality, and uninhibited vice." The notorious Franciscan Sixtus IV (1471) sired several sons and made his corrupt nephew Pietro Riario a cardinal. Sixtus licensed the brothels of Rome and, partly with this money, gave the Church the "Sistine" chapel. Sixtus, of course, paled next to the barbarian Rodrigo Borgia – Alexander VI (1492-1503), "the Tiberius of Christian Rome" as Gibbon called him. He had ten known illegitimate children. At age 58 he took a fifteen-year-old mistress whose brother became the future Paul III. His son, the notorious Cesare Borgia, became a cardinal at eighteen.

But we are slightly ahead of ourselves. As the Roman Empire crumbled and the Dark Ages ensued, monasticism grew confident that the ascetic celibate life was superior to marriage. Beginning in the Middle East, notably Egypt and Syria, celibate monks formed communities in staggering numbers. Female celibates also organized. Even here in an age of sexual pessimism, nature reared her insistent head. Convents became dumping grounds for unhappy daughters and, as Henry Lea states, "The blindly bigoted and turbulently ambitious found a place among those whose only aim was retirement and peace." Out of necessity monastic rules became tightened, allowing the Church to consolidate both her power and her property. And as for celibacy Lea dryly observes, "As to the morals of monastic life it may be sufficient to refer to the regulation of St. Theodore Studita, in the ninth century, prohibiting the entrance of even female animals." The omnipresence of "vagrants of the worst description" created sexual havoc and inevitably produced the genius who strove to mitigate the enfolding disaster, St. Benedict of Nursia (circa 500 CE), the founder of the Benedictine order and the Monte Cassino abbey.

Things never changed for the better. Ecclesial giants like St. Boniface (726 CE) seemed powerless to enforce the codes of celibacy and mitigate the promiscuity in the abbeys. "The clergy were still stubborn ... some defended themselves as being legitimately entitled to have a concubine." Boniface, the right hand of Pope Zachary, feared for his life as he attempted to discipline his unruly clergy. By the time of Charlemagne (800 CE), "unchastity remained a corroding ulcer," according to Lea. The failure was never-ending. Edicts prohibiting cohabitation of women and clergy were constant and absolutely ineffectual. Convents, as the Council of Aix-la-Chapelle (836 CE) states, "were rather brothels than houses of God." Infanticide of unwanted children became common. Part of the monastic discipline was the letting of blood in the hope of alleviating the effects of prolonged continence. And Sigmund Freud was still one thousand years away.

The eleventh and twelfth centuries were the absolute zenith of papal power. At the Second Lateran Council of 1139 all priestly marriages were declared invalid and priests' wives and children became the Church's property. Mass protests erupted to no avail. This was a massive change not understood by most people who think that clerical celibacy dates from the twelfth century. As we see from above, celibacy and priesthood had coexisted from the fourth century on. But now a priest was so set apart from lay people that marriage was inconceivable. Gregory the Great, in 602, had declared that a priest's marriage was valid, but now an ordinand had to choose. Ordination simply invalidated marriage.

Things only got worse and without the discipline of marriage, concubinage and promiscuity became rampant. Hear the frustration in the voice of one of the church's great saints, Bernard of Clairvaux (1135): "Take from the church an honourable marriage and an immaculate marriage bed, and do you not fill it with concubinage, incest, homosexuality and every kind of uncleanness?" From Norman times (eleventh century) at least until the sixteenth century the *cullagium,* a sex tax, was collected from anyone who wished to keep his concubine.

Hans Kung writes, "A church of celibate men established the prohibition of marriage. In the Eastern churches the clergy other than bishops remained married and were therefore more integrated into the structure of society. By contrast, the celibate clergy of the West were totally set apart from the Christian people above all by their unmarried state."

St. Ulric of Zell (d.1093 CE), a Cluniac monk whose feast day is July 14, spoke common sense to the issue. He simply argued for married priests on scriptural grounds and his witty comment survives to this day: "Some prelates are pressing the breasts of Scripture to make them yield blood not milk."

Council of Trent

It has often been said about the Council of Trent that it unnecessarily highlighted everything that the Reformers rejected – and so when it was convened, that which in a large part provoked the Reformation – namely celibacy – became the rigorous standard of the Catholic renewal. In classical arrogance which yielded not one whit to upstart heretics, Rome demanded instant obedience and refused to budge on celibacy.

Celibacy is about control and property. At a basic level a single man without a family and a partner is easier to control. The growing power of the bishops with families caused huge problems as valuable property and huge landed estates were handed down to family and other relatives. Boniface VIII (d.1303) is said to have given away one quarter of Church revenues to his family! A married priesthood simply had divided loyalties.

Unencumbered and isolated, a priest became a pawn in an ecclesiastical game, a loyal soldier in a clerical institution, expected to give absolute obedience to his episcopal overseer. Celibacy assured this loyalty – no more families to support, no more property to hand on. What Trent demanded once again was the single state (*caelebs*, Latin for alone). It could never guarantee chastity. You could break your vow hundreds of times and you would be welcomed back. Commit matrimony once and you were gone. To raise a family in a responsible way, cherish one woman and harness all your sexual energy into your work made more sense to Luther and the reformers than to keep imposing celibacy and denying everybody's natural right to wed. Such was the advice of the great priest Erasmus of Rotterdam in 1525. "I would like to see permission given to priests and monks to marry, especially when there is such a horde of priests among whom chastity is rare. How much better to make concubines into wives and openly acknowledge the partners now held in infamy! How much better to have children to love and rear religiously, as legitimate offspring of whom there is no need to be ashamed and who in turn will honour their sires." The admirable Dutchman was despised by the hierarchy, and his book burned the same year.

As we have noticed in the recent sex scandals, pathetic men used the power and prestige of the priesthood to destroy young lives. They gave up marriage but not chastity. Recent reports have linked sexual abuse to mandatory celibacy, and researcher Dean R. Hoge makes the point that "the celibacy requirement is the single most important deterrent to new vocations to the priesthood." The powerful spirit force of Vatican II with its universal call to holiness emptied seminaries and caused a huge exodus from priestly ranks. When the penny dropped that the laity had as much a claim on sanctity and holiness, the celibate life lost much of its allure. The "white martyrdom" which drained so much energy from celibates suddenly lost its rationale. The cultic purity of the priest, which at the same time degraded sex, has collapsed in our time. Celibacy and ministry turned out to be two different vocations. Similarly, the embarrassing arguments for an all-male priesthood are in fact the last gasp of a warped misogynist history. Scripture scholars have utterly demolished the apostolic origins of celibacy and priesthood, and cultural historians have ably unmasked the obvious conditioning of a patriarchal time.

Conclusion

Church leadership would have us believe that celibacy has a long and noble tradition within the Church. It doesn't. In these few pages I have merely scratched the surface of the terrible price we have paid for the imposition. In no way should these pages be seen as an attack on the marvellous ascetical discipline which some have voluntarily embraced and mastered. The question is, why do we still refuse to revisit the requirement of this discipline? That we do not have a priest for every second parish in the Catholic world appears not to bother some hierarchs. That the Roman Catholic Church appears willing to give up the laity's right to the Eucharist rather than dismantle the celibate male-only priesthood is sad beyond words. The greatest Catholic theologian of the twentieth century, Karl Rahner, gave that gentle Pope Paul VI some advice which the Church needs to hear. "If in practice you cannot obtain a sufficient number of priests in a given cultural setting without relinquishing celibacy, then the church must suspend the law of celibacy."

Not a few in and out of the Church link power and celibacy. Theologically the Catholic Church does not belong to the pope or the bishops – or for that matter, the laity. It belongs to Christ and this ultimately must demand a better way for non-celibate lay people to participate at every level of the church. The clericalized power of control presently lived out in the Church is not compatible with the vision of Jesus. The untenable continuation of priestly power accessible to celibates who then attempt to control the sexual lives of all the faithful can no longer be the *modus vivendi* of a healthy church. Lay people who comprise 99 percent of the Church are now much too educated, enlightened and democratic to allow this to continue. Endowed every bit as much with the gifts of the Holy Spirit, lay people are demanding the end of an autocratic structure and the end of the feudal clerical stranglehold on decision making. This is a natural evolution which can result in healthier modes of priesthood.

It has often been said that power is the aphrodisiac of the celibate. We have read enough of past history and observed enough of the present to see the harm done by celibacy: from the pathetic careerism of the upwardly mobile, who do not understand that the gospel is about downward mobility, to the repressed sexuality of so many good, gay men, to the alcoholism of the lonely celibate and the frigid asceticism of the poor pastor whose battle with celibacy has cost him his whole affective life. We have tragically observed the wrecked lives of the innocent, those who became the victims of too many who acted out twisted power relations with children, adolescents, and women. Lamentably we have watched the sorry codependency of the many who mistook holiness for a safe place in the comfortable arms of a bureaucracy.

Finally, one of the obvious benefits to a relaxation of the celibacy demand in the Church would be a much more wholesome attitude toward sex. The preoccupation of this holy and mysterious life force by a celibate priesthood has badly skewed Catholic morality. The end of celibacy and the deeper appreciation which only comes with experience will grace the Catholic Church with much more authentic wisdom in this realm.

THE
YOUNG FOGEYS'
ESCAPE FROM FREEDOM

The prolific Catholic sociologist Andrew Greeley, writing in the January/February 2004 issue of *Atlantic Monthly,* wrote about "the young fogeys," today's striking trend of conservative priests presenting themselves for ordination. Fr. Greeley observed, "These are newly ordained men who seem in many ways intent on restoring the pre-Vatican II Church, and who, reversing the classic generational roles, define themselves in direct opposition to the liberal priests who came of age in the 1960s and 1970s."

Analyzing this disturbing development, Greeley described the lamentable failure of nerve which characterized the immediate post-Vatican II period, the sad attempt to "quench the Spirit" (1 Thessalonians 5:19).

The backlash after Vatican II was swift. Church leaders, realizing that reform had slipped out of their control, grew increasingly convinced of the need for the Restoration – a movement in which the upper clergy would close ranks and reassert their authority. Newly-appointed bishops would restore the rules; theologians who disagreed would be silenced and the old order would be established. Today's young priests are rallying to the call.

In April 2002 the National Federation of Priests met in Toronto and I was present when the veteran "church" sociologist Dean Hoge led a seminar on "priests in the first five years." He then turned his findings into a book. Hoge's seminar was first unnerving because his findings were that the newly ordained priests believed a priest is fundamentally different from a lay person, "a man apart, 'ontologically' different," as the philosophers say.

One-third of the priest-respondents in Hoge's study felt that the laity needed to be "better educated to respect the authority of the priest's word."

Hoge's seminar in 2002 was helpful in predicting future fault lines in Catholic parishes. The veteran pastors were less than impressed with the attitudes of "the John Paul II brigade" of new ordinands. Words like "pompous," "arrogant" and "rigid" were used. One priest brought the house down with a description of a conversation he had with a priest ordained two years, complaining that he felt "burned out." The veteran quipped, "I thought his problem was ignition!"

Now Hoge's new study, "Experiences of Priests Ordained Five to Nine Years" (National Catholic Educational Association 2006) has become available and the results to anybody paying attention are not surprising. The new ordinands are "older, less educated, less thoroughly schooled in theology, and less likely to see its relevance to ministry."

Recent research confirmed by anecdotal evidence of seminary watchers reveals that a mere 10 percent of priesthood candidates are highly qualified while roughly 40 percent were substandard and, in several educational ways (poor educational backgrounds, learning disabilities, lack of facility in English and a poor grasp of North American culture), inferior to Vatican II priests. In the book *Educating Leaders for Ministry* (2005), from which the above stats were taken, the authors reported that seminary leaders "regardless of native abilities and educational experience" resist "the learning enterprise" because it "threatens their preconceived ideas of theology."

Greeley quotes Hoge and other surveys which show the wide gulf between the priestly generations on issues such as celibacy and the ordination of women. He points out, however, that 40 per cent of the newly ordained do not accept that birth control is always wrong, "a revealing failure of the Restoration efforts of the past thirty years."

He comments starkly: "Priests as a group are simply out of touch with the laity." A *Los Angeles Times* study found that only 36 out of 1,854 priests identified clericalism as one of the major problems facing the church's laity. Astonishingly, only 47 priests thought the sex abuse scandals worth mentioning. Priests of all generations are unable to see the clergy as responsible for the departure of disaffected lay persons.

Cultural Upheaval

Why the "young fogeys?" First, rigidity often accompanies lower intellectual standards. Confronted with a better educated laity, raised in highly democratic culture, young fogeys reach reflexively for the "authority" card. Desiring absolute certainty, they cannot tolerate any ambiguity. In a period of flux, people need clear and simplistic answers. These men are simply the Catholic analogue to the rising tide of fundamentalism around the world. After 9/11 and all the changes associated with the global restructuring of the economy, natural disasters (tsunamis, hurricanes) associated with global warming, the Fifth Horseman – Fear – seems to be riding tall in the saddle. Those seeking ordination have watched in dismay the rise of AIDS, nuclear numbing, environmental degradation, plummeting salaries and the accelerated cost of an education. Factor in as well the phenomenal increase in family breakdown in North America and one can readily see a deep hunger for structure and order. Into the breach leaps the absolute certitude of a global religious superstar like John Paul II and now the deeply pessimistic Joseph Ratzinger, Benedict XVI. In a time of great cultural upheaval there is always a turn to fundamentalism, quick and easy answers to difficult questions. "Pope-olatry" and ultramontane subservience to Rome are the Catholic variants of fundamentalism. Jesuit theologian John Coleman has described this time as "papal fundamentalism."

The "young fogeys" must be understood within the ambit of this historical moment. It takes a remarkably mature person to live with ambiguity in a sea of perceived chaos. How does one remain open to the authentic "signs of the times," those marvellous cultural breakthroughs, those Spirit moments when the Holy invades history and leads humanity into greater inclusiveness? Amidst the birth pangs "when all of creation groans with pain" (Romans 8:22), how does one stay open to the genuine thrust of the Holy Spirit of surprises? How does one separate the real from the transitory, the authentic from the faddish? The psychically immature seek out the institution – the Father figure – to tell them the answer. They wish, in Erich Fromm's prescient phrase, to "escape from freedom."

One can certainly understand the burdens that come with freedom. I believe this is what has happened to the young fogeys. Given the societal chaos which they see ("the culture of relativism") one can understand those who wish to surrender their power and autonomy to a higher authority. Faith to them is clinging to a shrine, remaining in a safe harbour, not Abraham Heschel's "endless pilgrimage of the heart." No "burning songs, audacious longings, daring thoughts," rather a soothing and secure bedtime lullaby before the sleep of the contented and secure. Many in the advanced capitalist world simply blend in with the herd and are buffeted by cultural trends. Here Ratzinger is correct. The authentic self disappears. Spontaneity and creativity evaporate. In Erich Fromm's words, they have given up the "freedom to." Mature Christians, however, maintain their "freedom in Christ" and maintain a loving but critical identification with the structure of the church. In Cardinal Newman's (d.1890) famous phrase, they toast the pope – but first conscience.

Young fogeys, then, cease to be critical of the institution on which they have staked their lives. The subliminal fear generated by the cultural upheaval drives them to seek not truth but security. They take refuge in prepackaged answers and dogmatic formulae. When challenged they become rigid and have a difficult time relating to better educated and more confident lay people.

In many respects, their timing could not be worse. Surrendering their identity to an institution which heretofore had all the answers and which offered the young "cheap grace" and instant respect which they had never earned, the newly ordained find themselves the brunt of jokes in a job which has fallen radically in public esteem. Their Roman collars no longer buy them "free passes" anywhere, and their simplistic answers to life's mysteries do not cut it with a highly educated laity which increasingly struggle to raise families with little of the security the priesthood offers. Many of these younger priests are stunned by their chilly reception, and, as one priest wag who has watched many of them, commented: "They are like Sea

King helicopters: very high maintenance. For every hour in the air, they need 25 hours of care on the ground." Many are deeply shaken when they arrive freshly minted from the cosseted seminary culture. Answers which satisfied inside the walls wither in the real world. Anecdotal evidence indicates that many become "Sea King helicopters."

What does this augur for the broader church? Certainly there will be more conflict in store as the young fogeys move, as the National Federation of Priests says in its study, "from a servant leadership model to a cultic model," one which seems more intent on shoring up clerical privilege than moving Catholicism into a more democratized era, an era which honours "the adult equality of all the baptized." The phenomenal growth of lay ministry and the huge numbers of women who have theology degrees are already changing the church, but for the near future the best we can hope for is civilized discourse, respect, dialogue. Maybe theologian David Tracy put it best when he said, "Conflict is our actuality; conversation our hope." – even with young fogeys.

A LIE CONTINUES

If you could hear at every jolt the blood
Come gurgling from the froth-corrupted lungs
Obscene as cancer, bitter as the cud
Of vile, incurable sores on innocent tongues, -
My friend, you would not tell with such high zest
To children ardent for some desperate glory,
The old Lie: Dulce et decorum est
Pro patria mori.
Wilfred Owen

On the general theme of war and the Church, there were three events, or points of discussion, which bubbled up a while ago and triggered some reflection. What spurred me to write on this theme was the powerful book *War Is A Force That Gives Us Meaning* (Public Affairs, Perseus Group, 2002), a brilliant extended essay by Chris Hedges. The son of a clergyman and himself a former seminary student, Hedges, from his many years as a war correspondent in Central America, Iraq and the former Yugoslavia, has written a powerful tome on the meaning of war. Much of it has been informed by his deep reading of the classics and his background in theology. I will comment on his book in my next essay. Suffice it to say, that this little gem helped me to try to discern the "signs of the times."

As one watches in disgust the growing Vietnamization of Iraq, and as the disgraced militant cold war ideology of George W. Bush implodes, one is forced at the same time to confront the radical impotence of Christianity as it fails to raise a counter-cultural voice on behalf of peace and the gospel of nonviolence. Polls conducted after the US President's call to war showed just how tepid was the response of American Catholic parishes to this illegal and unjust war. Preaching on the immorality of such a needless war was virtually non-existent and was hardly ever followed up by any serious resistance. It was just one more example of how corrupted the Church has become as it nestles slumbering by the fireside of an imperial Christianity. Once again in the heart of the world's wealthiest country we watched a Church utterly compromised by wealth, power and hubristic nationalism. The resounding ecclesial capitulation confirmed the adage that the religion of America is America. Hobbled by failure of episcopal leadership in the sex abuse scandal, the American Roman Catholic Church leadership stood mute and helpless as the "Christian born-again" president unleashed the dogs of war and then smugly stated, "Mission accomplished."

While organized religion seems marginally better on its statements about war's immorality, there is a growing global revulsion to such wanton murder. Spontaneously, around the globe humanity's inchoate desire for peace has erupted, often with the Internet acting as an electronic connecting spirit. Apparently the list-serves of resistance calling people to rallies never make it to bishops' offices or parishes formerly inundated by chancery appeals to support World Youth Days and other "Catholic" events. All the John Paul II Bishops, so intoxicated by orthodoxy, and guarding the communion rails from pro-choice Catholic politicians, became non-players in the great cause of peace.

Just the opposite, however, was the clarion prophetic voice of longtime Sojourners editor Jim Wallis. Like many of us, Wallis is fed up with the phony brand of Christianity peddled by the Bushites and their evangelical acolytes. So, in the middle of August 2004, in his book *God's Politics: Why the Right Gets It Wrong and the Left Doesn't Get It* (Harper San Francisco 2005) Wallis launched an appeal "to take back our biblical faith." This was his opening salvo:

"Many of us feel that our faith has been stolen, and it's time to take it back. An enormous public misrepresentation of Christianity has taken place. Many people around the world now think Christian faith stands for political commitments that are almost the opposite of its true meaning. How did the faith of Jesus come to be known as pro-rich, pro-war, and pro-American? And how do we get back to a historic, biblical, and genuinely evangelical faith rescued from its contemporary distortions?"

Now wouldn't you like to see something like this from any bishop's office, instead of the usual ahistorical pabulum which is a pale version of the Gospel challenge to be peacemakers?

Michael Moore: A Prophetic Voice

While the American episcopal failure of leadership is immense, it took a Catholic layman, Michael Moore, to prove just what righteous anger might look like. In his often-oafish everyman guise, Moore more resembled the ancient prophets of old than did the sad bishops. *Fahrenheit 9/11* became the number one movie in the country, the largest-grossing documentary ever, proving that there was insatiable hunger for some good old truth-telling. It turns out that there were more people who saw this withering critique of the Bush presidency in one weekend than all the people who saw *Bowling for Columbine* in 9 months. What an indictment for the mainline media that people flock to a movie knowing they cannot get near the truth on their television networks.

Moore, who grew up near the Canadian border, often heard the CBC and realized that he wasn't getting the facts on Vietnam, just as most Americans have been denied the facts in the present conflict. Now it is embarrassing to watch organs like *The New York Times* and *The Washington Post* sheepishly admit the fact. "We are inevitably the mouthpiece for whatever the administration is in power," said Karen De Young, a former assistant managing editor of the *Post*. Television networks like Fox and CNN were worse. At almost every turn they failed to challenge the lies spun by the Bushites. Formerly the press was considered the fourth estate, the defender of the public good. As corporate concentration grew in the last twenty-five years, the media appeared supine on bended knee to the US Presidency. It took the brilliant media columnist for the *Toronto Star*,

Antonia Zerbisias, to ask the impertinent question, "Since when is a presidential pronouncement the word of God?"

"White Folks Sending Black Folks ..."

Inevitably, the right wing landed on Moore for his supposed inaccuracies in his film, and while I am not going to defend everything in Moore's film as 100 percent accurate, his basic thrust is dead-on. In particular, I felt deep revulsion over the clip in *Fahrenheit 9/11* which showed the Marine recruiters head for the poorest part of Flint, Michigan, to entice alienated and often jobless cannon fodder youth into the maw of the American military. The strategy was simple: offer the poorest people in dead-end jobs a chance for an imperial adventure. Give them a job (killing for the state) or an education (which should be theirs by right), and hope they will become the new foot soldiers in defending the empire. Meanwhile the rich, white, frat boys like George W. Bush and Dick Cheney had both taken a pass on Vietnam. Cheney had four deferments, saying he "had better things to do." Bush Jr., using his Daddy's influence, ended up in the Texas Reserve – and even then he went AWOL. Now the great Commander-in-chief and his brave Vice President, safe on their ranches and in their winter homes, have no compunction about sending the poor to die in their crusade – for oil.

Nobody yet has improved on black comedian Dick Gregory's line about the war in Vietnam: "White folks sending black folks to kill yellow folks to defend the land they stole from red folks." The Gospel is about defending the face of the poor, but I must have missed the bishops' prophetic denunciation on the draft falling largely on the poor.

Truth Often Breaks Through

The Spirit appears in many places. Witness the brouhaha with Toronto Blue Jays slugger Carlos Delgado. Tired of millionaire flag-wavers like New York Yankee owner George Steinbrenner playing *God Bless America* during the seventh-inning stretch, Delgado refused to stand with cap in hand. He simply disappeared into the dugout. Delgado, a Puerto Rican, said he was tired of war. His protest was occasioned not only by the increasing death in

Iraq, but by the US Navy bombing raids on the Puerto Rican island of Vieques. Unknown to most US and Canadian citizens, Puerto Rico's churches – including Catholics, Protestants and Pentecostals – had long joined forces in an unprecedented ecumenical coalition against the continued use of Vieques for US bombing exercises.

Delgado was well aware that the 9,300 Puerto Ricans on Vieques had long suffered abnormal rates of cancer produced by uranium-depleted shells. His fellow citizens had already paid a high price for the testing of weaponry used in Iraq. "This is the stupidest war ever," said the Jays slugger, already bent out of shape by the situation in Vieques. Unknown to even Toronto fans, the low-profile Delgado, apprised of the situation by his father, joined other high-profile supporters like the Dalai Lama, Senator Hillary Clinton, singer Ricky Martin and *The West Wing*'s Martin Sheen in rejecting the ongoing bombing. Delgado helped pay for a full-page advertisement about Vieques in *The New York Times* and *The Washington Post*. He has also donated $100,000 (US) to youth sports, schools and activists on the island. In the summer of 2004 the issue came to a head and Delgado began his silent protest.

Vietnam: Still a Presidential Badge

The third incident which saddened me was the failure of US Presidential hopeful John Kerry to make an issue out of the war.

He came to look like a clone of the hapless Bush. What is worse is that Kerry prominently displays his medals gained in the worst example of imperial hubris in US history: Vietnam. Apparently, this is still a badge of honour in America. Maybe he should have listened to the other Kerrey, another medal winner in that evil war. When former Senator Bob Kerrey (Nebraska) was outed in 2001 for his part in the murder of 14 to 20 women and children, he had the courage to fess up. Apparently it shocked Americans. In a speech at Virginia Military Institute, the contrite Kerrey admitted he was haunted by this for 32 years. In an interview with *The Wall Street Journal* he said, "I'm tired of people describing me as a hero." Does that make Kerrey evil? I think not. He is every person caught up in the ancient lie that Wilfred Owen commented on in the opening quote. The drug of war, that ugly state myth which is dragged out incessantly to justify more slaughter, ultimately disillusions good people like Bob Kerrey. The lies of Nixon, Johnson, McNamara, all the best and the brightest who got caught up in this bloodlust, created a catastrophe which has haunted America to this day.

The United States dropped 6,727,084 tons of bombs in Indochina, a landmass no bigger than Nova Scotia. This was triple the tonnage dropped on Europe and the entire Pacific in World War II. Defense Secretary McNamara estimated that 3.4 million Indo-Chinese died during this war. Most were civilians. America is haunted, because it has never ever come to consciousness and dealt with this gross immorality. America's way of dealing with it was to elect Ronald Reagan, who swept Vietnam under the rug and produced cheap military victories in Grenada and Panama, and supported right-wing death squads elsewhere in Central America. George Bush Sr. received a tickertape parade down Broadway for his role in the mass murder in Gulf War 1.

Yet Vietnam still haunts. There is no Wall in the US for all those two million Indo-Chinese noncombatants McNamara refers to. No reparations and no apologies. The Empire never admits culpability and, as George W. Bush so arrogantly put it, "I will never apologize for anything America has done." The reality of such monumental evil, however, came back to haunt many in the US as psychic bombs began to explode in the lives of the returned vets. This statistic still shines out and haunts: 60,000 American soldiers took their own lives when they returned from Vietnam – 2,000 more than the actual number who died in combat. Each of those young men, icons of the Divine no less so than their Indo-Chinese cousins, were loved by their families; each death caused havoc and brought immeasurable grief and untold suffering; much like the many Iraqi civilian deaths which the US military refuses to count. And poor old John Kerry stumbled on, refusing to make this latest obscene war the major issue. How could he? He voted for it ... just as Canadians like Stephen Harper, Ralph Klein and Ernie Eves did.

As Pete Seeger still sings, "When will they ever learn?" And the bishops and the Catholic faithful, when will we disengage from war totally?

THE EFFECTS OF
THE WAR MYTH

After reading Chris Hedges' powerful tome *War Is A Force That Gives Us Meaning*, I was forced to rethink my own attitude toward war. His close proximity to the murderers and the murdered made him confront a truth: "The rush of battle is a potent and often lethal addiction, one I ingested for many years."

Hedges writes of this war fascination "peddled by mythmakers" (which includes the state) as "possessing excitement, exoticism, power, chances to rise above our small stations in life, and a bizarre and fantastic universe that has a grotesque and dark beauty. It dominates culture, distorts memory, corrupts language and infects everything around it."

In his introduction, the author says that his book is a call for repentance. Writing as an American, he utters a plea, "... not to dissuade us from war, but to understand it. It is important that we who wield such massive force across the globe, see within ourselves the seeds of our own obliteration." He maintains, "... we were humbled in Vietnam, purged for a while of a dangerous hubris ... offered a moment of grace."

It is fascinating that Hedges, while abstaining from theology and an overtly religious worldview, does use religious language. I see little evidence, however, that this "moment of grace" was seized upon by America. After the Lyndon Johnson and Richard Nixon administrations came Jimmy Carter, who for political reasons refused any apology over Vietnam. He was followed by Reagan/Bush and then the neo-liberal Clinton who, with the spectre of his own lack of military credentials, did little to reverse America's formidable and bloated military budget. The less said about the appalling record of George W. Bush the better. The pride-swollen face of empire is back.

It seems to me Hedges is correct when he says, "If the humility we gained from our defeat is not the engine which drives our response to future terrorist strikes ... we are lost." As an authentically religious person, he requests "humility and compassion." On the surface this should resonate with a country widely seen as the most religious nation on earth. So far, there is no evidence that the evangelicals behind Bush, nor Bush himself, get it.

Boston writer James Carroll thinks the reason many Americans back Bush's "relentless destruction of a small unthreatening nation" is that the American conscience has gone numb. He suggests as long as the suffering is somewhere else the horrific cost does not register with "our 60 year history of an accidental readiness to destroy the earth, a legacy with which Americans have yet to reckon." For him, "The Bush war in Iraq is only the latest in a chain of irresponsible acts of a warrior government going back to the firebombing of Tokyo. Something deeply sinful has us in its grip. We carefully nurture a spirit of detachment toward the wars we pay for. But that means we cloak ourselves in cold indifference to the unnecessary suffering of others."

The Myth of War

Hedges first analyzes the myth of war, the tendency "to imbue events with meanings they do not have. We see defeats as signposts on the road to ultimate victory. We demonize the enemy so that our opponent is no longer human." The sunny optimist Ronald Reagan cared little for the poor of Grenada, Panama, El Salvador, Guatemala and Nicaragua during his presidency. They were mere blips on a radar screen which lacked any human dimension, small countries to be crushed so that America could vanquish its "Vietnam syndrome." The mighty nation which had never lost a war had to get over its momentary embarrassment, its humiliation in the rice paddies of Vietnam. Reagan said, "America is back, and happy days are here again." The Vietnamese had already buried the two to three million non-combatant victims of an undeclared war. In Africa Hedges points out that Jonas Savimbi, the rebel leader the US backed in the Angolan Civil War, "murdered and tortured with a barbarity that far outstripped the Taliban." Five hundred thousand dead courtesy of the man dubbed "the Abraham Lincoln of Angola" by Ronald Reagan. More needless dead on the global chessboard. Another "signpost" on the road to the ultimate defeat of "international communism."

The poor in Latin America similarly paid with their lives. Prophetic voices like Bishop Romero, the Jesuit martyrs, Maryknoll missionaries and thousands of catechists could hardly make themselves heard among American Catholics who were moving from the Democratic Party to the party of achievement and power, the Republicans. The Gospel of the non-violent One, Jesus, was ignored and sidelined. American nationalism trumped faith.

In the late 1980s in the former Yugoslavia, Slobodan Milosevic ranted for years, filling his Serbian countrymen and women with propaganda and lies before the slaughter and ethnic cleansing began. He was met in kind by the equally destructive lies of Franjo Tudjman in Croatia. People who lived in close proximity for years turned on each other in an orgy of ethnic cleansing. Each side reduced the other to caricature. In the wake of this unfolding disaster, the very weak Orthodox Church in Serbia and the Catholic Church in Croatia were virtually as impotent as the US Catholic Church was to make a difference under Reagan/Bush. In fact they worked as state propagandists.

The myth of war "sells and legitimizes the drug of war," Hedges writes. US culture (more and more dominating the Canadian airwaves) has consistently fed the masses a diet of violence in film, television and computer games. As Michael Moore pointed out in *Bowling for Columbine,* the US is off the Richter scale in terms of violence compared to other nations. It still murders people by capital punishment as the rest of the world abandons it. Amnesty International reports the United States is the world leader in executing those under eighteen. Study after study has pointed out the correlation between violence in the media and violence in society. And war heroes, never peace heroes, are lionized in the media.

"The Nationalist is An Ignoramus"

Hedges' next chapter is entitled "The Plague of Nationalism." It could be summed up by Yugoslavian writer Danilo Kis' remark, that "The nationalist is by definition an ignoramus. Nationalism is the line of least resistance, the easy way ... he is not interested in others, they are of no concern to him." The horrific nationalist murders of the early 1990s in Yugoslavia, a country with high educational standards, was chilling to behold. Brutal thugs like Milosevic and Radovan Karadzic (a doctor, yet) manipulated Serbs, stoking hoary old nationalist myths of Serbia's supposed glory days of the fourteenth century. Taking over state television, both sides consistently inflamed the people with emotional propaganda.

Hedges appeared traumatized by his experience in another highly educated country, Argentina. During the time of the Falklands War (1982), Hedges reported that "overwhelming pride and a sense of national solidarity swept through Buenos Aires like an electric current and a populace that had agitated for change after the Dirty War (1976) now outdid itself and lionized uniformed killers. All bowed before the state." This taught Hedges a lesson that "lurking beneath the surface of every society, including ours is the yearning for a passionate cause that exalts us. It reduces the anxiety and erases the anxiety of individual consciousness." The same response took over in the United Kingdom. The war card, the time-old reference to the British bulldog and World War II, assured Margaret Thatcher that she could count on her fellow countrymen in the hour of need. It worked every time. As the author says, "There is little that logic or fact or truth can do to alter the experience."

Nowhere is the state myth worked more than in Israel. Hedges phrases it well: "To speak of the Israeli War of independence with many Israelis in which stateless European Jews established a country in a land that had been primarily Muslim since the seventh century, is to shout into a vast black hole. There is an emotional barrier, a desire not to tarnish the creation myth which makes it difficult for many Israeli Jews including some of the most liberal and progressive to acknowledge the profound injustice the creation of the state meant for Palestinians." For Jews, it was a glorious achievement; Arabs remember it each year as the Naqba (the catastrophe).

One would have thought that after the disaster of the state myth of Nazism and the fall of the Third Reich in 1945, countries would be well aware of the dangers of nationalism. But as Hedges says, this phenomenon is beyond logic. It was the exiled German theologian Paul Tillich who pointed out before leaving Nazi Germany that any political movement founded on a state myth of origin is dangerous, resulting in either external aggression (destiny) or internal oppression. While never denigrating a healthy nationalism (patriotism?), Tillich maintained it always must be subordinated to the norms of social justice, equality and international peace. If this does not happen, the result is usually xenophobia and tribalism in smaller nations (Rwanda) and the "arrogance of empire" (the US) in larger ones.

September 11, 2001 has become a watershed in the United States. The question is did it teach humility? Or did it produce more blind nationalism ready to swallow George W. Bush's nonsense that "they hate us because of our freedom?" Did it force Americans to delve into their history to understand how and why the world perceives them as they do? "Year after year," Muslim writer Shahid Alam (*Poverty From the Wealth of Nations,* Palgrave Macmillan, 2001) states, "Americans are kept in the dark, unaware of the actual, the real America – the only one kind seen by much of the rest of the world. This is the America that daily employs the might to mangle the lives of hundreds of millions, that pushes a globalization that devastates the economies of the Third World, that instructs and arms foreign tyrannies to terrorize their own people, that aids and abets an Israeli machine that is determined to extirpate the Palestinians." Although more recent polls (October 2006) indicate Americans have begun to question whether they were misled about Iraq, a *Newsweek* poll in 2004 found that 40 per cent of Americans still believed Iraq had something to do with 9/11. What can we make of such abysmal ignorance?

War Destroys Culture

Hedges' third point about war is that it destroys culture. Art, usually subversive, degenerates to kitsch in the service of the state. Our best example would be the awful "realism" generated in the Soviet Union. But those of us who grew up after World War II remember the horrible propagandized film industry wallowing in sentimental doggerel and utter dishonesty. Nobody refers to wartime as periods of great art. However, it is the debilitating lying that suborns a healthy culture. The Reagan years when the US was recovering from the Vietnam Syndrome gave us Sylvester Stallone's Rambo movies, appalling hymns to violence, starring a "war wimp" who, when he had a chance to fight on an actual battlefield in Vietnam, was instead in Switzerland as a chaperone at a girls' school. Schlock like this unfortunately deforms a culture and helps create a whole worldview. Demonic is too good a word for it.

Nowadays, one winces at the lies told by Condoleezza Rice, Colin Powell, Dick Cheney and George W. Bush – anything to justify a war proscribed by international law and the US Constitution, not to mention high ethical standards. "All is dedicated to promoting and glorifying the myth, the nation, the cause," Hedges writes. And woe betide those few who challenge the national consensus. So wounded was the United States by 9/11 that any contrarian hid below the radar line. Flags appeared everywhere and awful tribal anthems like *God Bless America* (and nobody else) become *de rigueur* at ball games. Everybody now sings from the same hymn book: we are the noble ones, the good ones. Our cause is just and if you are not for us, you are against us. Language, as Hedges states, "is reduced to code, clichés the only acceptable vocabulary." All out for the War on Terror!

The Allure of Heroism

"The myth of war entices us with the allure of heroism" writes Chris Hedges in his fourth chapter. Weaned on cultural lies and bankrupt state myths, working-class kids, cut adrift by the ruthless savagery of neo-liberal capitalism, flounder in dead-end jobs. Their sole area of psychic and spiritual enlargement is the vicarious pseudo-life of sports stars and the icons of the celebrity culture. A character in the insightful book and movie *Fight Club,* says, "We're all raised to think we'll be rock stars and celebrities and when this doesn't happen, we're pissed." The biggest "Fight Club" is the military and it seduces the working class with its false advertising of the macho, romantic life.

Michael Moore, a product of working class Flint, Michigan, gets it in his movies. He sees how victimized the poor are in the wealthiest culture ever known to humanity. Because post-secondary education – a virtual right in Europe – is so expensive in the world's wealthiest country, the military provides; the only price may be your life. You will take the place of a Dick Cheney or George W. Bush who know how to use the system. And the saddest thing is that they will skilfully manipulate you into believing that you are doing something beautiful for humanity. It is nothing but the old lie Wilfred Owen wrote about in World War I – "It is sweet and lovely to die for your country."

How unbearably sad to watch the poor uneducated victims used by the American military at Abu Ghraib, and the cannon fodder troops, disproportionately poor, roaring into battle with the cry, "Burn, m'f'er burn," – all pumped up to kill the "sand niggers" (the name they give to Iraqis). This was the testimony given by Jeremy Hinzman, a young war resister from South Dakota who fled to Toronto. All the bravado, of course, melts when they see the first casualty of one of their company.

Chris Hedges has written a powerful secular meditation on war. *War Is A Force That Gives Us Meaning* made me conclude that the Christian church is radically derelict in its understanding of the nonviolent Gospel. And to this I turn next.

THE DISCOURAGING SILENCE OF THE CHURCHES

Here is the test by which we can make sure that we are in him:
whoever claims to be dwelling in him, binds himself to live as Christ
himself lived.
1 John 2:6

On October 28, 2004 a chilling report was published online by *The Lancet* – a medical journal. Mr. Les Roberts of the Johns Hopkins Bloomberg school of Public Health made the astounding claim that 100,000 excess deaths had happened since the invasion of Iraq. Mr. Roberts also said that the claim was made "using conservative assumptions." He attributed the huge numbers to "the use of air power in areas with lots of civilians." Two-thirds of the violent deaths were reported in Fallujah, 50 kilometres west of Baghdad, a city which had been pummelled by US air strikes. Previous estimates had placed the Iraqi civilian death toll at 16,053. The public reaction was almost totally muted by the almost hysterical run-up to the American election less than five days away. In typical British understatement, Richard Horton, editor of *The Lancet* said, "These findings raise questions for those far removed from Iraq in the governments of the countries responsible for launching a pre-emptive war."

The killing in Iraq has continued. *The Lancet* revised the estimated number of Iraqi deaths to an astounding 655,000 as of October 2006. Even before that updated figure came to light Alan Simpson, a member of Labour Against The War, said, "Iraq has not seen this scale of slaughter since its war with Iran. At some point, the slaughter of civilians in the name of peace has to become a crime of war. This is not a matter of indifference but criminality. These figures are horrific, but it is a scandal that the world remains silent."

What any Christian might have said – with a scintilla of awareness of the Christian Gospel and the beatitudes of the murdered Christ in his hands – is that these stunning figures are putting a formidable challenge to the credibility of the Christian Church today. For Catholics, who represent the largest communions in both the United States and Canada, one might even venture to state the Church's credibility – already in tatters over the sorry performances of paedophile-enabling bishops – is now hanging by a thread in its failure to reject war in its totality. While the bishops did give notional rejection for the Bush administration's discredited reasons for Gulf War II, they did virtually nothing to organize against it.

Think of it for a moment. Six hundred and fifty-five thousand deaths. Six hundred and fifty-five thousand funerals. Vales of tears and mountains of anguish. Children weeping for their parents, grandparents for their grandchildren. One is driven to ask: cannot Christians, by virtue of their own humanity, grasp this intolerable suffering to another part of the Body of Christ? While the world stopped and shared the pain of American families in New York after 9/11, what kind of calcified hearts are unable to extrapolate and understand Iraqi suffering? Do Americans always have to get past their messianic pretensions that God is forever on their side? Isn't it the role of American Christians to protect the icons of God in other people no matter where they be?

In the dark years of the Reagan Presidency, and hiding behind the demonic state myth of its own holiness and righteousness, the US courted nuclear war by consistently demeaning the Soviet people. It turned brothers and sisters in Christ into "godless atheists," thus paving the way for their acceptable annihilation. The American people, while fighting valiantly in the Allied cause, lost not one life on their own soil (other than in the attack on Pearl Harbour in the US territory of Hawaii), yet there they were blaming and lecturing a former ally who, while it took Hitler's knockout blow, buried 16,000,000 sons and daughters under its own blood-soaked soil. Can we even now allow such unimaginable pain into our hearts? Do we care to even try?

One who understood this was Pope John Paul II who – caught between the Soviets and the Germans – knew in his blood what war does to a people. Maybe it helps us understand his own frantic efforts to bring George W. Bush and Tony Blair to their senses. Again and again he uttered Pope Paul VI's cry at the United Nations in the mid-1960s, *"Jamais plus la guerre!"* And a month after Gulf War I (1991), John Paul II added his own analysis of war: "It destroyed the lives of innocent people; it teaches how to kill; it throws into upheaval even the lives of those who do the killing and leaves behind a trail of resentment and hatred."

The Evangelical War Theology

The discouraging silence of the churches, along with the consistent polls which show that Christian evangelicals were the biggest backers of the war on Iraq, tell us that the non-violent voice of Jesus has been totally muted in our time. Catholicism, despite its institutional size and cultural clout, has become a silent accomplice to the horrific homicidal violence which has taken place in Iraq. In the case of the United States, several factors may be at work here. The first and major one is the massive and pervasive idolatry of the American state as worthy of ultimate allegiance. Canadians cringe at this frightening display of jingoism. Since the time of John Winthrop and the early Pilgrims, America has always had the naïve belief that she was the "shining city on the hill." A year before his murder, the prophet Martin Luther King Jr. attempted to pull off the mask of American blindness. As the B-52s rained death and destruction on Vietnam (one million civilians murdered) King described his country as "the greatest purveyor of violence in the world."

The Iraqi death toll evidences a horribly deformed and corrupted Christianity. In the Catholic lectionary the month of the Dead (November) begins with the Matthean reading of the Beatitudes, the powerful cry of the Galilean that his followers reflect mercy, compassion, peace and justice. Scholars agree that these were the values of the first three centuries after

Jesus. Until probably 200 CE, there is no record of Christian soldiers in the Roman legions, and up until 300 there were but a few. The reason is obvious: the non-violent witness of Jesus, his sacrificial death and his absolute refusal to countenance violence were still fresh in the Christian mind. There was no doubt they were following a Lord who taught them how to die but not to kill. Then, of course, the inevitable happened – the power and blandishments of Empire trumped the suffering servant Jesus. The lion of Rome devoured the Christian lamb and the faithful lost their salt. This Constantinian arrangement was but the first triumph of Caesar over Christ. In the year 382, Pope Damasus added the prefix Roman to Catholicism and the surrender was complete.

Following Constantine, the Church slavishly imitated the emperor and his bureaucracy, adopting fancy titles, living apart from the faithful and generally aping the secular power structure. Ambrose, Augustine's mentor, came to Milan as a governor and quickly became a bishop. The amazing Augustine is surely one of the great geniuses in church history. Nevertheless in 411, trusting that the Church would triumph over empire, he succumbed to using violence against the Donatists. The Gospel of Jesus became spiritualized, lost its savour again and ultimately witnessed its own demise in Africa. By the time of Justinian, (d.565) the historian Procopius reproved the latter for his fanaticism: "In his zeal to gather all men into one Christian doctrine, he recklessly killed all who dissented." Sound familiar? All in the name of the non-violent Jesus. Fast forward to the Crusades and the horrific shedding of blood under Pope Urban II, in 1095. Like George W. Bush he was a man of absolute certitude – *"Deus vult"* ("God wills it") – or the German soldiers who bore the frightening words in World War II *"Der Gott sei mit uns"* ("God be with us") on their belt buckles. God, however, is never "on our side" if we are violent.

Jesus Ratifies the Non-Violent Life

The late Jesuit bible scholar John McKenzie said it definitively. "If we cannot know from the New Testament that Jesus rejected violence, then we can know nothing of his person or message. It is the clearest of teachings."

This is so obvious that any attempt to portray Jesus otherwise absolutely fails. The very symbol of Christianity ratifies the non-violent life. The invitation to "follow me" sacralizes the pacifist way – to pick up the cross and follow the one who returned good for evil and prayed for his persecutors until he gave up his spirit. Yet his followers continue to reject the teaching as the hoary "righteous war" theory gets trotted out to justify every war and imperial adventure. Has there ever been a just war? Never.

After the war to end all wars (World War I) we saw a brief flurry of pacifist feeling. Ten million dead were not enough to stay the sword. World War II and 52 more million followed, almost half of them civilians. There have been more wars since then. The propaganda machines (us vs. them) manage to brutalize the enemy, then teach the young to deny the most deeply held truth of the human heart and to do harm to another, to smash the Divine imprint on our souls, to pervert the natural and divine law the Loving Parent has eternally carved inside us.

At Vatican II a mere 17 years after the horrible crucifixion of World War II, the Catholic Church, led by men who saw the slaughter up close, proclaimed that "an entirely new way of looking at war" is necessary.

In the year of our Lord 2007, the way of the Christ, the non-violent embrace of Jesus, God's word, has become almost totally corrupted by Christians in the US. The Roman Catholic Church there bears a massive responsibility for this dereliction of duty. Hundreds of thousands of dead Iraqis and a collective ecclesial silence bespeak Christianity's greatest failure in the modern age.

AN INSPIRATIONAL ECONOMIST

John Kenneth Galbraith, one of America's great public intellectuals, died on April 29, 2006. The bane of neo-conservatives, and a lifelong thorn in the side of market fundamentalists who could never accept the market intrusion of John Maynard Keynes, was 97. One would be hard pressed to name another person of the last century who had the public impact of Galbraith. As confidant and advisor of presidents from Roosevelt to Clinton, as ambassador to India, antiwar activist and prolific pundit, Galbraith's influence was felt in the groves of academe, the corridors of power and, most importantly, in the lives of ordinary citizens for whom he demystified the often arcane subject of economics. Perhaps his greatest gift was the latter. By the force of his logic he invited millions into national debates about economic priorities. University economists sputtered as the witty professor shattered their airtight mathematical models, broke into their closed graduate seminars and gave citizens the tools to raise obvious questions. Many jealous of his impact never forgave him, but they could never ignore him.

Born in the small southwestern Ontario town of Iona Station in 1908, Galbraith inherited the progressive politics of his farmer father Archie, who, from the time his son was age ten, dragged Ken to Liberal Party events. When the party became too accommodationist to the capitalist system, Archie helped form the United Farmers Party, whose electoral success in the Ontario of 1919 sent shock waves through the Canadian establishment. Before it imploded, the Farmer's Party (which had opposed conscription in WW I) enacted extraordinarily progressive social legislation which was not lost on Ken Galbraith – nor on his father's friend, Mackenzie King.

Galbraith graduated from the Ontario Agriculture College in Guelph in 1930 and, like many, was stymied by the failure of neoclassical economics in understanding the Great Depression. He headed off to the University of California on a scholarship in 1931 to study agriculture economics. Mixing with grad students who ranged "from liberal to radical," Galbraith imbibed the progressive thinking of Berkley professors and the much-discussed work of Stanford professor, Thorstein Veblen, convinced that the new capitalist world "was shrinking the possibilities of the universe." Receiving his doctorate in 1934, Galbraith moved to Harvard where he remained, on and off, for the rest of his life. The young economist learned much while at America's most prestigious university, but he learned more from the powerful expanded governmental interventions of Franklin Delano Roosevelt. This remained with him all his life, as did the impact of the book which revolutionized economics, John Maynard Keynes' *General Theory*, published at the height of the Depression in 1936.

Keynes refused to accept the inevitability of the market's adjustment capacities. He maintained that people suffering through years of the "short run" in the business cycle had every reason to distrust neoclassical economics. (His quip, "In the long run we're dead," aptly answered those who suffered little financial pain while counselling patience.) Canada's Depression Prime Minister, the wealthy R.B. Bennett, was a classic model of this wisdom. Investment was needed to boost aggregate income and expand purchasing power. But who would invest in a downturn? Keynes' response: the state, as FDR had shown. "Only active intervention by the state would keep the economy at or near full employment and ensure its steady growth," Galbraith commented in 1973. He advocated deficit spending while unemployment was high and the reverse when the economy was hot. Here was economics which was more than a bloodless intellectual theory; it was economics as if people mattered.

A Lifelong Liberal

For the rest of his life Galbraith kept the liberal creed. In book after book, in the thousands of articles he wrote, he never wavered. He kept his eye on the fundamental question: What is an economy for? Surely it is for the physical and moral good of citizens, to help sustain and build decent lives, healthy families and a sustainable environment, to create productive non-alienating work. If it failed in those respects, it must be rethought. If it continued to produce consumer goods promoted by mass advertising ("psychic rather than physical need"), to create pseudo needs and fulfill them while slums festered and obsolescent junk degraded the environment, economics must be challenged. Galbraith never stopped insisting that the so-called value-free market was never neutral. It was always radically influenced by ideology, power relations, corporate dominance and political power. These were the necessary lenses through which an economy must be viewed. He considered it ludicrous to think that individual needs make the consumer "sovereign" and that his "choice" will result in a self-regulating market.

Writing in *Economics, Peace and Laughter* (E, P and L, 1971), one of his over 40 popular books, the author stated, "For important classes of products and services – weapons systems, space probes and travel, a supersonic transport – decisions are not taken by the individual citizen and voter and transmitted to the state. They are taken by the producers of public services, by the armed services and the weapons firms. It is their goals that are primarily served. The Congress and the public are then persuaded and commanded to acceptance of these decisions ... there can be viewed men of accessible mind who have recently looked at the way weapons are produced without wondering if the notion of ultimate citizen sovereignty is above reproach. This is not a detail. It is half the Federal Budget."

Galbraith's genius (and the reason he was despised by the Milton Friedmans and the monetarists who gave us Reaganomics, massive deficits created by runaway military budgets and the growing global gap between the rich and the poor), was that he was able to pinpoint the deep cultural malaise the majority of citizens felt when they intuited that the public good was being eviscerated even as smiling leaders were crowing about "the economy" and the "bull market." By the sheer power of his formidable intellect and the grace of his felicitous prose peppered with memorable aphorisms, Galbraith convinced millions of citizens that indeed their instincts were right. The individual citizen was not sovereign nor was he in command, despite the assertion of the Friedmanites and "choice" gurus of corporate think tanks that the consumer cannot be at war with an economy he controls "for he cannot be at war with himself." This was the iron law of neoclassical economics, the theological straightjacket the average citizens untutored in economics had to wear. Galbraith gave them every confidence to resist this "conventional wisdom."

He wrote: "Sovereignty is exercised by large and complex organizations. Their exercise of power is to serve their own goals – goals that include the security of the organization and its growth, convenience and prestige, commitment to technological virtuosity as well as its profits. There is every probability that that these goals will differ from the aggregate expression of individual goals. Individuals are then accommodated to these goals not the reverse ... this normally will involve persuasion. But it may involve resort to the state ... it may involve power that is inherent in institutional position." (E, P and L)

As the citizen felt conflicted and found himself at odds with the accepted economics, Galbraith's work convinced him that he was not at odds with reality, but really was "in the grip of large impersonal forces whose purposes he senses to be hostile."

Whose "Choice?"

"The Pentagon pursues wars and builds weapons systems in accordance with its own dynamic. Similarly NASA ... General Motors as a producer of automobiles which threaten to smother cities ... so other industry as it subsumes countryside, water and air. This and the resulting discontent could not occur in a society in which the consumer or citizen is sovereign."

Galbraith's wide reading compelled him to reject the pure laissez-faire belief that "choice" produces "maximum levels of freedom, equality and welfare." It clearly wasn't so. As he watched the formidable power of the modern corporation grow in the 60s and 70s he continued to see the state as the "countervailing power." Regulatory agencies were created to balance competing interests. As the Cold War heated up Galbraith railed against "military Keynesianism," the astronomical military budgets seen as public spending but which produced high inflation and comparatively few jobs. As well, it fuelled McCarthyism and the military industrial complex which Eisenhower had warned against.

Galbraith watched in horror as the Reagan Revolution decimated America with its massive deficits and profligate military spending. He shook his head in disgust as deregulation undid public safeguards against reckless speculation. The Savings and Loans scandal epitomized the unleashing of greed in America. Financial speculation on a global scale wrecked several economies, skewed income distribution and created a new Gilded Age. Real income gains stagnated and people found themselves working longer hours just to remain even. In the world's richest economy of twelve trillion dollars, 45 million Americans went without health insurance and 33 million (the working poor) remained in poverty.

Perhaps Galbraith's greatest vindication came in the 90s, within the economics community itself. Surveys began to show radical disillusionment with mathematical models. One major survey by the American Economic Association showed that two thirds of respondents admitted to an overemphasis on "mathematical tools at the expense of substance." The conclusion found "an absence of an empirical and applied base in the entire economics curriculum." The influential brokerage house Morgan Stanley was more scathing: "The commission's fear is that graduate students may be turning out a generation with too many idiot savants skilled in technique but innocent of real world economic issues."

Autisme Economie

As the millennium turned, the criticism of neoclassical economics accelerated. Sorbonne economist Bernard Guérmien addressed a conference on the same theme – the disconnect between the teaching of neoclassical economics and reality. Shortly afterward, several students approached their professor and confessed the same disenchantment. The *autisme economie* (the Post-Autistic Economics Network, or "PAE") was born with the rallying cry, "We wish to escape imaginary worlds! We no longer want this autistic science pushed on us." The revolt stunned the media as well as the often-elitist French academy. Hundreds of students signed on, as well as many prominent economists. The wave moved throughout Europe, supported by France's leading economist Jean-Paul Fitoussi, who proposed new courses ignored by mainstream economists, namely unemployment and the environment. The movement found a similar response in Cambridge and Oxford. And with the same threatening consequences of professional marginalization that Galbraith himself had experienced battling for tenure at Harvard. The young turks this time were supported by Galbraith's son James, now a distinguished economist in Texas. PAE textbooks began to be printed and translated into Chinese.

However, it was at Galbraith's Harvard where the battle for an alternative economics really heated up. As students continued to exit bloodless economic courses, resistance accelerated. A challenge was launched against the doctrinaire offerings of the Economics 10 course taught by Martin Feldstein, a former Reagan advisor and "the scholarly mentor to Bush's team" as *The New York Times* called him. Rejecting Feldstein's decidedly Republican bias, and after sit-ins and petitions, students finally got an alternative course in 2003. It was taught by Stephen Marglin (Harvard '59) and appropriately called "Social Analysis 72." The Students for Humane and Responsible Economics (SHARE) could no longer stomach Feldstein's narrow brand of neoclassical medicine.

The proliferation of newer models of analyzing economy, the burgeoning institutional and structural questions which had consumed Galbraith, were beginning to proliferate in the wake of the disenchantment of the young and the obvious failures of neoclassical economics. While no new consensus has yet arrived, exciting new challenges are appearing as antidotes to a failed consensus. This is Galbraith's legacy.

Challenging the conventional wisdom of his day, and stimulated by the massive failures of capitalism and the attendant suffering caused by the Depression, spurred on as well by John Maynard Keynes and the brave interventionist moves of Franklin Delano Roosevelt, Galbraith avidly desired an economy which would work for the broad majority of citizens. To do this he had to break with the blind trust in markets and the tenets of the neoclassical consensus. Keynesian economics indeed had worked in stabilizing economies until it was sabotaged by a series of US presidents unwilling to challenge military spending which was masked as "Keynesian." In comparison to other spending it created few jobs but much inflation.

Catholic Social Teaching

Galbraith insisted that economics was never pure science, that it could never be captured and explained in mathematical formulae. In book after book and article after article he showed how economics was always embedded in power relations, inevitably skewed in corporate directions. Countervailing powers were necessary. This is where the state came in. In this sense Galbraith was absolutely in synch with Catholic Social Teaching (CST) which embraces a socially regulated capitalism. The massive failures of cowboy capitalism in Galbraith's adopted country have produced the most stratified society on earth, with the greatest maldistribution of income in the developed world. Galbraith, like CST, valued markets as producers of wealth but was leery of it as a distributor of same.

His witty remark that "In communism man exploits man; in capitalism it is just the opposite" spoke to the massive inequities in his own country. For him, pure self-interest could never produce a communal society. Market economies must never be allowed to become market societies.

At home and in the world where two billion live on less than a toonie a day and where the environment is ravaged, the common good cannot be served without massive intervention. Pope John Paul II spoke directly to this in *Centissimus Annus* (1991). "There are collective and qualitative needs which cannot be satisfied by market mechanisms." These needs –

like the natural and human environments – "escape the logic of the market ... and must not be bought or sold." Galbraith, while never using religious language or invoking a transcendent dimension, shared much of the core of CST, most especially the absolute rejection of economics as an abstract, pure science disconnected from culture, ecology and the state. Both Galbraith and CST were radically concerned with the common good and safeguarding the dignity of the most vulnerable. Both balked at modern economic reductionism which insisted that humans were strictly "interest maximizing" animals. Both understood that human choice often contains profound ethical dimensions based on human solidarity and, in the case of CST, altruistic options were summoned from a transcendent horizon. Both understood and responded to human suffering which unemployment, recession and Depression caused. Both Galbraith and CST insisted on the social nature of the human rather than the aloneness of the individual consumer. Both championed the obvious: we are all embedded in several social networks. For Catholics, created in the image of the triune God, we exist, thrive and are called forth within a society of persons.

The news is not bleak. Galbraith's long and consistent attack on neoclassical economics has reaped a rich harvest of new "countervailing" responses – many from within the United States. Galbraith's holistic thinking that economics is always socially embedded represents similar thinking in almost all of the social sciences as well as the life sciences. Atomistic thinking is dying everywhere. As the eminent quantum theorist David Bohm has stated, "Fragmentation (false divisions) is the hidden source of the social, political and environmental crises facing the world." In almost any scientific discipline the further you advance the narrower it gets. Tunnel vision is not germane to economics alone.

Perhaps Galbraith's greatest endorsement was that of Nobel laureate Amartya Sen, commonly regarded as the world's greatest development economist. Like Galbraith, Sen insists that economics be framed within moral and cultural concerns. The genius of both Galbraith and Sen lay in pointing out the obvious. As Galbraith relentlessly observed, it was producers rather than consumers who dominated markets and foreclosed on "choice." As well, Sen commented that famine has seldom resulted from market failure. Politics and ideology always intruded. The Cambridge professor, Sen, commented that his whole thinking had changed fifty years ago when as a young student he had read a book called *American Capitalism*. Its author was John Kenneth Galbraith.

TWO MARYKNOLL PROPHETS

In the halcyon days of that Spirit-filled decade of the 1960s when the Pentecost winds blew through the dusty corridors of the Church, that marvellous man who did so much to truly globalize the Catholic Church, Pope Paul Vl, wrote a powerful encyclical entitled *Populorum Progressio* ("On the Development of Peoples"). Released in March of 1967, it had an extraordinary impact on the universal church, focusing a spotlight on the huge problem of world poverty.

Pope Paul had been deeply affected by his trips abroad before he had assumed the barque of Peter. He had seen with his own eyes the grievous sores on the suffering body of Christ during his trips to Africa and Latin America. As pope he also had visited India and Palestine. Paul thus was able to internalize the pain he had experienced when confronted by so much needless misery. The result was this powerful encyclical.

"The seriousness and urgency of these teachings (Vatican II) must be recognized without delay. The hungry nations of the world cry out to peoples blessed with abundance. And the Church, cut to the quick by this cry, asks each and every man (sic) to hear his brother's plea. And answer it lovingly." And Paul was even more explicit. He requested all the religious orders and diocesan seminaries (at that time stocked with fresh fervent postulants) to send these eager apostles south.

In many ways the pope's plea was brilliant in its timing. For the first time ever, a new global awareness was being born via new technologies like satellites, fibre optics and television. As in no other era in human history, Marshall McLuhan's global village was becoming a reality. The whole world had grieved at JFK's assassination (1963) and Winston Churchill's funeral (1965), had seen the American invasion of Vietnam, and soon would experience the ultimate event which would bind us all together as co-inhabitants on the "big, blue marble," the Apollo flight of 1969. The world was indeed one. The People of God had gone global.

The response to the pope's entreaty was nothing less than phenomenal. Idealistic young men and women headed south to do what they could to alleviate human suffering and offer helpful suggestions. Thousands had heard the papal plea and the Catholic Church would never again be the same. A revolution had begun whereby the generous but naïve, cocooned by an ideological filter of northern superiority, would slowly begin to make the connection between southern poverty and the superabundance of the developed world. In a relatively short time, missionaries replaced the convenient lie of "there are rich and there are poor" with the maxim, "There are rich because there are poor." Less obvious was the growing understanding that, despite rhetoric to the contrary, the foreign policy of northern nations was actively engaged in perpetuating southern misery.

Roy Bourgeois and Lil Mattingly

The many missionaries who went south soon became appalled at the human suffering they saw first-hand. Encountering deplorable conditions where dignity was daily assaulted, they could not help contrasting this with their own privileged middle-class lives. Something was terribly wrong and something had to give. Two such idealistic religious were members of the Maryknoll order, one a priest named Roy Bourgeois and the other a nun, Sr. Lil Mattingly. Both would make a slow journey of discovery which would cause them deep suffering and a loss of idealism in their country, the United States of America. Both would later be arrested at the infamous School of the Americas in Fort Benning, Georgia.

Bourgeois, a Cajun from Lutcher, Louisiana, was born in 1938. By 1962, having worked in the Gulf of Mexico oilfields to finance his education, he was conflicted about marrying or seeing the world with the US Navy. The desire to travel won his heart and Bourgeois headed for the Caribbean, where he discovered real poverty for the first time in the ports of Trinidad and Jamaica. With each new encounter the young Cajun's world began to change. Sent to Vietnam and shore duty in 1965, Bourgeois, indoctrinated to the hilt with anti-communist fervour, saw death and mutilation up close. His oasis of sanity was an orphanage outside Saigon run by a French-Canadian Redemptorist missionary, Lucien Olivier. Bourgeois met the suffering Christ in the guise of legless orphans with bloated stomachs. As he began spending time with the orphans, his admiration for Olivier grew, as well as his desire to serve God as a priest. The company chaplain steered him to "the marines of the Catholic Church, the Maryknollers." He was told they work with the poorest of the poor. In the fall of 1966, Bourgeois entered the Maryknoll family.

In August of 1968, Bourgeois' superiors gave him permission to return to Vietnam. What he saw severely rattled him. The damage created by the massive bombing (more than all the tonnage dropped in World War II) was staggering. Chastened and humbled, his innocence shattered forever, Bourgeois began four years of study in the sylvan setting of the Maryknollers at Ossining, New York. It was here that the gospel of non-violence took seed with the former hawkish navy veteran. By 1970, much to the chagrin of his family, he was marching for peace. In 1971 he was arrested for the first time, and when he was summoned to the rector's office to explain his actions, Bourgeois asked him why he – the rector – hadn't been arrested. Six months later the rector, Tom Keefe, was signing petitions against the war.

Bolivia and the Banzer Plan

In 1972 Bourgeois was assigned to one of Latin America's poorest countries, Bolivia. There he joined Maryknoll Sister Ita Ford in Spanish classes. (The latter in 1980 would be raped and murdered by US-trained troops in EL Salvador.) Appalled by the poverty and the horrible abuse of human rights by the Banzer government, Bourgeois set up co-ops, clinics and schools to alleviate as much suffering as possible. In 1975, the Banzer government formulated its notorious plan which became a template for repressive governments in Latin America. It was Richard Nixon who, in the early 1970s, had warned the different agencies of the government that they could no longer count on the Catholic Church as agents of empire. The preferential option for the poor formulated at the Medellín conference of Latin American bishops in 1968 was having an effect.

The Banzer Plan thus was an attempt to undermine the effect foreign missionaries were having in aligning themselves with the poor *campesinos.* The modus operandi was to plant subversive documents on church property and, more crudely, to shut down progressive newspapers and radio stations. Eventually captured and briefly tortured, Bourgeois was expelled in 1977. He had begun to connect the dots between American foreign policy and its role in supporting domestic political repression to ensure the freedom of US capital. Roy Bourgeois was a changed man. For the next decade after the ghastly murder of his friend Ita Ford in El Salvador, he became involved countering US foreign policy in Central America. By 1990 he fastened upon what would become his burning obsession, connecting the dots by linking his country to the horrific violence in Latin America. He founded the School of the Americas Watch (SOAW), an office which monitors the US training of military officers, some of whom have been the most brutal in subverting democratic values. An official program of the US government, funded by the government, the School of the Americas (SOA) has been run to the everlasting shame of the US Armed Forces since 1946. SOA graduates again and again have been implicated in the most egregious human rights assaults in the southern hemisphere.

The SOA is called by some the "School of Assassins" (or *escuela de golpes,* "the school of coups"). It has turned out a "Who's Who" of murderers in several Latin American countries. Among its distinguished graduates have been the notorious Rios Montt (the psychopathic murderer of hundreds of thousands of Guatemalan Mayas in the 80s), Roberto D'Aubisson (the murderer of Oscar Romero), those responsible for the El Mozote slaughter of 900 *campesinos* in El Salvador in 1981, Byron Lima Estrada (convicted in 1998 of murdering Guatemalan Bishop Juan Gerardi), Argentina's Leopoldo Galtieri (the mastermind of the 1976-83 "Dirty War" in that country), Panama's Manuel Noriega, and a list of rogues too many to mention. They are literally present in the dark chapters of every Latin American country.

In 1990 Bourgeois stood, as an act of conscience, outside the gates of the SOA, to utter his 'No' to such an affront to both the Founding Fathers of the US and the Gospel of Christ. In November 2006, when the protest convened for the sixteenth time, a horde of 10,000 outraged Americans (together with busloads of Canadians) protested.

Sr. Lil Mattingly

One of those arrested at Fort Benning in November 2004 was a 63-year-old American nun named Lil Mattingly, a mature woman, suitably outraged at the degraded foreign policy of her own government. From a lifetime of Gospel service which had led to her six-month incarceration at Fort Benning, Mattingly in her courtroom submission described her gradual enlightenment in these terms:

"I came from a sheltered environment unaware of the extremes of US militarism used to economic and political advantage. Even when I joined Maryknoll in 1960 it was important that Russia be defeated. By 1970 I joined most of my nursing class on the streets to protest the war in Vietnam. I arrived in Bolivia at the time of the Banzer coup. His military grabbed, chased, shot, killed, imprisoned and tortured thousands during the seven years of dictatorship. Not only was he responsible for those horrible physical atrocities but he also received loans from the US banks in the millions, which grew into billions enslaving the Bolivian people.

"Judge Faircloth, if you have ever been to the SOA you may see Hugo Banzer's picture in the Hall of Fame! Can you imagine what an insult that is to the beautiful people of Bolivia who suffered terribly under his repressive regime? Bolivia has sent many officers to the SOA. In 1980 two of my Maryknoll sisters who were helping refugees were raped and killed ... hundreds and thousands died with them when our US policies funded and trained militaries in Central America to fight 'communism.' Most of them were SOA grads. In 1987 I lived in Nicaragua where the Sandinista government was trying to implement much-needed reforms as the US-backed dictator Somoza had stolen most everything. Can you see, Your Honour, how this process of awakening has impacted my soul?"

Sr. Mattingly finished her testimony with her conviction of "how misled many of our people are about our foreign policy." Like Roy Bourgeois, her long experience had enabled her to discern the truth and "connect the dots."

Just before Sr. Mattingly's conviction on January 25, 2005, there was one more obvious dot to connect. The Bush administration had just named career diplomat John Negroponte as its chief intelligence director, the man who would coordinate all US spy agencies. What the administration and most media outlets never told the American people was that Negroponte, the former ambassador to both Iraq and the United Nations, had a checkered past which should have excluded him from any government post. From 1981 to 1985 John Negroponte was America's ambassador to Honduras, from where he assisted the US-backed Contra rebels in their murderous attempt to unseat the legally elected Sandinista government. The Contras were notorious for their pillaging and burning of schools, co-ops and innocent civilians. *The Washington Post* deleted any reference to Negroponte's time in Honduras.

In 1995, *The Baltimore Sun* ran an exposé on the polished diplomat. Using as their source some members of the notorious Honduran death squad Battalion 3-16, the newspaper left no doubt about Negroponte's active meetings with the notorious General Gustavo Álvarez Martínez, the sadistic head of 3-16. Trained at the SOA, Martínez ruthlessly "disappeared" any one opposed to the US plans. One of those murdered by Martínez was the Jesuit priest Guadalupe Carney, who was thrown out of a helicopter by members of the death squad. In 2001 investigators exhumed 185 bodies at the El Aguacate military base. Before Negroponte's confirmation as UN ambassador in 2001, two ex-members of 3-16 were suddenly and conveniently deported from Florida to Honduras. Negroponte consistently defended Martínez as a "committed democrat" despite the evidence to the contrary. At the same time the ambassador ordered his aides to delete any reference to torture in the material for annual State Department human rights reports.

Roy Bourgeois has spent four years in jail for his non-violent Gospel convictions. Sr. Lil Mattingly did six months behind bars. With the Gospel as their guidebook, with their elevation of the poor person as their non-negotiable standard, they have managed to shine a light on the terrible moral cost paid by a country which has lost its once-shiny ideals. By linking "the degraded foreign policy" of their country to the victims defended by the one condemned and convicted in Jerusalem, Bourgeois and Mattingly show us once again the price which all of us might pay when we begin to connect the dots.

CONTEMPORARY STATIONS OF THE CROSS

Almost thirty years ago, saddened at our own Catholic parishes' failure to make the links between the crucifixion of Christ and the ongoing suffering today, a few teachers, myself included, decided that a new approach was necessary. The Good News had become endangered by a stultifying lack of imagination which rendered the perennial Story lifeless, almost an exercise in nostalgia. In one downtown Toronto parish, the parishioners enacted the Stations of the Cross by dressing up as the biblical characters and walking through the neighbourhood, replicating a southern Italian tradition based on a theology which would find its apotheosis in Mel Gibson's *The Passion of the Christ*. Two thousand years ago God demanded the sacrifice of a perfect son and made everything right. To many thinking Christians this story is not only incredible but barbaric, turning God into a sadist. It is based on St. Paul's attempt to understand the shocking death of Jesus. As a Jew, Paul already had a metaphor available – the sacrificial lamb offered up at Yom Kippur. But what kind of a God is imagined here? In this scenario death is glorified and not contested. A cursory look at the 20th century should have disabused anybody who thought that everything is all right. This sterile theology anchored everyone in the past and left little room to understand the Crucifixion as contemporary and ongoing. It was a Jesusolatry with little room for the Spirit.

We felt the time had come for a new, contemporary Stations of the Cross.

On April 13, 1979, we began our little walk through the streets of downtown Toronto, stopping to pray and meditate, as our flyer said, "on five contemporary wounds of the suffering body of Christ." The sole sponsor of that walk was the Teachers for Social Justice (TSJ), a small group in the Toronto Catholic School Board who were committed to the social vision of the Church.

The Litton Years: Nuclear Weapons as the Nails

The following year, it was revealed that Litton Industries, a Canadian subsidiary of a larger US company, was making the guidance system for the deadly Cruise Missile. It seemed Litton was overjoyed at new employment opportunities: fourteen hundred new jobs and $1 billion dollars in new business. The only problem was that the business was mass murder. Here was a new weapon 10-15 times as lethal as the Hiroshima bomb, which had killed 85,000 innocents and 2,000 every year since, because of the deadly effects of radiation.

At Vatican II the arms race had been condemned as "an utterly treacherous trap for mankind." It was not a huge leap for us to shift our locus from downtown Toronto to suburban Rexdale, to shine a light on Canadian complicity in the arms race and how it added to the forces of death in our world. We agreed with Pope Paul VI who said: "It is unthinkable that no other work can be found for hundreds and thousands of workers than the production of instruments of death."

There was no better place to pray, no more important place to be on Good Friday, than a discreet piece of suburban real estate, hidden behind barbed wire where mass murder of our fellow humans was being prepared, where a veritable modern Golgotha was being fashioned right in our backyard. Our flyer maintained that: "The Gospel is violated here since it affirms nonviolent love and rejects such massive destruction and suffering of the innocent." We were insisting on a consistent ethic of life. The previous year we had prayed at the Toronto General Hospital where abortions were being performed regularly. Now, we chose to target this factory and pray for its conversion. The money spent on such needless weaponry was already diverting precious resources from the global poor. We were in solidarity both with the poor of the world and in touch with our prophetic Catholic teaching which called the arms race "a crime against God and against humanity which must be condemned firmly and without hesitation."

I will never forget the tears streaming down the face of a hardened CityTV reporter while I held the microphone for Setsuko Thurlow. As a young schoolgirl in Hiroshima, Setsuko had survived the unconscionable atomic blast. She implored all of us to say "No" to this weapon.

Our TSJ group had been joined by the dynamic Youth Corps team of Fr. Tom McKillop, the unparalleled Youth Ministry team of the Toronto Archdiocese. As well, we were supported by the Diocesan Office for Social Action and by Project Ploughshares and the Christian Movement for Peace, ecumenical church groups which were focused on peace. The pastor of the nearest Catholic Church, a veteran Vatican II priest, Fr. Gerry Cochrane happily turned his church over to us so we might devise a prayerful liturgy fitting for the solemnity of the day.

The Good Friday Witness caused an uproar in the city. Many people were shocked that Christians would dare to spend Good Friday like that. When the negative criticism came, the Cardinal's director of social action, Fr. Brad Massman, strongly supported this imaginative attempt to make the Gospel live. In a defence of our actions I wrote in the *Catholic New Times,* "The Good Friday walk to Litton was an attempt to enact another symbolic freedom march – to Jerusalem on Palm Sunday. Like Jesus, we too came in peace. He rode a donkey, the symbol of poverty and humility. We walked defenceless too, to say, "our hope is in his Spirit not in any weapons system.'"

Many More Good Fridays

And so twenty-eight more Good Fridays have come and gone. The memories are fresh and sustaining. The faces of such a cloud of witnesses appear before me. Our prayers were becoming more and more ecumenical, more truly catholic. Many have left us, greats like former United

Church moderator Clarke McDonald, Anglican primate Ted Scott, that marvellous Quaker activist Nancy Pocock, the indefatigable United Church minister Floyd Honey.

Over the years, there have been ups and downs as more and more people came on board to add their energy to the day. A wide variety of social justice issues were addressed including: homelessness, Aboriginal suffering, poverty, and corporate dominance. The Good Friday story came alive and forced more people to realize that this major Christian holy day belonged in the public domain. Like the life and death of Jesus, it had radical social ramifications. Ecumenical Christians were inspired by each other's presence to carry on God's transformative work and confront the violence in society.

In 2004, "Compassion in the Balance" became the theme. The Ecumenical group wanted to "name the violence whose terrible face darkens our world, our city, our community." In what was to become a terrible irony, the Christian Peacemaker Team led by Fr. Bob Holmes and James Loney staged a mini-play about the plight of Iraq detainees, blindfolded and gagged. Barely three weeks later graphic pictures of the notorious Abu Ghraib prison were flashed around the world – and one of those playing the role of an innocent gagged Iraqi would himself become a hostage in Iraq but two years later. James Loney, a Catholic Worker and a member of the Christian Peacemaker Team, had been attending these alternative Good Fridays for several years.

In 2005 the theme of the Stations was "Women at the Foot of the Cross." It was particularly inventive. Violence against women was enacted through drama, song and prayer at four downtown stations. The First Station in Holy Trinity set the theme with a slide show of images. We walked to the new city core, Dundas Square, a perfect place to meditate on the objectification of women by the media. Surrounded by huge neon billboards where L'Oréal assured us that "we deserve it" and the television escape series *Survivor* was promoted, Christians remembered the many ways women were used by the advertising business. *"Kyrie Eleison"* ("Lord, have mercy"), we sang as we proceeded to Old City Hall to listen to Sandi

Hill, an Aboriginal woman, speak about her lost sister Elaine, who had disappeared without a trace 26 years previously. Like 500 other natives in the
past 30 years, Elaine seemed to have walked off the face of the earth with
little concern from the broader society. At this third station we learned
about the Sisters in Spirit Campaign supported by The United Church,
which is making common cause with these women. The fourth station at
the City Hall Peace Garden told the story of Jesus in the persons of women
suffering economic exploitation. "Jesus remember me when you come into
your kingdom" was sung as we arrived back at Holy Trinity for the final
station, Women, Sexuality and Justice, a powerful meditation on the disproportionate suffering of women under the AIDS epidemic.

"AIDS is more than a disease," we chanted. It puts the onus on women
as prime caregivers who are forced to barter sex for food and medicine,
women who bear the brunt when Structural Adjustment Programs in poor
countries slash safety nets. We were all then raised up by the Watoto
Children's Choir of Uganda, young people successfully dealing with AIDS
in the terribly poor country. As always, we ended with the symbolic bread
and soup sharing of solidarity amid old and new friendships. Ironically,
the one serving me my soup was Jeremy Hinzman, the young American
serviceman who fled to Canada after refusing to serve in the immoral, illegal and unjust Iraq war.

Good Friday 2007

Over the past twenty-nine years the Good Friday Walk for Justice has
attempted to zero in on a particular theme or issue. Participants return
again and again, nurtured by the imaginative presentations they experience. It was natural that 2007 should be the year of the Crucified Earth.
Participants had become aware that a new movement in theology called
"Creation-centred theology" had pointed out that the churches had seemingly forgotten the Divine presence beyond and before the human, that of
the earth, the sky, the air, the very universe itself, the ultimate sacred community. While we believed that the primary revelation had taken place in

the life, death and resurrection of Jesus, it had become obvious that "God's body" was being crucified as well.

In the opening slide show various images of the earth were projected on the wall, the theme being "Every part of the earth is sacred." We then processed out into the downtown core of Toronto.

What struck me was that our very city bears the name taken from the original inhabitants of the area, our aboriginal people. As we moved out onto the streets of "trees standing by the water" (in the Mohawk language, Tkronto) it became abundantly clear how alienated we had become from our natural environment. Our First Peoples who lived here had no problem relating to the great Mystery they called *Gitchee Manitou, Orenda* or *Wakan Tanka*. It was clear to them that the Holy Spirit moved through the trees, the winged ones and the finned ones, the rising and the setting of the sun, birth and death. They danced first, then chanted their unison with the Great Spirit. In this city we now cannot see the evening sky or the stars. Our First Peoples had an extraordinary capacity for relatedness, for profound respect for the magnificence of the created order. They intuitively knew and understood that they were part of a Sacred Story which had little to do with a saviour figure offered up to an angry god. Collectively they possessed the wisdom of the mystic.

Here we were in 2007, Christians, members of different communities, seemingly out of touch with the sacred dimensions of our planetary evolution and the role of the Creator in that evolution. We were coming to understand that the original sin was not that of Adam and Eve but our own separation from the bigger story. In this great city we had become disconnected, alienated from our deep mystical roots. We needed to come home again to that ancient spirituality of the earth and the cosmos, because in 2007 we were crucifying our nurturing mother. We needed to stop the abuse and reconnect with the great life force known throughout creation. The first station on this Good Friday was called Wounded Earth: Mining on Holy Ground. Here we heard how Canadian mining companies operating in the global south were abusing the environment and engaging in serious human rights violations. Another station was entitled From

Poisoned Earth to Life Giving soil. The soils had become a place of suffering. Jesus suffers in the soils of the earth. His body was laid to rest in the tomb of the earth. A soil litany was proclaimed. The people responded by saying, "Creating God help us never to forget." And so, creation was honoured in the 2007 Stations of the Cross.

A Contemporary Theology of the Cross

The question continues to rise about just what this *theologia crucis* means for us and the broader Church. If it ends up with the appalling triumphalism seen in the US after 9/11, where a war crusade was presided over by the President and Billy Graham in the Washington National Cathedral, the Gospel and Christianity will continue to be betrayed in the name of a church in the service of empire. If the cross continues, à la Mel Gibson, to be subjectivized and internalized as a private event, then the church will continue to repel serious disciples. Peter asked the first-century followers of the Way not "to be surprised by the fiery ordeal" (1 Peter 4:12) which comes upon them, but in this respect only a few churches really come to mind. The Confessing Church in Nazi Germany is one. Two others are the black church of the civil rights movement and the anti-apartheid struggle, both of which contained many whites in active solidarity. Most Christian churches have disappeared into middle-class conformism and suburban captivity, too often reflecting the prevailing cultural values and mores. The most egregious example in memory has been the embarrassing silence of US churches in the wake of both the death-dealing embargo and the bombing of Iraq. Sad to say, too many churches are riddled with "cheap grace" and content with odd doses of charity. And no one will ever be murdered for charity.

The cross is about justice and the price that must be paid for God's reign to come into existence. And God's reign, as was stated in the 2007 stations, must include a healthy earth. As Salvadoran theologian Jon Sobrino reminds us, a church which forgets itself and turns toward history's victims, a church actively engaged in taking people down from the cross and not merely giving them a drink of water, such a church will inevitably stand against the executioners in a conflictive opposition. Becoming an enemy of empire, it may itself become a victim of state power. No church today, certainly in North America, is ready for this – even though historically it is consequence of serious discipleship. The church is simply too well established, though periodically we have seen some powerful examples (Oscar Romero's Salvadoran witness) south of the Rio Grande. The fact remains that it is very difficult for the church to set aside its *theologia gloriae* for a *theologia crucis*. Yet the future viability of our ecclesial life will hinge on our understanding this. Nobody put it better than Dietrich Bonhoeffer when he said that Christianity is about being human and "it is not the religious act which makes the Christian but participating in the sufferings of the world." And that suffering includes the air, the earth, the sky and the soil, constituent parts of God's body.

The Ecumenical Stations of the Cross challenge us to reclaim the cross as the authentic mark of the church.

As we walk, we journey together with Jesus enacting a hope for all people and all that lives in this biophilious universe. Good Friday never stands alone, it is simultaneously Easter, a spirit dimension which still has the power to confront the myriad forces of death and overcome them in all their forms. Abundant life for all no longer refers to the human, and that's what Good Friday Ecumenical Walk 2007 was proclaiming.

A CHALLENGE TO BISHOPS

One of the many side effects of the last pontificate has been the disappearance of what the apostolic Church called *parrhesia* or free speech, the type of plain talk which characterized Paul's challenge to Peter at the Council of Jerusalem. The word went out very early in John Paul II's tenure that even in non-infallible areas of Church teaching, no dissent would be brooked. Over one hundred theologians were muzzled and a veritable chill descended on the Church. Fear seemed to stalk the ecclesial landscape, the irony being that the mantra of the last pontificate was "Be not afraid."

This fear seeped all the way down to local levels and any diocesan priest brave enough to proffer a different opinion was disciplined or reprimanded. In Cobourg, Ontario (an hour east of Toronto) parishioners were outraged at the treatment of Fr. Ed Cachia in the fall of 2005. The much-loved pastor was quoted in the local paper as saying that he welcomed the women priests who had been "illicitly" ordained the previous July on the St. Lawrence River. Furthermore, he said the Catholic Church needed to open up the priesthood to women. That Cachia was echoing the sentiments of a broad majority of his flock was irrelevant, that this "idea" might be the *sensus fidelium* of God's people at this moment in history seemed inconceivable to Cachia's bishop and the blind loyalists around him. And then the inevitable happened: An alternative Catholic community was set up in the Peterborough Diocese with Cachia as its pastor. But I digress.

Bishops today seem to be answering to a constituency of one, the Roman pontiff. That they should also be listening to the baptized in their own dioceses seems to have eluded many of them. The highest teaching in the Church, the Vatican Council (in this case, Vatican II) reminded us that, "the holy people of God share in Christ's prophetic office" and that "it is the people as a whole" who share in this infallibility. The Spirit is the head of the Church, and all are under obedience to the same Spirit. In the last quarter-century the institutional leaders have arrogated to themselves the sole interpretation of scripture and Church tradition. All this despite the profound advance in theological literacy among lay people. As of yet, the celibate hierarchy has not accepted the lay *sensus fidelium* as an authentic prophetic charism. As Pope Pius XI put it two weeks before he died in 1939: "The Body of Christ has become a monstrosity – the head (the papacy and Curia) has far outstripped the Body" (the vast majority of lay people). And this was over 65 years ago!

The terrible silence of the last twenty-five years has so bothered Capuchin priest Michael Crosby that he wrote a book about the disappearance of prophecy in religious life. The book was entitled *Can Religious Life Be Prophetic?* As a member of a religious order, Crosby was particularly saddened by what had transpired in the last two decades.

In his judgment the religious orders have defaulted on their charisms. Religious life is not purely functional. It exists as a "sign" and a "privileged witness to God's reign particularly among the poor." This "experience of the Spirit" precedes fidelity to the Magisterium. Religious orders, particularly after Vatican II, re-founded themselves to come closer to the poor and marginalized and "to read the signs of the times and return to the Gospel according to the charism of their founders." As the late Pope John Paul II said, these men and women in the history of the Church "have carried out a pastoral ministry, speaking in the name of God even to the pastors." This, of course, is a reference to the traditional role of the biblical prophets who spoke both to the king, and to the Temple and synagogue.

Crosby maintains, "We began to reinterpret our lives as revolving around the poles of prophecy and contemplation, with solidarity with the poor and marginalized and commitment to social justice as the benchmarks of the authentic expression of these two poles in our lives." All of us can name several in religious life who did this. They moved out of huge houses and confronted institutions with God's challenging word.

There is not much of that activity left, according to Crosby. While proclaiming publicly this prophetic charism, the orders, illuminated by their own internal polling, realized that they had been assimilated into the dominant culture too. The blandishments of worldly success and power, the toxicity of rampant individualism, the loss of energy of aging clerics unsupported by the more conservative confreres and sisters, the episcopal swing to the right, and in the United States the overwhelming presence of American civil religion – all took their toll. Yet many religious kept on, faithful to God's reign of justice and the Church's fading claim that it was semper reformanda (always in the process of renewing itself).

But something happened in Canada in March of 2006 which would bring a smile to Crosby's face. The Canadian Religious Conference (CRC) found its prophetic voice once again.

Enter The Canadian Religious Conference

In June 2004, the CRC assembly, obviously disturbed at the diminished involvement of the Canadian bishops in the social sphere and their seemingly utter capitulation to Rome, expressed a desire to speak out more publicly and to engage the faithful (both lay and clerical) in a deeper discussion. A survey was then sent out to the 230 religious congregations representing 22,000 priests, nuns, and brothers. On December 13, 2005 the Administrative Council approved the "Message to the Bishops" and sent the results out to its members. According to Sr. Donna Geernaert, the CRC vice-president, the responses were meant to be private, but were leaked to *La Presse,* a Montreal newspaper. On March 18 they found their way into *The Globe and Mail,* Canada's national paper of record.

The results are dramatic and are slowly causing a buzz among Catholics.

In a letter to all CRC members, president Allain Ambeault, a priest of the Clercs de Saint-Viateur, a Quebecois order, stated, "We have the firm conviction that this message reflects the thinking of religious communities in Canada as well as the majority of the men and women religious throughout the country ... We can expect it to evoke criticism, perhaps even strong criticism ... At times solidarity expresses itself in disquieting words."

While always respectful, the CRC document pulls no punches and Ambeault, in his letter, asked the bishops to "carry with them to Rome in their upcoming *ad limina* visit what the People of God are saying ... Our Church is isolated by its language and its attitudes. It moves away from being a meaningful force in our world."

A Blunt Report

The 26-page letter is blunt in its description of the Canadian Church's defects. Divided into five parts and sub headed by "Recognitions, regrets and hopes," it is a model of prophetic clarity and would dearly cheer Michael Crosby. Prophecy is back – at least in the Canadian Church.

Under the heading "The Church and the search for meaning," the document faults the Church for its failure to advance in areas of sexual morality, for its legalistic, rigid, and intransigent position. The Church is not a player among the young; its message is out of synch with their search for meaning. There is little freedom and theologians seeking pastoral responses are condemned much too quickly. The John Paul II ordinands' theological training is not "bringing valid answers to today's problems." This is not a listening Church, the document states, and there is no training for collegial relationships. In the view of the CRC the Canadian bishops are supine to Rome, too afraid to defend general absolution and raise the issue of married priests and the role of women.

And This is Just The Start!

Always attempting to name the positive achievements of the Church, the second subheading of the report deals with "Community Life in the Church." After listing nine positive steps, this section laments the loss of collegiality 40 years after Vatican II – the failure of integrating more lay people in the area of Church governance and too much clerical domination. What is the hope here? More dialogue without arrogance, more collaboration and lay consultation, and more openness to the world and dialogue with other churches.

"Solidarity with the Church," the area dealing with social justice concerns, acknowledges the Canadian Church's well-deserved reputation for progressive justice stands in the years after the Council, but laments the poor follow-through in those same areas in the last few decades. Charity is not enough. The hope is that the Canadian Church will "position itself closer to the major issues of the world-environment and inequality etc." and that "a true partnership will be established with social organizations and groups involved in the struggle for humanitarian causes ..." The Canadian Church has been notorious in this regard. If it's not leading the justice parade, it's not in it, much to the embarrassment of engaged laity.

Finally, an interesting section on "Prophecy in the church" challenges the bishops. It is very pointed and, from my long experience, absolutely correct. "We regret the timidity of the prophetic voice of the Canadian church: fear of change, lack of encouragement of various initiatives by lay people." The most egregious example of this was when the well-known grassroots Christian Peacemaker James Loney went missing in Iraq. It took the institutional Church two full weeks to wake up to the fact that Loney was a Catholic and that prayers should be offered up in each parish for his release. Phone calls to the out-of-touch Toronto chancery office finally shook it from its torpor. Still not one member of the hierarchy showed up at weekly vigils for Loney while he was held hostage. This autistic avoidance of justice issues has long been the norm.

A Prophetic Challenge

The document concludes with "profound solidarity with you ... even if some of our statements may be difficult to receive."

Make no mistake about this challenge to the bishops. Coming from such a respected group it can only be ignored at the bishops' peril. It names – in no uncertain terms – the deep problems of the Canadian Catholic Church. It zeroes in on an overly timorous episcopate. While the broad *sensus fidelium* has been badly marginalized, frustrated, and leaving the Church in droves, the CRC has been listening and is acting on what they have learned.

Fr. Ed Cachia has since returned to the Church but his case reflects a top-down clerical institution which has sadly forgotten to listen deeply to the "signs of the times," to the Holy Spirit incarnate in all its members and not just a privileged clerical caste. Until it remembers to do so, it will continue to devolve into a closed-command society, a lifeless feudal rump where the structure remains but the Spirit of truth, inclusion and deep listening has departed.

The brave but faithful initiative of the CRC should be the basis of a new conversation with the broader Catholic community. It probably will be ignored. If it is taken seriously it could serve its purpose of regenerating a Church which has ceased to be salt in this predominantly Catholic country.

A GRACE-FILLED JOURNEY
DOWN THE KINGDOM ROAD

One of London's major tourist attractions is a famous monument designed and erected by Sir Christopher Wren, to commemorate the Great Fire of London in 1666. The monument is near St. Paul's Cathedral. You can easily visit both in an afternoon. Climbing the 311 steps of the monument, you will get a breathtaking view of one of the world's great cities.

Not far from St. Paul's there is a spot equally rich in history – an extraordinary hidden marker to the magnanimity of the human spirit and a testament to human hope and dogged perseverance. Two George Yard is not difficult to find, even though it bears no visible blue marker, the usual signpost to an important site in London's fascinating history.

On May 22, 1787, a dozen determined men sat down in a now-vanished print shop with one idea in mind: to eradicate the stain of the slave trade from human history. It was their collective will to bury the chains forever, to relegate to the dustbin of history, the odious and dehumanizing practice of the international slave trade. Their declaration was simple and to the point. At a meeting held for the purpose of taking the slave trade into consideration, it was resolved that the trade was both impolitic and unjust. In retrospect, their declaration was both staggering to imagine and impossible to conceive. Slavery was a given in the mindset of most Britons and, more importantly, slave-grown sugar was a major engine of the British economy, employing tens of thousands of people. In our postmodern era of jaded worldviews, cynical asides and apathetic, non-engaged pietism, Adam Hochschild's riveting story *Bury the Chains* (Houghton

Miflin, 2005) will add a refreshing chapter to the ongoing and evergreen triumph of the human spirit.

Lately, we have witnessed the fall of the Berlin Wall, Tiananmen Square and the end of apartheid. Now another narrative encourages us to remember that history is the collective decision-making of human beings.

In the 18th century in England, a small maritime country with a global empire, the slave trade was an acceptable way of life. It was a commercial ticket to unbelievable wealth and influence in society. One dreamer was 11-year-old John Newton, who in 1736 followed his sea-captain father into the lucrative business of providing slaves for the sugar plantations of the British West Indies. The business, as one trader wrote, was "the foundation of our commerce and the support of our colonies."

Canadians may be deflated to know that in 1773 the small island of Grenada created eight times the wealth that Canada produced for the mother country. Jamaica alone produced five times the wealth of the thirteen American colonies. Among the maritime nations, Britain ferried 40,000 chained men, women and children across the ocean from Africa to the West Indies. This was more than all the other countries combined. Newton wanted a piece of the action. His is one lens through which Hochschild spins his riveting tale. John Newton, second only to John Wesley, became the most prolific Christian hymn-writer in England, the same John Newton who gave the world the classic "Amazing Grace." It would take Newton until middle age to awaken to the shocking immorality of his earlier life.

Granville Sharp and Thomas Clarkson

Granville Sharp played oboe and flute in the Granville Family Musicians, a precocious brood, eight brothers and sisters, who provided glorious music to, among others, King George III. The son and grandson of Anglican clergymen, Sharp's life dramatically changed in 1765 when a black man named Jonathan Strong appeared at a free clinic of Sharp's physician brother. Beaten beyond recognition by a slave trader, Strong was taken by the Sharps to the famous St. Bart's hospital where he was nursed back to health in four months. Two years later, another slaver tried to kidnap him and send him back to Jamaica. That was it for Sharp. For the next 50 years, he became an untiring enemy of the slave trade.

Olaudah Equiano (also known as Gustavus Vassa) was a former slave living in England. In 1783, he spied a small article in a London paper about a shocking case being heard in the courts. Captain Luke Collingwood, the master of the slave ship Zong, had claimed the maritime principle of "jettisoning," tossing overboard cargo (human beings) to save valuable produce. The *Zong*'s owners filed an insurance claim ($500,000 in today's money). Many of the humans were tossed overboard shackled together.

The shock for Granville Sharp, to whom Equiano had run for help, was that this was not a homicide case, but a civil insurance claim. Equiano spent the rest of his life giving dramatic readings about his own life as a slave.

Granville Sharp waxed indignant, firing letters across the British Isles. One letter reached the vice-chancellor of Cambridge University, who made the morality of the slave trade the subject of the prestigious Cambridge Latin essay contest. The winner was a 25-year-old divinity student named Thomas Clarkson. Six feet tall, with flaming red hair, Clarkson had a "Damascus" moment on his horse near Wades Mill, Hertfordshire (where there is a historical marker).

Heading to London to begin his life as an Anglican clergyman, Clarkson was struck by the realization that "if the contents (of his essay) were true, someone should see these calamities to their end." He would take his essay and turn it into a pamphlet demanding an end to the slave trade.

At that time the Quakers were virtually alone in combating the slave trade in Britain. Anglicans by and large were mute, as well as being the owners of the biggest plantations in Jamaica.

A Quaker friend took Clarkson to the printing shop of James Phillips in George Yard. A pamphlet was printed and a movement was born. Clarkson became the greatest catalyst and "a veritable moral steam engine," as Samuel Taylor Coleridge called him. For the latter, Clarkson became "my friend, my exemplar, my saint. How highly I revere him."

The novelist Jane Austen fell in love with him from afar. The Quakers admitted that they had long had their eyes on the Anglican, Clarkson. They were wise enough to realize that few would trust the idiosyncratic Quakers, widely mocked as a fringe religious group at the time. Though deeply dedicated in their faith, they were viewed, with their "thees" and "thous" and broad-brimmed hats, as odd sticks.

Clarkson set off into the belly of the beast, the ports of Bristol and Liverpool. Liverpool was the chief port from which ships would carry 300,000 Africans into slavery during the years 1783 to 1793. The town council was controlled by slavers hostile to Clarkson. He later wrote that he did not think he would leave Liverpool alive. He received death threats in the taverns and opponents tried to toss him off the pier in the harbour. His bodyguard, Dr. Alexander Falconbridge, followed him throughout Britain as he collected 680 pages of first-hand testimony from slaves, doctors and ship captains. This evidence was later used by abolitionists in America. Step by step the movement was carried forward.

The Society of Friends (Quakers)

The Society of Friends was – and is – the least hierarchical religion in the western world. In a period of rigid class stratification and an established state religion, Quakers had little public acceptance. What they did have was a passion for justice and a fundamental belief that each human carried the *spermatikos,* the divine spark. Hence Quakers were never hidebound by rigid structure and paternalism. Anyone could get up and speak at a Quaker meeting. In theological terms, the Spirit could more easily penetrate groups and not be sidelined by clerical authority. Even today Quakers' impact on justice and peace movements is far out of proportion to their small numbers.

Quakers brought to the Abolitionist movement a century of articulated activism. With their central insight that they were part of the Divine movement in history, they got on with the job. They were cowed neither by parliamentarians nor by bishops. Since everybody had human dignity, the males refused to take their hats off to any man, not as a sign of disrespect but with the confidence that all were equal in the sight of God. Catholics and other religious activists today would be wise to emulate this well-founded confidence.

Fired with evangelical zeal, these men and women fearlessly and confidently approached royalty with deputations, parliamentarians and other people with petitions. They were street-smart and spirited people who never surrendered their intelligence, as they organized the campaign which they knew would take years – if not decades – to come to fruition.

In their practicality, the group understood that their aim could not be abolition, but rather the curtailing of the slave trade. Clarkson said this was "to lay the axe at the root of the problem and abolition sure must follow."

Clarkson and Granville Sharp would be the leaders of the new movement. In Parliament the great ally of the anti-slavers was the silver-tongued William Wilberforce, who again and again took the cause to the House.

At 5 p.m. on April 18, 1791, Wilberforce began his famous speech on the slave trade. Lasting four hours, it was described by Edmund Burke as "the greatest eloquence ever displayed in the House." Wilberforce never stopped his efforts inside government. His role is undisputed. "I have attached my happiness to this cause and shall never relinquish it." Good to his word and bolstered by evangelical Anglicanism, he persisted until the slave trade was outlawed in 1808.

Clarkson, Sharp and Wilberforce became the public face of the movement, but it was the "dissenting" Quakers who supplied the energy and network throughout the British Isles. In many ways, they pioneered the age-old justice techniques for public education: broadsheets, essays, boycotts, petitions and direct-mail fundraising.

The Midlands potter, Josiah Wedgewood, even produced his Slave Medallion, a fashion accessory which adorned hat pins and brooches. It showed a black man in a supine position looking up at his captor saying, "Am I not a man and a brother?" Wedgewood shipped some to Benjamin

Franklin, the president of the Pennsylvania Society for Promoting the Abolition of Slavery.

A Female Contribution

In this epic battle for human dignity, we see the beginnings of a strong feminist component. The battle for justice was waged everywhere, including at dining room tables. It was women who controlled the family hearth and who organized the boycott of sugar in English homes. The young Quaker poet Mary Birkett wrote: "If we the produce of their toils refuse, / If we no more the blood-stained luxury choose …"

By the thousands, women began purchasing Indian sugar rather than that from the West Indies.

In Jamaica, as more evangelical churchmen began to preach the evils of the trade, the plantation owners, desperate to protect their ill-gotten gains, ratcheted up the fight. The power of the righteousness of the abolitionist cause proved too strong. The liberationist message drawn from the Exodus story inspired the slaves, who were convinced that the God of the Bible was on their side and desired their freedom. Christianity grew for the simple reason that a disenfranchised people were now convinced of their innate dignity. Twenty Methodist and Baptist chapels were burned to the ground after an uprising in Montego Bay. Portraits of Clarkson and Wilberforce continued to be hung in the shanties of Jamaica.

In 1832, legislation was finally passed outlawing the slave trade. Forty years of pushing Parliament had paid off. The government, still dominated by financial elites, paid compensation to the slavers and insisted that the freed slaves would be indentured for six more years until August 1, 1838.

One of the most active clergymen in the struggle, William Knibbs, returned to Jamaica to preside at a church service celebrating the end of the barbaric practice. As the hour moved toward midnight the congregation sang: "The deathblow is struck / He cannot survive till the dawn streaks the sky / In one single hour he will be prostrate and lying / Come shout o'er the grave."

The children of Wilberforce wrote a massive biography of their father, by all accounts one of the loveliest men ever to sit in the British Parliament. The contributions of men like Clarkson and Granville Sharp were minimized as the historiography of the "great man" school dominated Victorian England. Such a narrow view of social change would have embarrassed the great Wilberforce, who had always been lavish in the praise of his contemporaries. It was not until 1989, in England, that a biography of Thomas Clarkson was published. Now, Adam Hochschild has helped restore Clarkson and others to their rightful place in this titanic struggle.

Our Role in the Drama

In the pages of *Bury the Chains*, we have proof that the arc of the universe does bend toward justice, that we all have a role in the redemptive drama. All stand on the shoulders of those who have gone before in an extraordinary communion of saints, those whose own "Yes" to the divine summons has given us our cue to enter stage left and do our part, however small we think it to be.

One brave soul hearing the trumpet call of conscience rejects the received wisdom of his culture and, yes, sometimes of his church. Step by step a tiny group advanced a small mustard seed watered by God's Holy Spirit of justice. It is a profound lesson for postmodern cynics who despair of social change.

Wedgewood's grandson was Charles Darwin. Wilberforce's great ally, William Smith, was the grandfather of the Victorian feminist Barbara Bodichon. Another abolitionist, Bristol's Sam Blackwell, had a granddaughter who was the first female physician in Europe. Robert Goulden's granddaughter was Emmeline Pankhurst, one of the most significant suffragettes. James Stephen's great-granddaughter was Virginia Woolf.

Clarkson was the sole member of the 1787 meeting to see the end of the slave trade. At his funeral in 1846, the Quakers took off their hats in respect to the role that he had played in the movement. Clarkson went to his grave knowing that he was not alone in one of the great moral struggles of his age. His witness already had lit a spark across an ocean, in the lives of the great abolitionists William Lloyd Garrison and Frederick Douglass. His indefatigable witness should inspire all of us to carry on down the Kingdom road of our time in history. The issue may be different, but the divine summons remains the same.

THE CHRISTMAS POEMS

For 35 years now, I have been sending Christmas poems out to close friends. A number have found their way to anthologies in Great Britain. None have appeared in print elsewhere, though several people have asked me if they could use them in church bulletins. I never refuse.

These prose poems are consistent in that they take seriously the idea that the Christmas stories are not for children. Christians have for far too long treated the Infancy Narratives as myth or as pretty harmless legends for kids. They are anything but. They are evangelical dynamite, brilliantly polished nuggets brimming with radical theological import. They challenge the Roman claim that the powerful Emperor Augustus is Lord and rules as *"dominus et deus,"* a common inscription of the time. In an absolutely outrageous claim, the evangelists point to the itinerant rabbi, murdered by the state, as *"Dominus et Deus."*

Roman writers of antiquity could not grasp the dynamic spread of the Jesus Movement. Men like Tacitus, quoted here, were beside themselves as the *exitiabilis superstitio* (pernicious superstition) continued to make inroads in the vast empire long after Jesus' public execution. The description of this great Roman historian is typical of the time – shocking disbelief that a *"dominus et deus"* could come out of Galilee, part of a backwater Roman province.

These few poems I have chosen attempt to unpack the good news for our time. In the words of the great German theologian, Johann Baptist Metz, these are "dangerous" stories. I have simply tried to let them speak to our era. Each year demands a new interpretation. If the four gospels do not reproduce a "fifth" for our age, they are simply "old news" and not "good news." I have tried to be faithful to the contemporary manifestation of the Spirit, the Divine Disturber. I am indebted to my great teacher in England, Hubert Richards, who set me on this path in 1971.

The essay, "The Lost Cry of Liberation," sets the theological table for the poems.

THE INFANCY NARRATIVES:
THE LOST CRY OF LIBERATION

You still persist in sending us angels
to teach us unfear
to steel us sufficiently to stare back
at the darkness in love
and playfully purse our lips
into a royal raspberry —
convicted of your constant Presence.
The baby is born, the rest are pretenders
and we have every right to sing:
Gloria in excelsis deo.
Ted Schmidt (1986)

Christmas is the Catholic feast par excellence. Despite its paling by theological contrast with Easter and Pentecost, we nevertheless have said otherwise with our lives. Canadian Catholics, specifically, insist on the centrality of Christmas. There is something wonderful about the snow, the warmth inside, the decorating of the tree, the family reunions, the aroma of the Christmas meal, the midnight mass. In the midst of this, we once again feel right, secure, loved. In so many ways we feel "religious." Who can quarrel with this idealized portrait?

And yet, something is not quite right.

Sensitized to the plight of the global family we feel increasingly uneasy about the commercial hype around the season. Somehow we resent the pressure to spend outrageous sums to prove our devotion to loved ones. Rather than seeing Christmas as a time to count our blessings and share them with the marginalized, we become hostage to the worst aspects of this time: selfishness and greed. The countervailing trend to simplicity is to be fostered.

And what of Jesus, "the reason for the season?" How will the Prince of Peace be honoured among the Christians in the US? Their silent night and lack of outrage over the obscene murder of hundreds of thousands of Iraqi innocents will hardly make a dent in their festive bacchanals. Sadly, the hymn of Christmas cash registers will once again usher in; in the regal style he has become accustomed to, the birthday of the one who died in disgrace in the royal city's garbage dump. The hosannas of retailers welcome the nativity of the Messiah who, the stories tell us, was born in the poverty of a cave, the king of the stable, Jesus Christ.

What do these stories mean to us anymore? They were learned by rote in a simpler time. Is it not time to move away from what Mircea Eliade termed the "first level of naïveté?" Is it not high time to stop trivializing these potent gospel invitations to conversion? The answer is obvious. The world can no longer afford our adolescence and our ignorance. We need to recover the depth of social and political criticism contained in these familiar accounts. This essay, I hope, will be a modest contribution in regaining the serious challenge of the infancy narratives.

Threat and Promise, Life and Death

It has long been accepted by scripture scholars that the infancy narratives are more interested in proclaiming the meaning of Jesus' birth than giving us verifiable historical details. Unknown to the first evangelist Mark and written at least three generations after the event, these powerful stories attempt to interpret for first century people the significance of the life, death and resurrection of Jesus.

Matthew and Luke, writing in the glow of the resurrection and knowing the end of the story, rightly insist that even the birth of Jesus is significant. The best way to communicate this, given the nature of the audience and the historical period, is by narrative. People love stories. Ultimate truths, in fact, are best proclaimed by stories. These carefully crafted myths, written by Matthew and Luke against the background of the Hebrew Scriptures, contain the eternal themes of life-death, threat-promise, power-weakness, etc.

It was at the end of long theological reflection that the beginning of the Christ emerged. In a sense, Jesus was raised before he was born. To this day these brilliant narratives continue to fire our imaginations. Yet, the latent power has long been domesticated. Perhaps the perennial consumer onslaught has deadened their impact; certainly bad theology has for too long trivialized them.

Let us turn to Luke. He begins his account of Jesus' birth with the moving account of Mary's visitation to Elizabeth. In response to the latter, Mary proclaims her famous *Magnificat*. Based on Hannah's prayer in 1 Samuel and a host of other Jewish biblical texts, the *Magnificat* (Lk. 1:46-55) is the great hymn of praise to Israel's Lord, Yahweh, whose history is replete with examples of God's preferential option for the poor. This God has a long and consistent track record for showing "the power of his arm" (v.51). Luke shows us not a pious illiterate teenager but a young woman who has pondered Israel's history:

The madonna's smile signifies something
Only understood in Israel's blood
Soon the hungry will be filled with all good things (TS-1980)

Mary knows this Exodus God is one who "has pulled down princes from their thrones and exalted the lowly"(v.52). Luke, of course, is writing from the perspective of one who knows the end of the story. He wishes to tell us that many of the themes that will follow his Lord throughout his life are present right from the beginning of his life. Even while in his mother's womb, Jesus is being prepared to imitate his Father. Mary remarks that this God, in the past, "has filled the starving with good things and sent the rich away empty" (v. 53). So the Son as presented by Luke will reaffirm later in his life, "How hard it is for rich people to enter the kingdom of God" (18:24).

Luke's gospel consistently speaks of the honoured place of the lowly ones and the danger of riches. Maybe this is why we privileged Christians of the North, complicit in the crimes of the New World Order, feel so uncomfortable with the *Magnificat*. Ernst Fuchs, the great German scholar, has pointed out why we often miss the power of these challenges. He says, "We have not yet captured the meaning of biblical words in our present day sermons and lectures until it is as dangerous in our situation as it was for the original biblical spokesmen." Where it is dangerous and where the spirit of the *Magnificat* is captured is of course in the Church of the marginales: Guatemala, Soweto, Peru etc. It is they who read this infancy narrative with the same eyes as the early Christians: with the eyes of those longing for liberation and ready to risk martyrdom.

Latin American campesinos live out of the hope, "mindful of his faithful love, according to the promise he made to our ancestors" (Luke 1:54, 55). What God has done in the past he will surely do again. The assorted Pharaohs who have brutalized Guatemala and El Salvador for decades will suffer the same fate of the biblical pharaoh. Was it not Yahweh's son, the Lord Jesus, who began his ministry in Luke's gospel by saying that

> "He has sent me to bring the Good News to the poor
> to proclaim liberty to the captives ...
> to set the downtrodden free ..." 4:18

Matthew's Story: More Radical Political Criticism

A similar theme is seen in Matthew's story. Using a Moses typology (five blocks of teaching similar to the five books of Torah, the teaching received and proclaimed on a mount similar to Sinai, birth as threat to a ruler – Pharaoh and Herod), Matthew implies that a liberator greater than Moses is here; the ultimate Exodus has arrived. Like Pharaoh, Herod is afraid that he will become a prince who is pulled from his throne. Matthew tells us that, "He was perturbed and so was the whole of Jerusalem." (2:3)

Herod had a right to be perturbed.
So does every Herod who sits on a throne
Of his people's bones
Who drinks his people's tears as
Unrighteous wine. (TS-1980)

Implicit in these stories is radical political criticism. Both evangelists are in fact saying that any world governed by imperial values, which makes war on innocent children, is contrary to the will of God and in fact must be resisted. Should we maybe look forward this year for a dramatization of "the slaughter of the innocents" in our children's pageants? It might not be a stretch to link the death of half a million Iraqi children in the blockade of 1991-2003 as grist for the gospel mill. It might ruin our Hallmark Christmas if we somehow made the connection. It is irrelevant where or when that world happens: in Egypt in 1250 BC, in Palestine in 30 AD or in Iraq from 1991-2003. In the Reagan-Thatcher decade of greed, the 80s, war was increasingly made on the global poor; the gap between rich and poor widened. It is not a coincidence that this decade as well saw the rise of liberation theology, a powerful cry of human dignity from the underside of history. This resistance to the humiliation of so many in the human family was called "opportune, necessary and useful" by John Paul II (April 9, 1986, Letter to Brazilian bishops).

It was the poor and their spokespeople who pointed out their similarity to Jesus. Did not Luke as well contrast the humble birth of Jesus, the nobody born in a cave, with the wealth and status of imperial power (Tiberius Caesar, Herod, Philip, and Lysanias: (Luke 3:1)? How can the naked Jesus, born outside the inn at a forsaken outpost of the Roman Empire ever compete with these? Luke, the consummate gospeller, is already getting us ready for the baby's tragic end – he will die as he was born, naked – a shameless death, one reserved for revolutionaries. Murdered by the state, he will have no funeral rites; he will hear no soft words of assurance. There will be no elaborate eulogies, no marble sarcophagus in an imperial court. He will die as he was born, Jesus the perpetual outsider.

This Jewish kingdom peddler will, like the poor of Latin America, be scorned by Annas and Caiaphas, those "imperial flunkies, high priests of accommodation to imperial power." Latinos in particular pointed out the similarity of the humble origins of their Lord, his special love for *los pobres.* They would correctly deduce that this Jesus was more like their slain martyrs than their powerful oppressors. It is all there in the infancy narratives: God's reign is modelled and begun in weakness.

Luke knows that the baby, locked out the day he was born, will pretty much live like that the rest of his life:

Down the road, the only room he found was in a whore's heart
a madman's psyche, room only in the lives
of the broken and the bent, the vulnerable and the
uncool (TS-1977)

Challenge to Imperial Propaganda

Raymond Brown, in his exhaustive study *The Birth of the Messiah,* comments: "It can scarcely be accidental that Luke's description of the birth of Jesus presents an implicit challenge to this imperial propaganda, not by denying the imperial ideals but by claiming that the real peace of the world was brought about by Jesus."(415)

To those with the eyes of faith it is not Augustus who is *"dominus et deus,"* but the baby "wrapped in swaddling clothes" (Lk.2:7). It is the very one who will wear another crown and initiate another kingdom. It is he, the member of a despised race, not the architect of the *Pax Romana,* who will become the Son of God. Similarly, it will be poor campesinos, not George Bush, who will ultimately construct the New World Order. The incarnation of God, spoken about in such a simple yet sophisticated way by Luke, is nothing less than confrontation. It simply says "No" to all imperial ideologies, since they all contain record unemployment, underemployment, suppression of minorities, racism and hunger, premature death. As it always has, incarnation will resist gulags, psychiatric hospitals, and worldwide military bases. It will not celebrate peace without justice or

New World Orders without human dignity. It will resist the lie that shalom can be purchased by mass murder. Even the nails of the Empire will not break God's power first known in the weakness of Luke's baby. It is the Empire, not the Kingdom, which will be convicted on Calvary.

Luke's ironic contrast between these two dramatically opposed kingdoms warns us very early in the gospels not to look to Caesar for peace. He cannot give it. The angels proclaim that it is the infant, not Augustus, who will give "glory to God and peace to all who enjoy his favour" (2:14). Only the infant's naked vulnerability, which ends in non-violent redemptive love, can be "news of great joy to be shared with the whole people" (2:10). No heavenly host will sing for any Commander-in-Chief. The "saviour born to you, Christ the Lord" (2:11) will soon die at the hands of the Commander.

Similarly, Matthew in another reading (the slaughter of the innocents), insists that while Caesar cannot bring in the final shalom he has it in his power to bring in the final solution.

Finally, it is Luke who presents us with the mystery of God's unseemly habit of revealing himself to the poor and humble of heart. In this case it is the far from cute rustic gentlemen we have traditionally pictured on our cards. No, the shepherds in biblical times were

the niggers of religious Palestine,
Jews who worked the midnight shift
and could not observe the Mosaic laws ...
poor men invisible to Rome,
forgotten by Jerusalem,
a despised class. (TS-1974)

Yes, the shepherd first sees. What is Luke telling us? Simply, that the religious experts missed the salvation of the world. Not only did they miss it at birth but they missed it during his life. In fact, the religious had Jesus murdered. If God surprised then, what now? Should we not be looking away from the centres of power for rebirth? Do we expect to find salvation in the heart of this consumer darkness or institutional sclerosis? Will God not once more reveal herself to the perceived outsider? What is happening here? Could these cute stories be more than they seem? Are the infancy stories really for grown-ups? Should we begin to move beyond the crib, the star and the shepherds? Can we begin to hear the new summons in the oldest of stories?

Are we ready for the unspeakably new?
Or are we resigned to the weary, the worn out,
locked into a determined cosmos
where there are no surprises?
We believe Novelty comes, always comes
breaking us, remaking us?
Are we ready? Fine.
Let us go to Bethlehem and see this thing
that has happened. (TS-1974)

CHRISTMAS 1986

They were terrified but the angel said to them: Do not be afraid.
Luke 2:9, 10   Gospel reading: Christmas Day 1986

We are reminded again of the risks involved.
The fair weather boys will not buck the prevailing winds
and this month we remember Merton's Chinese monk's monitum:
There are no structures:
there is only spiritual self-reliance on God.
Indeed we would be fools to ignore
the hobbled old emperor and his greedy Herodians
north of the 49th,
the chuckling commissar on the Steppes,
the white fascists, the fundamentalist theocrats
and the bored multitudes.
No, we are not naïve but apprehensive.
In our night of confusion
you still persist in sending us angels
to teach us unfear.
You steel us sufficiently to stare back
at the darkness in love
and playfully purse our lips into a royal raspberry –
convicted of your constant presence.
The baby is born, the rest are pretenders
and we have every right to sing:
Gloria in excelsis Deo.

CHRISTMAS 1998

The people who walked in darkness have seen a great light.
Isaiah 9:2   Mass during the night, Christmas 1998

Isaiah man, you walk with me all through dark December
moon-mad with hopeful visions
wolves as guests of lambs all peoples feasting on rich foods
death swallowed forever
and tears wiped away for good.
(Keep it up, I'm really digging it.)
Awash as I am by leveraged buyouts
blinkered men shouting hosannas to the free market
while socializing the risks
bankers and business driving inflation to zero
and unemployed workers to their knees.
(Oooh Isaiah, don't stop now)
You tell me the eyes of these blind bastards will be opened? When?
Trust in the Lord forever, you repeat.
He humbles those in high places
and the lofty city he brings down,
levels it with dust.
It is trampled underfoot by the needy,
by the footsteps of the poor (26:5, 6)
I wanna believe the meek shall obtain fresh joy in the Lord,
the poor and humble shall exult in the Holy One (29:19)
I burn with shame today:

"The UN has condemned Canada – one of the wealthiest countries – for
the way it treats its most vulnerable citizens – the poor, the homeless and
our First Peoples." (*Toronto Star,* Dec. 5, 1998)

Last month the good news was the top 10% make 314 X more
than the poorest.
The neo-liberal assault continues:
the three unwise men, Chrétien, Harris and Manning
come bearing gifts of food banks, attacks on the common good
and tax breaks for the rich.
But still I'm with you, brother Isaiah. As Jimmy Rushing used to say "sent
for you yesterday, here you come today."
And I'm shakin' those winter blues already
gettin' ready for the big one once again,
warmed into believing that Emmanuel is truly with us
"amid the bread of adversity and water of affliction" (30:20)
I know "when you turn to the right or when you turn to the left
your ears shall hear a word behind you saying,
"This is the way, walk in it." (30:21)
Christus natus est! Hallelujah!

CHRISTMAS 2000

In the fifteenth year of the reign of Tiberius Caesar, when Pontius Pilate was governor of Judea, and Herod was tetrarch of Galilee, and his brother Philip tetrarch of the region of Ituraea and Trachonitis, and Lysanias was tetrarch of Abilene, during the high priesthood of Annas and Caiaphas, the word of God came to John the son of Zacharias in the desert.
Luke 3:1, 2

Luke reminds us that the Good News is concrete
fleshed out (literally in carne) in place and time.
Timeless abstraction is utterly foreign to the Bible.
This Christmas baby winds up down in the dumps
where Jerusalem's garbage was collected.
Luke insists that salvation is located
at the edge, on the margins of empire
in a Palestinian backwater.
So why are we so shit convinced that the answers
are in this "world-class city" wired up to our wazoos in
Bill's global village?
Does Pontius have his palm pilot
and does Caiaphas answer his cell phone?
Will the Word reach you in your SUV
while the Magi cross the desert in their Hummers
to pay homage to the newborn king?
Can you dig Nasdaq and the Dow or is it the Tao?
"The workers of the world, according to a U N Report
are united in just one thing: record levels of stress.

What is more," the report warns, "anxiety levels are set
to dramatically rise in the coming years
as globalization continues its relentless march." (*Guardian,* Oct. 12, 2000)
Dark Advent. Whence comes the light? What saith the Church?
The northern Body looks inward, inviting believers to consolation,
pandering to the market Christians, the suburban captives.
Bring on the ermine-lined crib of a crossless saviour.
Jesus, God's word is back in the tabernacle, or is he?
I swore we met him in Chiapas, Seattle, Washington
among the irrelevant.
He chuckled as he wiped the mace from his eyes.
"Are you all right man?" I asked.
"Yeah, yeah. I'm OK."
"What should we do Lord?'
"We need to make a structural adjustment," he said simply.
Then this: "If you aren't on the edge, you're taking up too much space."
Come, Advent Spirit, Resister, complacency shatterer. Lead us out of
empire, out of comfort, out of boredom, out of certainty.
Send us to the margins so that we may be truly born again this Christmas.

CHRISTMAS 2001

The people who walked in darkness have seen a great light:
Those who lived in a land of deep darkness – on them light has shone.
Isaiah 9:2   First reading for Mass during the Night

In the refugee camp of Masiakh, the largest in the world
Christ is born again.
His teenaged mother who can neither read nor write
has been on the road for weeks, hoping to lay her priceless
jewel on a soft bed beside her.
It is not to be for this is Afghanistan,
"the poorest most miserable state in the world." (World Bank Report)
Having walked in the darkness she too has seen a great light
a 15,000 pound bomb called "daisy cutter" which flattened her home in
a place called Kandahar.
Every 30 minutes a woman like her dies from pregnancy-related
complications. (World Health Organization)
She does not understand this "War on Terrorism" which has
already killed the same number who died in the far-off towers.
She will be dead in 47 years.
The fly boy who has dropped the light
hopes to be home for Christmas
to tuck in his precious children
and get them up on this long-awaited day
so they can celebrate in the land of the free
and the home of the brave.

Unwitting dullard, he has served the new imperium
and paved the way for theme parks, the golden arches
and cheap gas for his SUV.
They will go to church and hear the holy story
of the Christ child born in a manger
and praise God for their good fortune.
"Afghanistan has the highest infant mortality rates,
the lowest literacy rate and life expectancy in the world,"
says the Asian Development Bank Report.
God of Masiakh, God of Bethlehem help us birth the Christ
who slumbers in our warm stables.

CHRISTMAS 2002

For all the boots of the trampling warriors
and all the garments rolled in blood
shall be burned as fuel for fire
for a child has been born for us, a son given to us
authority rests upon his shoulders; and he is named ... Prince of Peace.
Isaiah 9:5, 6   Mass during the Night, December 24, 2002

(For Phil Berrigan Oct. 5, 1923 – Dec. 6, 2002)

You first torched paper instead of human flesh as the B-52s
poured napalm down in the land of the Burning Children.
Next, you wielded Isaiah's hammers with single determination,
swords into ploughshares,
spears into pruning hooks.
Each blow you hoped to recast the molten metal of empire
back into God's order and design,
a newer Jerusalem of sisterhood and brotherhood.
Tossed into Caesar's stocks, you waged peace in prison –
organizing, teaching, fasting, counselling.
There was no tug of the forelock, no genuflection
to a state which resembled Mars, a Church resembling upper management.
Ripped from family, friends, you never blinked, did your hard time
and returned to the fray more gentle than ever.
Once again you picked up the hammers and sparks flew;
some flashed briefly, disappeared as quickly.
Others took flight and scorched our faces as we turned away

like Peter in the courtyard, frightened of the price we might
have to pay in Christ's nonviolent army.
Some sparks lit dry faggots and other resisters picked up your hammers.
And so it went till the end and on the feast of St. Nicholas
you gave your life back, Christmas-wrapped in righteousness, to
the God of Peace.

CHRISTMAS 2003

How beautiful on the mountains are the feet
of the messenger who announces peace, who
brings good news.
Isaiah 52:7   Mass during the Day, Christmas 2003

The myrrh gift given to the Virgin by the magi
will be used as sweet balm for the feet of the Christ child who will
crawl in the dirt of his Palestinian home;
similar nard will be lovingly kneaded on his bloody body
as he is stripped from the wood of his Roman executioners
and carefully laid in Joseph's tomb.
The mere sound of those feet on the dusty roads of Galilee
and the cobblestones of Jerusalem will be an alarm to
the Occupiers;
hardly beautiful as well, to the stopped ears of the oppressor, will be
the sound of his voice announcing "Malkuth Yahweh"
the day of the Lord's reign when the rich will be tumbled from their
thrones
and the inside traders will be outside looking in.
The Prince of Peace comes once again, our crucified pied piper
announcing the ever elusive, always hopeful dream of Shalom.
How beautiful indeed are the feet of the messenger who announces peace.
How great the price to be paid to build the peaceful city.

For the Women in Black of Israel and all doers of Shalom.

CHRISTMAS IN FALLUJAH,
AMNESIA IN AMERICA 2004

When Herod saw that he had been tricked by the wise men, he was infuriated, and he sent and killed all the children in and around Bethlehem who were two years old or under ...
Matt. 2:16

M. C. Mrs. Veritas, principal:
Welcome to our Christmas pageant everybody.
We are so glad that you have joined us at St. Valentine's Catholic school.
As you know our school was named after a doctor who was murdered for his
faith on the Flaminian Way, in Rome, on Feb.14, 269 CE
Most of you are familiar with the principal actors in our beloved
Christmas story: Jesus and the Holy Family, the shepherds, the wise men and, of course, the Star of Bethlehem. This year we know you will be pleased that we are dramatizing that long overlooked part of the holy tale: the slaughter of the innocents. The cast is contained in your programme beneath the words to Silent Night.

Narrator:
Fallujah, "city of mosques", is located on the banks of the Euphrates, the largest river in Southwest Asia. The city of Ur, found at its mouth, was the birthplace of Abraham. On its banks stood the city of Babylon.

First child:
The British online medical journal *The Lancet* reports that over 100,000
Iraqis have perished in this war.

Chorus:
Forgive us, O Lord, we are the new good Germans
who see nothing, hear nothing and do nothing.

Second child:
They dropped 1,000 and 2,000 pound bombs; AC130 Spectre gunships
demolished city blocks and cut off our water and starved civilians. All
of these are condemned by the Geneva conventions

Chorus:
Forgive us, O Lord, we were too busy haunting malls getting ready
for the Holiday season.

Third child:
Our loved ones were buried under rubble and wild dogs
feasted on our families

Chorus:
Forgive us, O Lord, while we decorated our sanctuaries and
prepared for midnight mass.

Fourth child:
Our Sunni city, which refused prayers for Saddam, watches
in despair as a massive military machine sends us the message: this is
the price you will pay for defying us.

Chorus:
Forgive us, O Lord, for our pallid resistance, for fighting an

election where this mass murder was not even an issue

Mrs. Veritas:
Thank you, thank you children, for such a lovely re-enactment of Matthew's Gospel.

CHRISTMAS 2005

The spirit of the Lord God is upon me
because the Lord has anointed me
He has sent me
to bring good news to the oppressed
to bind up the broken hearted.
Isaiah 61:1   3rd Sunday of Advent, Gaudete Sunday

(For Jim Loney, kidnapped in Baghdad)

Is he crazy? Are they naïve?
What were they trying to prove?
I mean, it was a war zone.
They got what they deserved.
"I love it when left wingers run up
against reality." (Rush Limbaugh)

Driven by another dream, dying in the sweet molasses
of the fun culture, incomprehensible in the steely
logic of the market,
clear eyed they marched to Baghdad
bearing the same armour the Bethlehem babe wore
as he walked to Jerusalem –
ready to be refined in the fiery furnace
for the righteous reign.
Hearts are still broken.
Bad news the daily fare of the oppressed.

Herod still sits on his throne
sacrificing ghetto kids and Appalachian poor
to Moloch, Mars and black crude.
"Mission accomplished"
Nos morituri te salutamus.

Yet, yet the old story, defused and sentimentalized
again comes to life
this Christmastide,
it still has power to raise up
four worthy disciples of the Prince of Peace.

ANOTHER AMOS

A catastrophic, disproportionate Israeli assault on Lebanon began in July of 2006. This assault would see Lebanon turned into a wasteland with 700,000 internal refugees, civilian deaths totalling over one thousand, and Israeli deaths numbering thirty-seven. As this assault began, the words of a Jewish prophet were read aloud in Christian churches.

Amos of Tekoa (a town near Bethlehem) had made his way to the famous northern shrine of Bethel, 19 kilometres north of Jerusalem. The humble prophet, "a dresser of sycamore trees," was there to speak truth to state power legitimated by a co-opted priesthood. The year was circa 750 BCE. The king was Jeroboam II. Amos' perennial message was simple: "Let justice roll like living water." (5:24). Do not become Pharaoh; stop being Goliath. Amos was told to leave.

Invited to preach on this text at the historic Anglican church of Holy Trinity on July 19, I reminded the congregation that once Toronto had its very own Amos in the Jewish community, Rabbi Reuben Slonim (1914-2000). The latter's stormy career among his people fully entitles him to be reckoned among the modern Jewish prophets. Further, his unflagging insistence on Judaism's universal values has, in my judgment, placed Slonim in the pantheon of the greatest Jewish witnesses of the past century. Despite his lonely exile from mainstream synagogue life, the Winnipeg-born rabbi persevered in reminding his people that the deepest ethical values of Judaism were being jeopardized and betrayed by Israel's blatant ghettoization and suffering inflicted upon another Semitic people, the Palestinians.

McCaul Street Shul

Slonim arrived in Toronto from Winnipeg in 1937, a newly minted rabbi. Beginning at the McCaul Street Shul, the first Canadian to head a Canadian congregation, he spent fifty years reprising the theme of his first sermon. "I wanted a decent community organized for justice, mercy and peace," he commented in his autobiography *To Kill a Rabbi* (ECW Press, 1987). His goal was "to be the first to lead a congregation out of the darkness of Orthodoxy into the light of Conservative Judaism." To this end Slonim spoke English, not Yiddish, from the pulpit, and rejected the segregation of women in the synagogue. He believed that the Bible was neither literal nor divine, but was a human document spanning centuries, and that after the war, Jews would have to develop compassion for Germans. "They wanted a soothing message not a challenging one," he remarked.

The postwar years at McCaul Street dramatically changed Jewish life. The knowledge of the Holocaust and the creation of the state of Israel increased Jewish self-awareness and self-affirmation, bringing a newfound pride to the community. Slonim could not abide the cry of "Never to forgive, never to forget" which increasingly defined the Jewish community. "Never to forget yes ... but never to forgive? No Jew should be capable of hewing to an eternal hardness of heart. The Jews survived because they were compassionate." The rabbi came to believe that: "The Holocaust did more than annihilate six million Jews; it invaded Jewish thinking and tradition and wrought alienation from Judaism's true nature."

As the Jewish state became a reality in 1948, the Zionist Slonim, influenced by the moderate voices of Martin Buber, Judah Magnes and Ahad Ha'am, insisted that Israel must develop the land for all its inhabitants. As a youngster, Slonim had deeply imbibed the spiritual and cultural Zionism of his teacher Shimon Frankel (his *"Moreh,"* meaning guide or mentor). The latter was a lover of Asher Ginsburg, a Russian-born Hasid, who wrote under the pseudonym, Ahad Ha'am. Ginsburg died brokenhearted in 1927, in Tel Aviv, as he watched the spiritual basis of Zionism unravel over the treatment of local Palestinians.

In letters home Ginsburg exploded the myth that the Holy Land was virtually empty. He rejected the growing insensitivity to Arabs. "I can't put up with the ideas that our brethren are morally capable of behaving in such a way to humans of another people ... what will be our relation to the others if in truth we shall achieve at the end of times power in Eretz Israel? And if this be the Messiah I do not wish to see his coming."

For Slonim, the new state would rest upon the foundations of liberty, justice, and peace as envisioned by prophets like Amos and enlightened Zionists mentioned above. To his shock and near devastation, he was reviled as a "Jew hater" and "Arab lover." He had perceived in his own community "an astigmatism, a supreme egoism ... this new state was their monument, their pride was in the externals, the army, consulates etc."

1967 and Jewish Empowerment

Following the merger of the McCaul and University Avenue shuls in the early 1950s, Slonim served a small conservative synagogue, Congregation Habonim. At the same time he caught the eye of John Bassett, the publisher of the *Toronto Telegram,* who sent him to Israel to write on the new state of which he was much enamored. As the Six Day War broke out in 1967, Slonim, visiting his daughter in Israel, spent time with his daughter's friends in a bomb shelter. As the Israeli victories accumulated he shared his consistent opinion with them that Israel might win the war, but it would lose the peace if it did not show magnanimity towards the Arabs. He was accused of dreaming.

On his return to Toronto, Slonim shared these same sentiments with his congregation. It exploded in recriminations. He was branded once again as an "Arab lover" and "an enemy of the Jews." He became depressed that this attitude seemed to pervade much of the entire community. He wrote: "The victory had plunged modern Jews into an orgy of chauvinism from which they have never recovered."

From Slonim's angle, the empowerment of Jews after the Six Day War, the rise of the "tough Jew," had severely compromised Jewish ethics. By opting for power, too many Jews were unable to see that the price paid –

the displacement, then the cruel oppression and ghettoization of the Palestinian people – had wreaked havoc with the deepest values of Torah. The universal lessons of the Holocaust had not been internalized to include the suffering of others.

Like the prophet Jeremiah, torn apart with anguish at his people's infidelities in the 8th century BCE, Slonim became "sick at heart" over what he considered the betrayal of the Covenant. For him, Torah transcended tribe. He was chagrined that "ethnic loyalty had replaced ethical obligation." He regretted the use of the Holocaust to stifle legitimate criticism of Israel. "It invaded Jewish thinking and tradition and wrought alienation from Judaism's true nature," he said.

With the growing postwar affluence, Slonim grew increasingly disenchanted with the loss of the inner spirit of Judaism. Religion seemingly had become an adjunct to the market, a placebo and a therapeutic substitution for the prophets' clarion call for justice. Israel without Torah was an empty shell. Jewish existence was not to preserve the state of Israel at any cost but to reduce suffering. For him Israel's power had bewitched many diaspora Jews and turned their eyes from the displacement and continuous subjugation and humiliation of the Palestinian people. The prophets of old had called this idolatry.

In describing synagogues as "country clubs for the wealthy," Slonim was simply naming the change which secularization and consumerism had wrought in Christian and Jewish communities. As Canadians grew wealthier the prophetic voice of synagogue and church were muted. Torah and Gospel had been compromised. The spirit of commerce had invaded the sanctuary and sacristy of both communities. Both had become hostage in a suburban captivity. Both had been suborned by affluence, comfort, and spiritual lethargy. Church and synagogue attendance along with sterile ritual observance had replaced the divine summons of solidarity with the oppressed.

For American Catholics, it was the postwar silence over the depredations of the American empire from Vietnam to Guatemala – and latterly, its complicity in the war on the Iraqi people. America had abundantly rewarded immigrant Catholics as well as Jews. The quid pro quo was silence and conformity.

Losing the Universal Spirit of Judaism

In 1983, looking back on his stormy life in Habonim, Slonim wrote in his memoir *Grand to Be an Orphan:*

"Today we Jews are losing [the] humanism and universalism of Judaism, all for the sake of Jewish statehood. We love Israel, and so we should, but we are so blinded by that love that we are willing to pay a prohibitive price for it. We condone acts we would declare unconscionable anywhere else in the world: nuclear weapons are wrong but necessary for Israel; apartheid is wrong, but for the sake of Israel's survival we will tolerate it; human rights are critical, but not for the Palestinians; we have a right to a state but Palestinians do not. Our racism towards Arabs would be regarded as anti-Semitism if others spoke of us in the same light. In all things we need to remember that the Jewish people and the Jewish state are but instruments, not ends in themselves; that what is good for the world is good for the Jews, not what is good for the Jews is good for the world; that the ultimate goal of the Jew, if he be truly Jewish, is to serve humanity."

Leaving Habonim, Slonim founded the Association of the Living Jewish Spirit to continue to promote Judaism's ethical values, speak out against Israel's growing oppression of the Palestinians and champion the spiritual legacy of his Zionist heroes – Martin Buber, Ahad Ha'am and David Ben-Gurion, Israel's founding Prime Minister. The latter, at the end of his life (1973), had become the most hated man in Israel for daring to say that he would return all of the Occupied Territories for peace.

Slonim assuredly had become the most despised Jew in Toronto by the mid-1980s. Hate calls and poison-pen letters were his daily portion. Invitations, which logically should have come to a wise elder, were withdrawn. The pages of Jewish newspapers were closed to him. Bookstores would not carry his writings and he was regularly condemned from the pulpit. Reuben Slonim had become your classical pariah, a prophet exiled from his own community. As one senior Toronto rabbi said to me, "He is our Job."

On a personal note, it was at this time I came to know Reuben, and my frequent calls blossomed into a warm friendship. What I loved about him was his equanimity and acceptance of his fate. Often we would frequent a kosher restaurant on north Bathurst Street in Toronto, and as he moved toward his 80th birthday, invariably he was greeted with friendly salutations. "Good morning, Rabbi" was a frequent greeting. Reuben would chuckle at the ever-so-small thawing. "It must be my age," he once quipped to me. Still, twenty publishers turned down his felicitously written and important autobiography.

He Heard Deeply

Reuben Slonim paid a ferocious price for his principled defence of Judaism's universal values. Like his forebear Amos, he "felt fiercely" because in the words of the great Jewish theologian Abraham Heschel, "He heard deeply." And what he had heard was the same voice that the biblical prophets heard – the voice of the victims. His many trips (thirty in all) to Israel had given him a privileged view of Palestinian suffering, which hometown Jewish audiences never saw and refused to hear.

What would Reuben Slonim think of the recent shocking events in Lebanon and Gaza? I believe he would substantially agree with Israeli historian Tom Segev: "Many Israelis tended to look at the Qana incident primarily as a media disaster and not as something that imposed on them any ethical responsibility. Just like in Iraq, the lessons of Vietnam have been forgotten. It is hard to avoid the impression that the routine brutality of oppression in the Gaza Strip and the West Bank is also reflected in the unbearable ease with which Israel has forced out of their homes hundreds of thousands of Lebanese and bombed civilians."

Haaretz, August 3, 2006

The good news is that moral voice is alive and well in Israel itself – in the pages of the daily newspaper *Haaretz*, in the organization B'Tselem, which monitors the widely disproportionate human rights abuses, in the Rabbis for Human Rights, in the lives of thousands of brave Israeli and diaspora Jews who see the ongoing humiliation and devastation and can no longer bear it. Quite possibly the Covenant is being carried forth largely by secular Jews.

It is this flowering of the authentic Jewish spirit which Reuben Slonim would have loved. That such a rabbi existed in the heart of Canada's largest Jewish community is something to be grateful for. A modern Amos, he suffered the prophet's fate. Like Ezekiel, he had become "a watchman for the nation of Israel" (3:17). He passed on the warning and watched in horror as the shock of the Palestinian Nakba (catastrophe of 1948) inevitably turned to resistance. As the decades passed, words morphed into stones, stones to homemade bombs, and bombs to Katyusha rockets raining deadly fire on Israel. As he wrote in 1987, "Few heard; fewer even listened."

The words of his beloved Moreh he took to his grave:

"Outspokenness will bring you loneliness but don't be afraid of being lonely. Everybody is. There are no pills to cure that, no formulas to charm it away. If you retreat from it, you end in a darker hell, yourself. But if you face it, you will remember there are millions like you who want to speak out and for one reason or another, cannot and in the end you will be lonely no more."

Reuben Slonim's life was a mitzvah to the entire Canadian people. May his memory be blessed.

SHATTERING THE MONOLITH:
ISRAEL, APARTHEID AND CHRISTIANS

Then justice will dwell in the wilderness and righteousness abide in the fruitful field. And the effect of righteousness will be peace and the result of righteousness, quietness and trust forever.
Isaiah 32:16

The state of Israel ... will be based on the principles of liberty, justice and peace as conceived by the prophets of Israel; will uphold the full social and political equality of its citizens.
The Declaration of Independence of the State of Israel, 1948

On November 14, 2006, former President and Nobel Prize winner, Jimmy Carter, eschewed the self-censorship which has bedevilled most Americans around the state of Israel. He called his latest book *Palestine: Peace Not Apartheid* (Simon & Schuster, 2006). Speaking on the American version of the CBC, National Public Radio (November 28, 2006) Carter did not run from the "A" word, nor did he accuse Israel of racial policies inside the Jewish state. These are part of his remarks:

"The alternative to peace is apartheid, not inside Israel, to repeat myself, but in the West Bank and Gaza and East Jerusalem, the Palestinian territory. And there, apartheid exists in its more despicable forms, that Palestinians are deprived of basic human rights. Their land has been occupied and then confiscated and then colonized by the Israeli settlers. And they have now more than 205 settlements in the West Bank itself. And what has happened is, over a period of years, the Israelis have connected settlements with highways, and those highways make the West Bank look like a honeycomb and maybe a spider web. You can envision it. And in many cases, most cases, the Palestinians are prevented from using the highways at all, and in many cases, even from crossing the highways."

In his book, Carter has written: "Most Arab regimes have accepted the permanent existence of Israel as an indisputable fact and are no longer calling for an end to the State of Israel, having contrived a common statement at an Arab summit in 2002 that offers peace and normal relations with Israel within its acknowledged international borders and in compliance with other U.N. Security Council resolutions."

Nobody can doubt Carter's *bona fides* in the area of Israel/Palestine. Along with his Nobel Prize for negotiating peace between Israel and Egypt in 1978, the deadly serious Christian has continued his intense interest in the area for 30 years monitoring election after election. His frank analysis is important and a major part of the rapidly crumbling political correctness around Israel.

The Israel lobby unleashed its firepower on the former president, but to little avail. As writer Alexander Cockburn sardonically remarked, "All this is starting to lose its hold on the broader public debate. Why? You can't brutalize the Palestinian people in the full light of day, decade after decade, without claims that Israel is a light among the nations getting more than a few serious dents ... But once a book by a former president with weighty humanitarian credentials makes it into bookstores, it's hard to shoot it down with volleys of wild abuse." The wild attacks only succeeded in shooting Carter's book into #4 on the Amazon bestseller list.

In these days of the Internet, globalized conversation and exposure tours, the appalling treatment of Palestinians is no longer a secret. It appears that the days of craven self-censorship are ending. This paralyzing hypnotic state, endemic in most of the West (and virtually the entire US Congress), came about originally through Christian guilt for the Holocaust. Christians bent over backwards to give the new state of Israel every benefit of doubt about what is now recognized as the ethnic cleansing of the Palestinian population. Since 1948, a spate of Israeli historians has documented the forcible expulsion of the Arab majority. This exodus amounted to about 800,000 people. Communications in the late 1940s were in their infancy and a state for dispossessed Jews seemed a small price to pay in recompense for the losses of the Shoah. But there was one small problem. The local Palestinian population, forcibly exiled, bore no blame for that mass murder.

Before proceeding, however, we must do a capsule political-historical background of the issue.

Zionism, the return of Jews to Zion (the name given to Israel in the Jewish Bible and in particular the Psalms), arose in the late nineteenth century, not as a religious movement but as a nationalist political movement. The zeitgeist of this period was decidedly nationalist, an era when several nations began agitating for independence. It was also a white-hot period of imperialism, though the establishment of a Jewish homeland cannot be viewed in that way. It certainly wasn't economics that drew European Jews to Palestine. Western imperialism (France, Britain and the US), however, did have a particular interest in the Middle East, largely because of the growing importance of oil. Israel, in time, became an important proxy for US interests in the area.

Theodore Herzl, the founder of the Zionist movement, was a secular Jew who was willing to consider other places for a Jewish settlement – but for obvious historical, emotional reasons he settled on Palestine. The ugly Christian cancer of anti-Semitism (the Dreyfus case, Russian pogroms) had become virulent. Zionism had many supporters among British politicians who had been nourished on literalist readings of the Bible. Those obscure prophecies, untouched by serious biblical criticism, had resulted in millenarianism, a wild idea that Jews should return to their native Israel before they are converted and the new final age of redemption is ushered in. This literalist abuse of scripture, perpetrated by American fundamentalists like Jerry Falwell and Pat Robertson, has greatly complicated matters in the Middle East to this day.

What is fascinating is that Zionism during this period had few converts among religious Jews. Even today ultra-orthodox Jews have set their face against it, calling it presumptuous and saying only the Messiah could usher in the final age. Reform Jews, in a famous meeting in Pittsburgh in 1885, rejected land as central to Judaism. "We consider ourselves no longer a nation, but a religious community, and therefore expect neither a return to Palestine …"

Yitzhak Epstein

From the earliest years of Zionism several Jewish voices raised the prophetic flag. Among the first was Yitzhak Epstein, a Russian-born teacher who emigrated to the Galilee in 1886. Epstein would have largely been forgotten had not his speech in 1905 coincided with the Seventh Congress of the World Zionist Organization. The noted educator had the knack which many great teachers possess – that of asking the hidden question which was the name of his speech. He opened his stunning oration with these remarks:

"Among the difficult questions linked to the idea of the rebirth of our people on its land there is one question that outweighs all others: the question of our attitude toward the Arabs … this question has been completely hidden from the Zionists and scarcely mentioned in the literature of our movement."

Epstein then put his finger on the source of most human social intercourse – the inability to embrace the common human face of the Other, her basic co-humanity: "They did not know the country and its inhabitants – and even more, they lacked human and political sensitivity … This shows the superficiality that dominates our movement … We forget one small detail, that there is in our beloved land an entire people that has been attached to it for hundreds of years and has never considered leaving it."

Epstein's prescient observation was akin to the famous remark which the eminent philosopher Martin Buber related about a prominent German Zionist, Max Nordau. When the latter heard that indeed Palestine was inhabited by Arabs, he ran to Herzl exclaiming, "I didn't know that. We are committing an injustice."

Epstein also challenged the myth that only Israelis made the desert bloom. While it is true new methods of farming greatly improved the country, Epstein wrote, "The time has come to dismiss the discredited idea spread among Zionists that there is in Eretz* Israel uncultivated land as a result of lacking of working hands and the indifference of the inhabitants. There are no empty fields ..."

Bear in mind that when he gave this speech Epstein had been farming for nineteen years in the Upper Galilee and knew the country well. The Zionist plan, untempered by cultural Zionism with its deep humanistic sensitivities, was a recipe for disaster.

"In general we are making a flagrant error in human understanding toward a great, resolute and zealous people. While we feel the love of homeland in all its intensity toward the land of our fathers, we forget that the people living there now also have a feeling heart and a loving soul. The Arab, like any person, is strongly attached to his homeland ... I am averse to the idea that in our land we need to grovel and submit to the inhabitants ... but we will sin against ourselves and our future if we thoughtlessly cast away our best weapon: the justice of our action and the innocence of our way."

Yitzhak Epstein was chillingly prescient about the future relationships between these "two proud *peoples.*"

"The Jewish *yishuv** has already bestowed considerable bounty on the country's inhabitants ... but all of this will not compensate for what we have subverted. Our name is not inscribed on the good, but is engraved on the bad, the memory of which will not perish."

He finished his prophetic clarion call by saying, "Our watchword must be live and live. God forbid we should harm any people ... how can we establish ourselves in Eretz Israel without sinning against justice. We are complete illiterates in anything concerning the Arabs and all of our wisdom about them is folk wisdom. It is time to get smart!"

From the very beginning of the Zionist movement, we notice heartbreaking tensions. When we observe the almost unbearable conundrum of today's "Middle East" problem, Christians need "to get smart" and contextualize the whole issue. This would begin with historic reality of Jewish homelessness, the understandable *idée fixe* of the Zionists. The famous

*Eretz means "land" or "country."
*Yishuv means "settlement."

mantra of "a people without a country needed a country without a people" became the somewhat disingenuous slogan, untested by history. So intent were the Zionists on a homeland that they could not see the native population. This was of course exacerbated by the white-hot cultural zeitgeist of nationalism.

On the other hand the Arabs could not see any historical rights of the Jewish people. To them the Jews were simply invaders, colonialists, albeit ones who purchased their land from absentee Arab landowners. Here we have a clash of two legitimate claims – the natural rights of the Arab population and the historic rights of the Jewish people who were flooding into their new home (not yet a country). There was no reciprocity from the Arab side. One of the main reasons was Arab unemployment. The Zionist colonists attached a mystical element to the land, now being redeemed purely by Jewish labour. This total way of living almost precluded any serious dialogue with the indigenous population.

The Cultural Zionists: Asher Ginsburg

Asher Ginsburg (1856-1927),who wrote under the pen name of Ahad Ha'am ("one of the people"), was a Ukrainian Jew who lost his Hasidic faith to the Enlightenment. Ginsburg, however, maintained the necessity of a secular spirituality, one which would permeate the new settlement with the deep ethical values of Judaism. These then would flow out from the new home to the Jewish diaspora. In Ginsburg's words, this is what makes "a Jewish state" and not simply "A state of Jews."

It would be the cultural Zionists who would provide the living spirit, the *sine qua non* of the new settlement.

"We have to treat the local population with love and respect, justly and rightly. And what do our brothers in the land of Israel do? Just the opposite. Slaves they were in their country of exile and suddenly they find themselves in a boundless and anarchic freedom as is always the case with a slave who becomes a king and they behave toward the Arabs with hostility and cruelty …"

In 1912 he protested the exclusion of Arab labour:

"Apart from the political danger, I can't put up with the idea that our brethren are morally capable of behaving in such a way to humans of another people and unwittingly the thought comes to my mind: if it is so now, what will be our relation to the others if in truth we shall achieve at the end of times power in Eretz Israel? And if this be the Messiah, I do not wish to see his coming."

At the time of his death in 1927, Ginsburg was shattered as he watched the increasing violence: "My God, is this the end? ... is this the dream of our return to Zion, that we come to Zion and stain its soil with innocent blood. It has been an axiom in my eyes that the people will sacrifice its money for the sake of a state, but never its prophets."

Judah Magnes

Similar to Ginsburg was Judah Magnes (1877-1948), an American Reform rabbi who emigrated to Palestine in 1922. Indefatigable in his commitment to Arab and Jewish reconciliation, he became president of Hebrew University where he consistently promoted the universal values of Judaism. Magnes believed in a binational state with equal rights for all. For him a state was irrelevant to the ethical mission of the new homeland. There were two options. The first, political Zionism, would be based on militarism ("bayonets and oppression"); the second would be cultural Zionism or the "pacific" option focusing on all those efforts which would make for peace and harmony with the Arab neighbours.

"Palestine would become a country of two nations and three religions, all of them having equal rights and none of them having special privileges, a country where nationalism is but the basis of internationalism, where the population is pacifistic and disarmed – in short, the Holy Land."

With his profound knowledge of the Hebrew scriptures, Magnes held out two choices. Jews could opt for Palestine, conquered as in the time of Joshua, or a more ethically developed choice, a land of the Psalms, the prophets and the rabbis, one which would reflect the words "not by right and not by violence but my Spirit, saith the Lord"(Zechariah 4:6). If this was not possible, "I should much rather see this people without such a 'National Home.'"

In the midst of the Holocaust, Magnes argued for a home, even a state in Palestine – if it were empty. If it was not, this "would be like a declaration of war against them. No code of morals can justify the persecution of one people in an attempt to relieve the persecution of another. The cure for the eviction of Jews from Germany is not to be sought in the eviction of Arabs from their homeland." This would be the constant argument of Palestinians for decades.

Martin Buber

Arguably the most famous "cultural Zionist" of all was the renowned twentieth-century philosopher and theologian, Martin Buber (1878-1965). A Zionist from the age of twenty, Buber's thinking evolved dramatically. By the 20s he was arguing for a binational state with equal rights for all. In 1938 he left Nazi Germany to settle in Palestine where he worked tirelessly for reconciliation. This is typical of Buber:

"We considered and still consider it our duty to understand and to honor the claim which is opposed to ours and to endeavor to reconcile both claims. We have been and still are convinced that it must be possible to find some form of agreement between this claim and the other; for we love this land and believe in its future; and seeing that such love and faith are surely present also on the other side, a union in the common service of the land must be within the range of the possible."

Buber grew extremely disenchanted with the levels of violence after the new state came into being. In a famous address on his 80th birthday in 1958, he appeared near to despair that the advice of colleagues like Judah Magnes had gone unheeded.

"… the majority of the Jewish people preferred to learn from Hitler rather than from us. Hitler showed them that history does not go the way of the spirit but the way of power, and if a people is powerful enough, it can kill with impunity as many millions of another people as it wants to kill. This was the situation that we had to fight."

For Buber, the only possible way forward was by "an internal revolution to heal our people of their murderous sickness of causeless hatred ... It is bound to bring complete ruin upon us. Only then will the old and young in our land realize how great was our responsibility to those miserable Arab refugees in whose towns we have settled. Jews who were brought here from afar; whose homes we have inherited, whose fields we now sow and harvest; the fruits of whose gardens, orchards and vineyards we gather; and in whose cities that we robbed we put up houses of education, charity, and prayer, while we babble and rave about being the 'People of the Book' and the 'light of the nations' ..."

The Balfour Declaration to the Nakba

The now famous Balfour declaration of 1917 gave the political go-ahead for the new Jewish home. Lord Balfour, the British Secretary for Foreign Affairs, in a letter to Baron Rothschild stated, "Her Majesty's Government views with favour the establishment of a National Home for the Jewish people." Britain named a Jew, Herbert Samuel a committed Zionist, as the first British High Commissioner (1920-1925) of mandated Palestine. The die was cast. Arab revolts right through the 20s and 30s never ceased until the state of Israel was proclaimed on May 14,1948. It is beyond the purview of this essay to delve into the internecine politics of the contiguous Arab states (Syria, Jordan and Egypt); suffice it to say Abba Eban's famous dictum that "The Arabs never miss a chance to miss a chance" has a ring of truth. These quarrels, along with their military inferiority and lack of diplomatic cohesion, have gravely injured the Palestinian cause, despite its justness. The noted historian Arnold Toynbee in 1961 described this cause in these terms. For him the Arabs had been "robbed" and cruelly treated. "Though not comparable in quantity to the crimes of the Nazis, it was comparable in quality."

David Ben Gurion, Israel's first Prime Minister, hinted at this. "Were I an Arab, and Arab with nationalist political consciousness ... I would rise up against an immigration liable in the future to hand the country and all of its [Palestinian] Arab inhabitants over to Jewish rule. What

[Palestinian] Arab cannot do his math and understand what [Jewish] immigration at the rate of 60,000 a year means to a Jewish state in all of Palestine."

For several years, the Palestinian population – about 150,000 – remained. Suddenly there was land and there were villages for Israel to use as incentives to European Jews to emigrate. Four hundred Arab villages were bulldozed, discouraging any repatriation. According to historian Don Peretz, more than one third of Israel's Jewish population lived on absentee property. For the indigenous Arab population this was the period of the *Nakba,* the catastrophe. There was massive crowding in the remaining Arab homes, massive Jewish immigration and the growth of the "temporary" camps in the Gaza and West Bank. In 1949 about 1 million refugees were registered by the UN in the West Bank and Gaza. By 1982 this had grown to 2 million. The UN since 1948 has consistently supported the principle that these refugees have the right of return to their homes, a claim Israel has steadfastly denied. For 50 years Palestinians have never ceded their national rights, surviving in semi-squalor only because their educated children kept sending money home. This alone is a heroic story of resistance and national consciousness. Not only did Israel wish they would disappear, but contiguous Arab states for their own reasons did as well.

In the West, it was as if the Palestinian people were non-existent until the late 1960s when an organized Palestinian resistance was formed. This was the Palestine Liberation Organization (PLO), almost universally condemned everywhere because of its initial "terrorist tactics" – the hijacking of El Al planes and the brutal murders of Israeli athletes at the Munich Olympics of 1972. The latter reprehensible and despicable act was actually carried out by a renegade group, Black September expelled by Fatah (the main PLO group under Yasser Arafat).

For the next 10 years, the PLO grew in respectability. The more the world learned about the issue, the more fair-minded people acknowledged that the Palestinians had a case. The UN in 1975 officially voted 89-7 to recognize the rights of Palestinians to self-determination and sovereignty.

One of those countries which voted against this (and would continue to reject the Palestinians with catastrophic global consequences) was the United States. The ultimate acceptance for the Palestinian cause was that of the Vatican in 1994. When Pope John Paul II visited Bethlehem in March 2000, he explicitly stated the Palestinians have "a natural right to a homeland." The Vatican's position was that of the ancient prophetic injunction of Isaiah, that there would be no peace without justice. In this case "stable guarantees of the rights of all peoples" based on UN resolutions must be observed. These resolutions, particularly 242, stipulated that territory won in war must be given back. John Paul II deplored Palestinian suffering and advocated "a home of their own."

At this juncture, it is worth pausing before we move on to an early defining moment in the world's changing perception of Israel. I am referring to the invasion of Lebanon in 1982.

Jewish Empowerment

In the light of the post-1967 war, historians are unanimous on this point: The terrible destruction of European Jewry (the Shoah) which until this time had not figured greatly in Israel's narrative, suddenly became dominant. Jewish suffering led to a new Jewish empowerment. A number of influential theologians leapt into the breach, foremost among them Irving Greenberg. The latter's thought is too nuanced to do justice here, but one of his themes is the move from powerlessness to power. For him the euphoric victory of 1967 (the Six-Day War) is a visible sign of redemption. Hope is now possible. The weak Jew who went to his slaughter in the Holocaust has been supplanted by the new "tough" Jew who does what he must to survive and flourish. The cardinal ethical question is: Is it good for the Jews? No apologies necessary. Israel may have to use immoral means to its fundamental end: survival. Power is the name of the game in today's savage world. Anything that diminishes power is to be eschewed. Jewish survival depends on it. Greenberg recognized that ethical compromise may be the result, but so be it. The Palestinian people and their rights are radically subordinated to Israel's well being.

Israel then began to hitch its wagon to the American imperium and diaspora Jews were expected to follow suit. America would defend Israel and Jews must mute their criticism of America who would then stand tall for Israel. In the post-1967 era, "check-book Judaism" took off. Financial support for Israel began to replace religious obligation. No criticism of Israel would be tolerated. The Likud Party of Menachem Begin and Yitzhak Shamir was shameless in demanding total allegiance to whatever policies Israel engaged in. More on this later.

Begin, who was Israel's sixth Prime Minister (1977-1983), was a very tough Polish-born Jew, the leader of a terrorist group called the Irgun. In 1946 he had ordered the demolition of British headquarters in the King David Hotel. Ninety-one people were killed. Shamir followed Begin as Israel's seventh Prime Minister (1983-84 and 1986-1992). He too had been a member of the Irgun, engaging in assassinations of prominent figures of the British Mandate in Palestine. Both embodied Jewish empowerment. The price, however – as history has shown – has been steep. It is this tension which has been at the heart of Israel's dilemma to this day. The blindness and the inability to hear another's pain has shamed Jews of conscience around the world. Theologian Marc Ellis phrases it this way: "We have not recognized the formation of other peoples and their struggle for freedom to be as important as our own and a legitimate demand on us … we may be in danger of becoming a people void of ethics."

In a famous letter to *The New York Times* (December 2, 1948) Albert Einstein (and several other prominent Jews) warned Americans of the dangers of Menachem Begin and his new Freedom Party, " … a party and social appeal closely akin in its organization, methods, and political philosophy to the Nazi and Fascist parties … formed out of the former Irgun, a terrorist, right-wing chauvinist organization in Palestine."

The group warned Americans not to be fooled by this new party. It then described the slaughter (April 9, 1948) in Deir Yassin, a small Arab village of 750 inhabitants. This day of trauma is still remembered by Palestinians yearly. Einstein's letter reflects the tension even then in the Jewish community:

"Most of the Jewish community was horrified at the deed, and the Jewish Agency sent a telegram of apology to King Abdullah of Trans-Jordan. But the terrorists, far from being ashamed of their act, were proud of this massacre, publicized it widely, and invited all the foreign correspondents present in the country to view the heaped corpses and the general havoc at Deir Yassin. The Deir Yassin incident exemplifies the character and actions of the Freedom Party.

Within the Jewish community they have preached an admixture of ultra-nationalism, religious mysticism, and racial superiority. Like other Fascist parties, they have been used to break strikes, and have themselves pressed for the destruction of free trade unions. In their stead they have proposed corporate unions on the Italian Fascist model.

During the last years of sporadic anti-British violence, the IZL and Stern groups inaugurated a reign of terror in the Palestine Jewish community. Teachers were beaten up for speaking against them, adults were shot for not letting their children join them. By gangster methods, beatings, window-smashing, and wide-spread robberies, the terrorists intimidated the population and exacted a heavy tribute."

Both Begin and Shamir were brilliant at "intimidating the population" – this time diaspora Jews. On their many trips to North America they became famous for laying guilt trips on fellow Jews. Their line of reasoning was simple: You here in America are living the good life. You have chosen not to come to Israel – okay. Pony up. Write a substantial cheque and shut up. Christians and non-Jews had no right to speak either, because of the Holocaust.

In the 60s and 70s Christians in North America were slow to criticize Israel. One of the reasons was a hidden anti-Arab racism, subtle to be sure, but present nevertheless in stereotypes which were not flattering to a people few of us had come into contact with. Jews had neatly assimilated into North American culture and politics and many were slowly eschewing their labour, working-class values for more conservative ones. This is a natural evolution for any community, though Jews by and large continued to espouse liberal, secular values.

As the Middle East and the PLO become hot topics, Arabs were further hampered by their inability to connect with the increasing global techno culture. Arafat wearing a kefiyah (traditional headdress) at the UN was simply no match for the urbane spokesmen like Abba Eban and Oxford-educated Jews. In North America, Jews were overrepresented in the media, particularly in the global hub, New York City. In those years Canada and the US had not yet the massive Muslim immigration which would later give voice to a more balanced view of the Middle East. Arab leaders are generally more volatile and fiery in their style. Israeli spokespersons on the other hand are urbane, reasonable and often utterly duplicitous. Watching the oleaginous Israeli talking heads during the Lebanon War in the summer of 2006 would make an excellent example for journalism students. As the shocking disproportionate bombing of Lebanon increased and even as Israel murdered UN observers (including a Canadian), it was instructive to watch the crocodile tears and pathetic bromides trotted out for Western video consumption.

Before the debacle in Lebanon Christian theology was dominated by guilt for the Holocaust. People like the Eckhardts, Franklin Littell and Paul Van Buren often were very good on the Christian history of anti-Semitism – but for all of them, the Palestinian people were simply absent. I am sure all of them today would be embarrassed by such glaring omissions. I would prefer to think that they all were captivated by an ideological blindness, as I certainly was. For these people Jewish suffering was absolutely unique, catapulted into a Sinai-like status, absolutely incomparable to, say, the 10 million Africans murdered in the slave trade or the American indigenous population wiped out in several ways as the US moved west. To even compare these sufferings was blasphemous. And then came Lebanon in 1982 and the first Intifada of 1988.

The Shift to the Right

The War in Lebanon (1982) stunned many diaspora Jews. The killing of 19,000 Arabs became Israel's Vietnam. The war was a blatant attempt to deal a death blow to the burgeoning Palestinian nationalism. At that time the PLO was headquartered in Lebanon. The war brought 400,000 Israelis into the streets to protest, and it helped raise the consciousness of Palestinians. The world was becoming aware of Palestinian dispossession. The war prompted another Jew, Roberta Strauss Feuerlich, to write her powerful book *The Fate of the Jews: A People Torn Between Israeli Power and Jewish Ethics* (New York Times Books, 1983). Heartsick over the shocking revelations of Israeli complicity in the Sabra and Shatila massacre (under Ariel Sharon), she wrote, "Perhaps Israel is too heavy a moral burden to bear." She went on to quote with approval Alexander Schindler, the then leader of American Reform Jewry: "We do ourselves irreparable harm when we make Israel our surrogate synagogue."

The Lebanon War destroyed Menachem Begin. He virtually never recovered from the public outcry and descended into a deep depression. The Kahan Commission called by Begin placed the blame on Ariel Sharon. As Israeli professor Baruch Kimmerling wrote in his devastating portrait of Sharon, *Politicide: Ariel Sharon's War Against the Palestinians* (verso, 2003): "Ariel Sharon – after the findings and unequivocal conclusions of the Kahan Commission of Inquiry – was considered to be political deadwood from a moral and even a legal point of view." The fact that such a brutal despiser of Palestinians would be resurrected as premier in 2002 indicates how far Israel has fallen from its visionary Zionist beginnings. As Kimmerlimg succinctly puts it: "The man who many consider a war criminal by any standard, and who had been Israel's most notorious politician for twenty years, had become the country's most popular and highly regarded premier."

Despite Lebanon, the world community did not pay too much attention to the ongoing Occupation and the rise of the illegal settlements. The West Bank and Gaza were but names to most observers. It was the Intifada of 1988, the "shaking off" of Palestinian despair, which again focused the international gaze on Israel. Many North American Jews became visibly upset by the shocking level of violence imposed on stone-throwing, Arab, young people. As more and more church delegations arrived in the Occupied Territories and Gaza – as media increasingly reported on the massive disproportionate violence visited on the Palestinian populace, the humiliating checkpoints, the bulldozing of homes, the targeted assassinations and extrajudicial murders, the land seizures and destruction of Palestinian olive groves, and latterly the building of Separation Barrier which steals even more land – people of conscience have broken silence and said, "Enough."

As many North American Jews began to shift politically to the right, fellow Jew Earl Shorris (*Jews without Mercy*, Anchor Press, 1982) outlined their neo-conservative opinions:

- The state of Israel can do no wrong
- The Palestinian people have no right to exist as a state
- The killing of an Israeli civilian by a Palestinian is an act of terrorism
- The killing of a Palestinian by an Israeli is a justifiable act of self-defence
- Occupation and colonization of foreign territory by Israel is not imperialism.

Post 9/11

9/11 was a temporary boon to Israel. The Israeli spin machine had a brief success linking the word "terrorist" to Palestinian resistance to the Occupation. The 2006 summer war in Lebanon, however, and the staggering overkill of Israel's superior firepower disgusted the rest of the world. Then came the stunning revelation that according to UN officials the Israeli military fired 90 percent of the bombs during the last 72 hours of the war when they knew a ceasefire was imminent. Those one million cluster bombs continued to kill three civilians per day. As member of the Knesset, Ran Cohen, a reservist colonel who commanded an artillery battalion during Israel's first Lebanon war, said: "This is a very serious matter. If cluster bombs were used in populated areas, this constitutes an indescribable crime." They were and it is. Canadians got a rancid taste of Israel's overkill in late July, 2006 in Lebanon when one of our own, Major Paeta Hess-von Kruedener (part of the UN observer team) was killed by an Israeli air strike. The observers' outpost was clearly marked, and they had communicated ten times with the Israeli Defence Force.

The latest disgusting murderous assault was in early November 2006 in Beit Hanoun, where 19 members of a family were blown to smithereens in Gaza. The usual disingenuous hand-wringing occurred for North American consumption. "Accident," "tragedy," "event," "mistake," and "incident" were words used to describe this. Former Knesset member, Uri Avnery cut to the chase in an article. "No it is a M-a-s-s-a-c-r-e," the ex-Irgun writer wrote. "The entire choir of professional apologists, explainers-away, sorrow-expressers and pretext-inventors, a choir that is in perpetual readiness for such cases, sprang into feverish action."

The Israel Lobby

One is literally staggered at the level of denial still extant in North American Jewry about the failure to give justice to the Palestinian people. Certainly there have been a lot of frightened journalists, newspaper owners and media barons, not to mention parliamentarians, unwilling to buck the formidable Israel lobby. In March 2006, the *London Review of Books* published John Mearsheimer and Stephen Walt's essay "The Israel Lobby" (now in a book, *The Israeli Lobby and U.S. Foreign Policy* – Farrar, Straus and Giroux, 2007). It was wonderful to see so many discussing this "elephant in the room." The two American researchers, in prose suitable to academic journals, laid out the obvious. This well-organized Israel lobby group, American Israel Public Affairs Committee (AIPAC), vigorously targets any one brave enough to criticize Israel. Their barely legal thuggery is well known in the US. They have thousands of trained seals whose mission in life is to stem any legitimate criticism of Israel and, as one former Israeli ambassador said, his greatest achievement was to get people to think that anybody who dared criticize Israel was an anti-Semite. The essay created a media firestorm. Valuable material, however, came to public consciousness perhaps for the first time. Such as the following:

"Since the October War in 1973, Washington has provided Israel with a level of support dwarfing that given to any other state. It has been the largest annual recipient of direct economic and military assistance since 1976, and is the largest recipient in total since World War Two, to the tune of well over $140 billion (in 2004) dollars. Israel receives about $3 billion in direct assistance each year, roughly one-fifth of the foreign aid budget, and worth about $500 a year for every Israeli. This largesse is especially striking since Israel is now a wealthy industrial state with a per capita income roughly equal to that of South Korea or Spain."

and this:

"Since 1982, the US has vetoed 32 Security Council resolutions critical of Israel, more than the total number of vetoes cast by all the other Security Council members. It blocks the efforts of Arab states to put Israel's nuclear arsenal on the IAEA's agenda. The US comes to the rescue in wartime and takes Israel's side when negotiating peace."

and this obvious fact:

"More important, saying that Israel and the US are united by a shared terrorist threat has the causal relationship backwards: the US has a terrorism problem in good part because it is so closely allied with Israel, not the other way around. Support for Israel is not the only source of anti-American terrorism, but it is an important one, and it makes winning the war on terror more difficult. There is no question that many al-Qaida leaders, including Osama bin Laden, are motivated by Israel's presence in Jerusalem and the plight of the Palestinians. Unconditional support for Israel makes it easier for extremists to rally popular support and to attract recruits."

Then there's the canard of David and Goliath:

"Israel is often portrayed as David confronted by Goliath, but the converse is closer to the truth. Contrary to popular belief, the Zionists had larger, better equipped and better led forces during the 1947-49 War of Independence, and the Israel Defence Forces won quick and easy victories against Egypt in 1956 and against Egypt, Jordan and Syria in 1967 – all of this before large-scale US aid began flowing. Today, Israel is the strongest military power in the Middle East."

or that Israel is a shining democracy:

"Unlike the US, where people are supposed to enjoy equal rights irrespective of race, religion or ethnicity, Israel was explicitly founded as a

Jewish state and citizenship is based on the principle of blood kinship. Given this, it is not surprising that its 1.3 million Arabs are treated as second-class citizens, or that a recent Israeli government commission found that Israel behaves in a 'neglectful and discriminatory' manner towards them. Its democratic status is also undermined by its refusal to grant the Palestinians a viable state of their own or full political rights."

and these gems:

- The bottom line is that AIPAC, a de facto agent for a foreign government, has a stranglehold on Congress, with the result that US policy towards Israel is not debated there, even though that policy has important consequences for the entire world.
- Key organizations in the Lobby make it their business to ensure that critics of Israel do not get important foreign policy jobs.
- The Lobby doesn't want an open debate, of course, because that might lead Americans to question the level of support they provide.
- The Lobby's perspective prevails in the mainstream media: the debate among Middle East pundits, the journalist Eric Alterman writes, is 'dominated by people who cannot imagine criticizing Israel.' He lists 61 'columnists and commentators who can be counted on to support Israel reflexively and without qualification.' Conversely, he found just five pundits who consistently criticize Israeli actions.

Professor David Noble of York University, himself a Jew, showed in the November 2005 edition of *Dimension Magazine* how the Israel Lobby works in Canada:

"This is not about Jews. It is not about race, ethnicity or religion. It is about power. The new Israel lobby in Canada – the Canadian Council for Israel and Jewish Advocacy (CIJA) – has enormous power, derived from abundant resources, corporate connections, political associations, elaborate and able organization and a cadre of dedicated activists. Since its inception several years ago, this hard-line lobby has used its power, first, to gain political hegemony and impose ideological conformity on the matter of Israel within a heretofore diverse Jewish community, and second, to influence government decisions and shape public opinion regarding Israel – ostensibly in the name of all Canadian Jewry."

Noble went on to name prominent Toronto Jews like the power couple Heather Reisman (Chapters) and Gerry Schwartz (Onex Corp.) whose friendship with Paul Martin helped tip Canada's heretofore even-handed Middle East policy toward Israel (Reisman later quit the Liberals and joined the Tories over Michael Ignatieff's critical comments during the Lebanon War), Larry Tannenbaum of the Toronto Maple Leafs, and others. According to *The Toronto Star,* some members of the community believed that the CIJA "will put control of Jewish lobbying efforts in Canada into the hands of a few wealthy and powerful individuals."

As a personal aside, because of my often critical comments about Israel when I was editor of *Catholic New Times* (which were always coupled with an absolute rejection of Palestinian suicide bombers and the right of Israel to live with safe and secure borders) the knee-jerk Israel lobby, represented by a small anonymous group of intellectual knee-cappers, several times attempted to have my talks in Jewish venues cancelled. Regrettably they were successful in a few instances. In general they had a difficult time smearing me, because of my lifelong pioneering commitment to Holocaust education and awards I received from the Jewish community, for this.

I did enjoy one occasion when I was supposed to give a talk on my memoir *Shabbes Goy,* my loving account of growing up among Jews in downtown Toronto. The subject of Israel never came up on these occasions in many different Jewish locales. All my readings were received very warmly. However, this one time a very nervous rabbi was bullied into cancelling a lecture. The place was packed but he told his all-Jewish audience that I could not make it. Three friends who attended, e-mailed me, wondering where the hell I was. When I told them the truth they were furious. One, the well known Canadian folksinger, Jerry Gray of "The Travellers," stormed up to see Rabbi Craven the next day and tore a strip off him, telling him I was the best friend the Jewish community had in Toronto.

That meant more to me than the lecture. In the 50s Jerry had had his own battles with the thought police.

My line of reasoning when it came to discussing Israel was simple. It was a state (certainly important for Jews as a symbol) but still a state that was doing terrible things. I never once worried about criticism. After all, I had been to Israel and seen for myself. And it broke my heart. It's not that Israel is demonic. It long ago ceased to be *lor goyim,* "a light unto the nations." States, as the well known truism says, have interests and sometimes values. This state had expropriated land from an indigenous people. It expelled them from their centuries-old homeland. It humiliated a proud people on a daily basis. This was a tragedy and remains one. It is not anti-Semitism to say this. The same thing can be said of Israel's protector, the United States. It has been a terrible imperial power, turning its back on its founding principles. It is not anti-American to say so. Vietnam, Chile, Iran and El Salvador are but four examples of ugly American interference. Uncritical and blind support of any state is the greater crime.

Though few Jews live in Israel, the state represents the embodiment of continuation, of Jewish survival. It stands as the enfleshment of the late Emil Fackenheim's addition to the 613 commandments of Torah. The 614th reads: Thou shalt not grant Hitler any posthumous victories. When bombs go off in Israel, when missiles fly (even those pathetic Qassam rockets) diaspora Jews immediately feel a sense of solidarity.

The sad fact is that so few Jews in the North American Diaspora have any first-hand knowledge of Middle East realities. Simplistic slogans ("The Arabs want to drive us into the sea," "Arabs only understand force," etcetera) with virtually no experience of the Palestinian reality is a poor substitution for clear-headed analysis. Massive propaganda from a series of neo-conservative Israeli governments, much of it deeply cynical, is shoehorned into an automatic "pro Israel" stance. The war in Lebanon was a classic example of mainline Jewish reaction. It was rightly condemned by most of the world as appalling and excessive. The Diaspora response, largely manipulated by mainline Jewish organizations, was overly defensive. In another article in this book, I examined the tragic life of Rabbi

Reuben Slonim who had been 30 times to Israel and could not break through the chauvinism of congregants who had never seen or tasted the historic and ongoing brutal occupation of the Palestinian people. Only Jewish suffering appeared to matter.

Knee-jerk defence of Israel among some Jews is similar to the lockstep behaviour of ultramontane Catholics. The farther they get from Rome the more vigorously do they defend Vatican policies, often without seriously examining them. In many ways, some aspects of Judaism resemble Christianity – in that both went from marginal status to state power and paid the price for it. Constantinian Christianity and Constantinian Judaism were both the sad result, a triumph of power over ethics.

What always encouraged me, however, were the great brave Jewish voices in Israel. Like Reuben Slonim they embody the living spirit of ethical Judaism. I mention a few here.

Amira Hass and Shulamit Aloni

The daughter of Holocaust survivors, Amira Hass is the only reporter of an Israeli daily (*Ha'aretz*) who actually covers the Occupied Territories and Gaza. Like any good reporter she writes what she sees – and she asked her fellow citizens on August 30, 2006 precisely this question: Can you not see?

"Let us leave aside those Israelis whose ideology supports the dispossession of the Palestinian people because 'God chose us.' Leave aside the judges who whitewash every military policy of killing and destruction. Leave aside the military commanders who knowingly jail an entire nation in pens surrounded by walls, fortified observation towers, machine guns, barbed wire and blinding projectors. Leave aside the ministers. All of these are not counted among the collaborators. These are the architects, the planners, the designers, the executioners.

"But there are others. Historians and mathematicians, senior editors, media stars, psychologists and family doctors, lawyers who do not support Gush Emunim and Kadima,* teachers and educators, lovers of hiking trails and sing-alongs, high-tech wizards. Where are you? And what about you, researchers of Nazism, the Holocaust and Soviet gulags? Could you all

*Gush Emunim (Block [of the] faithful) was an Israeli political movement that encouraged Jewish settlement of the land they believed God has allotted for Jews. Kadima ("Forward") is a political party in Israel; it became the largest party in the Knesset after the 2006 elections, winning 29 of the 120 seats.

be in favor of systematic discriminating laws? Laws stating that the Arabs of the Galilee will not even be compensated for the damages of the war by the same sums their Jewish neighbors are entitled to?"

Then Hass asks the scalding question asked of Germans in the Holocaust years: "Could it be that you do not know what is happening 15 minutes from your faculties and offices?"

"Where were you when this massive dehumanizing was taking place?"

These are scenes which no diaspora Jew is likely to ever see, so sheltered are they and indeed all of us who go to "the Holy Land" to look for the biblical stones but miss the human stones crying out for solidarity.

How is it that Hass "sees" while other Israelis do not? For her it was the witness of her extraordinary parents who had a history of "resisting injustice, speaking out and fighting back." In her book *Drinking the Sea at Gaza* (Metropolitan Books, Henry Holt & Co., 1999) , she recalls an indelible story of her mother's. Having just arrived at the death camp of Bergen-Belsen, she saw a group of German women slow down as the strange procession of emaciated people walked by. All of these women watched with "indifferent curiosity." For the daughter, Amira: "These women became a loathsome symbol of watching from the sidelines and at an early age I decided that my place was not with the bystanders."

Another Israeli woman, Shulamit Aloni, 78-year-old human rights lawyer, former education minister and descendant of a Polish rabbinical family, wrote an article about this time, even more to the point. In vigorous language which can only come from visceral human disgust at the observed treatment of fellow human beings, she stated that Israel's leaders must change their mindset:

"Over the years we deported, robbed land and stole water, destroyed crops, uprooted trees, turned every village and town into a detention camp, and set up hundreds of communities on land that doesn't belong to us ...

We paved roads for Jews only, a case of blatant apartheid, while defending it using witty Jewish self-righteousness in the absence of fair and public reporting of the budgets involved, deeds committed, expropriation of land, and disregard for vandalism ...

But as we usually present it – we're the victim, while they're the murderers with blood on their hands. We never report the number of Palestinians we murdered from the sky and killed by fire – women, children, the elderly, whole families, thousands of them.

No wonder they hate us … the time has come for the government of Israel to start talking peace, and end the excuses for disqualifying and boycotting Palestinian representatives."

Diaspora Jewry, of course, does not see what these women see. Nor does it appear they want to.

Jeff Halper and Arik Aschermann

When I asked Jeff Halper, the American-born founder of the Israeli Committee Against House Demolitions (ICAHD), why North American Jews (who in the past have had a strong justice perspective) seem so blind when it comes to Israel – he said it was simple. Most are ignorant of the situation. Their idea of Israel is still from the movie *Exodus,* the Jew as eternal victim.

I asked Halper, who has spent 30 years in Israel and is a retired anthropology professor, about the Israeli pull-out of Gaza in August 2005. Did he agree with another well-known critic, the aforementioned Professor Baruch Kimmerling, who called it "emotional exploitation" and "the evacuation trauma?" The whole event – "the most expensive production yet" – was to portray Sharon and the state of Israel as "heroes of peace." Kimmerling maintained it was to show the world that so much was invested in this – that there is no chance of evacuating the huge population in the West Bank.

Halper replied to my question: "Yes all this is true. This is part of the narrative of Jews as victims. One of the things I am working on is reframing the conflict because the way Israel frames it, which has been accepted by the public and media, is a framing based on security and terrorism, where there is no Occupation. After 9/11, this resonates with people. Now, the story is that Israel is doing a wonderful thing. Look how it evacuated the settlement. These poor people lost their homes. I think every Israeli in Gaza was interviewed three times. This was not pathos, but bathos.

We present an alternative reframing. First you start with the Occupation. Two, Israel is the stronger party. Three, the Occupation is pro-active, a claim for the entire country. Everything is a ploy to claim Judea and Samaria. We're claiming the entire country and we're going to lock the Palestinians into a Bantustan (the name given to the 'homelands' of Africans in the apartheid era). We must do this in a clever way because the world does not like apartheid these days. At all costs, you want to preserve your image as the victim. This is very convenient, as no one will hold you accountable."

And we have no right to despair when such men as Rabbi Arik Aschermann, the head of Rabbis for Human Rights, regularly befriend Palestinian families who have had their homes bulldozed and their human rights crushed. At one of his trials, Aschermann said simply, "I am very deeply affected when the Torah which I am sworn as a rabbi to uphold is being trampled on. In a piece which I wrote immediately after the demolition of the Da'ari home I noted that my kippah* was lost in the rubble. I wondered whether this symbolized what was being done to Jewish values and/or whether it would be found some day so that it would be known that somebody had stood against this evil in the name of Torah."

The statistics, however, still speak volumes. B'Tselem, the Israeli Human Right group, provides these figures up until December 31, 2006:

29.9.2000 - 31.12.2006

Palestinians killed by Israeli security forces: 3,944
Israelis killed by Palestinians: 464
Palestinian minors killed by Israel: 809
Israeli minors killed by Palestinians: 119
Palestinians who were objects of targeted killings: 336

These stats are not the full measure of Palestinian suffering. They do not include the house demolitions, the destruction of olive groves, the humiliating border checks, the sonic booms which traumatize the children, the

---

*The home of the Da'ari family was one of the demolished West Bank homes. A kippah (sometimes called a yarmulke or a kepel) is a thin, slightly-rounded skullcap traditionally worn by Jewish men.

small acts of discrimination like the "small dose" of ill-treatment – a slap, a kick, an insult, a pointless delay at a checkpoint, or degrading treatment of a similar ilk. These acts have become an integral part of Palestinian life in the Occupied Territories. From time to time, cases of severe brutality and murder like the ones mentioned above occur. Add to this 780 Palestinians in administrative detention. Most of them are held in facilities run by the Israel Prison Service (IPS). Administrative detention is detention without charge or trial, authorized by administrative order rather than by judicial decree. It is allowed under international law, but, because of the serious injury to due process, rights inherent in this measure and the obvious danger of abuse, international law has placed rigid restrictions on its application. Administrative detention is intended to prevent the danger posed to state security by a particular individual. However, Israel has never defined the criteria for what constitutes "state security." Then there is the apartheid wall, the Separation Barrier, which has leached 10% of Palestinian territory. And so it goes.

Now with the Carter book piled on top of simply too much Israeli violence, the world has become abundantly aware of Israel's moral deficit. This was put in simple terms on November 22, 2006 in a report in *The Toronto Star* that said: "Israel Worst Brand In World Says US Survey." The National Brands Index (NBI) survey showed that Israel is suffering from the worst public image in the world. "Israel's brand is by a considerable margin the most negative we have ever measured in the NBI, and comes at the bottom of the ranking on almost every question," states report author Simon Anholt. The survey also indicated there was nowhere respondents would less like to visit than Israel. Worse yet, Israel's people were also voted the most unwelcoming in the world.

Within Israel we may be coming to a moment of truth. As Jimmy Carter says in his book, the vast majority of Israelis yearn for a solution as do Palestinians. At a deep level Israelis must be tired of being viewed as a pariah state. Recently two Nobel Laureates grieved publicly at the malaise that has gripped their country. Yisrael Aumann and Aaron Ciechanover bemoaned the "fatal disease: the depletion of spirit ... that has spread through Israeli society."

David Grossman

The leading Israeli novelist David Grossman, who lost a son in the Lebanon war, gave a powerful speech on November 4, 2006. He used the occasion of the Rabin anniversary to lament the deep malaise in his country. This is part of his speech:

"In particular, we discovered that Israel faces a profound crisis, much more profound than we imagined, in almost every part of our collective lives.

We have interred, time after time, young people in the prime of their lives. The death of young people is a horrible, outrageous waste. But no less horrible is the feeling that the state of Israel has, for many years now, criminally wasted not only the lives of its sons and daughters, but also the miracle that occurred here – the great and rare opportunity that history granted it, the opportunity to create an enlightened, properly functioning democratic state that would act in accordance with Jewish and universal values. A country that would be a national home and refuge, but not only a refuge. It would also be a place that gives new meaning to Jewish existence. A country in which an important, essential part of its Jewish identity, of its Jewish ethos, would be full equality and respect for its non-Jewish citizens.

Look what happened.

Look what happened to this young, bold country, so full of passion and soul. How in a process of accelerated senescence Israel aged through infancy, childhood, and youth, into a permanent state of irritability and flaccidity and missed opportunities. How did it happen? When did we lose even the hope that we might someday be able to live different, better lives? More than that – how is it that we continue today to stand aside and watch, mesmerized, as madness and vulgarity, violence and racism take control of our home?"

The outstanding Egyptian novelist Ahdaf Soueif responded to this soul-searching alienation in *The Guardian* (November 17, 2006). Her answer I believe gets to the heart of the matter and a potential place for healing:

"The secret rotting at the core of the state of Israel is its refusal to admit that the Zionist project in Palestine – to create a state based on the dispossession of the non-Jewish inhabitants of the land – was never noble: the land it coveted was the home of another people, and the fathers of the Israeli nation killed, terrorized and displaced them to turn the project into actuality."

Soueif writes that the Palestinians live on, clinging to their dream and hopes for justice. They have survived even in a sewer like Gaza (my words). Soueif continued, saying:

"Meanwhile, Israel insists it is civilized, decent, and peaceable. How can a society caught in such delusion thrive? And how can people living within the Zionist project as privileged Jewish citizens bewail their embattled lot or be puzzled by it? Israel will not be well until it acknowledges its past and makes amends for it. The process has a name: truth and reconciliation."

Avi Mograbi

My wife and I were privileged to attend a recent (Fall 2006) screening of Avi Mograbi's film *Avenge But One of My Two Eyes,* a Cannes selection of 2005. Despite wide coverage on the CBC (where we heard the director speak) none of the Diaspora was present at Ryerson University the night of the Toronto screening in early October.

The affable Tel Aviv professor and filmmaker takes two Israeli "myths," the Samson story, where the blinded Jewish hero pulls the temple down on all, killing hundreds of Philistines, and that of Masada, where in 73 CE over 900 Jews died by their own hand rather than submit to Rome. The message: Death is preferable to domination. The film is excruciating to watch. The constant humiliation of Palestinians is only matched by the stunning arrogance of the Israeli Defence Force (IDF). At one point

Mograbi (in the film) loses his patience at the soldiers humiliating school-boys.

In the question period after the film, Mograbi admitted that he is able to show his film in his native Tel Aviv, but few come. Nevertheless it is a powerful contemporary understanding of the end result of humiliation: suicide bombing. This time it is the Palestinians who are both Samson and those who despair in Masada by inflicting violence on themselves.

I still believe in Israel because of the brave Israelis who struggle for jus-tice there. The above-named people represent a minority snapshot of con-temporary Israel. But they number in the thousands, and they include both those young men who refuse to serve the IDF in the Occupied Territories, and those Women in Black who have participated in vigils on behalf of Palestinian rights for years. Their voices are small, but they are present, tiny shoots of hope.

I have often wondered what those signs outside of synagogues mean when they say it is time to "stand up for Israel." I make the following anal-ogy. If I had an alcoholic brother, I would want to stand up for him. I would not bless his destructive activity. I would try to intervene and set him on a healthy course. Would this make me "anti-fraternal?" By giving in to his every self-defeating whim, am I loving him? I think not.

Diaspora Jewry rightly feels strongly about the survival of Israel. I believe we all should. Jewish empowerment in the state of Israel is a fact, but the question we must ask is this: Does the Holocaust not have univer-sal meaning, and should not that meaning be: No massive suffering upon anyone else?

So Where Does That Leave Us?

We are beginning to see the gradual but decisive transformation of the global view of Israel vis-à-vis the Palestinians. An unrelenting media, com-puters and Internet, the rise of the Arabic news network, *Al Jazeera*, decades of hard slogging by fact-finders to Palestine/Israel, the extraordi-nary persistence of moral Jewish voices in Israel and abroad, all have con-spired to disclose that the emperor is naked. For Jewish theologian Marc

Ellis, the symbol for Israel is a gunship hovering over a defenceless people; for Jewish historian Tony Judt the symbol is the Star of David emblazoned on a tank. The world now gets it. Palestinians have replaced Jews as the persecuted minority. Power inevitably corrupts ethics.

The tired and utterly unhelpful cry "Everyone hates us" no longer works when David has become Goliath. The Holocaust as an ideological prop to deflect criticism of modern-day Israel has outlived its usefulness. Guilt no longer works here or in Israel. As Judt so cryptically says, "The fact that the great-grandmother of an Israeli soldier died in Treblinka is no excuse for his own abusive treatment of a Palestinian woman waiting to cross a checkpoint. 'Remember Auschwitz' is not an acceptable response. The era of Israel as eternal victim is over."

The overwhelming onus for peace in Israel/Palestine must be placed on the broad shoulders of the more powerful party, Israel. Several Jewish thinkers have embraced this vision – notably distinguished rabbis like Arthur Hertzberg, Arthur Waskow and Michael Lerner of *Tikkun* Magazine. Probably the most prolific writer in this area is theologian Marc Ellis, now at Baylor University in Texas. All have moved beyond the Holocaust theology of the 60s and 70s. It totally missed the palpable suffering of Palestinians.

Today Israel, the fourth largest army in the world, armed and supported by the United States, is no longer innocent. The only way forward is to understand its own historical suffering, universalize its meaning and enter into the pain of Palestinian life. To keep on using Auschwitz and Yad Vashem, the Holocaust museum in Jerusalem (where every foreign dignitary is taken) as sacraments which only look inward and not outward is to profane those heartbreaking deaths of the Shoah. Human solidarity with other undeserved suffering must be the response. This will bring Israel face to face with that suffering which she herself is causing.

Nobel laureate Desmond Tutu was denied permission by Israel to go as a fact-finder to Beit Hanoun, the northern Gaza town mentioned earlier, where 19 innocents were killed in November of 2006. For the bishop, like the brave Jews mentioned above, human suffering is suffering. It should inevitably lead to solidarity with others in the same predicament. My vision of a redemptive Israeli future would be to see a Jewish Prime Minister take a foreign dignitary to Yad Vashem, to embrace the particular pain of his own people, then go with him by car to Gaza and embrace Esau his biblical brother in his particular Palestinian suffering. Peace will be near when Israel starts bringing young Jews to Yad Vashem and Masada, then billets them with a Palestinian family in the world's largest prison, a rancid ghetto called Gaza.

The Zionist dream has turned to bitter ashes. Europe's unwanted ended their exile in another land and sadly created internal exile for another people. This has been a disaster for a Judaism which has insisted on hitching its wagon to an exclusive Jewish state. As Michael Lerner has said, "A Judaism that has lost its moral teeth and becomes an apologist for every Israeli policy, no matter what its moral context, is a Judaism which not only betrays the prophetic tradition but also risks the adherence of the Jewish people." This oppression of the Palestinian people has also generated much toxic anti-Semitism around the world and fuelled Muslim anger everywhere. Israel's conversion is the key to Middle East peace.

For Christians, a double solidarity must be engaged in. It begins with our solidarity with the global Jewish community in whose hearts Israel has an especially cherished place. It must begin here because of Christianity's horrible historical role in the victimization of the Jewish people. This will mean a non-negotiable commitment to the safety of Israel and its right to live with secure borders. It will further mean a rejection of violent means of overthrowing the Jewish state, in particular, the death of innocent bystanders. This is the non-violent Jewish Jesus ethic. The Church has come a long way from Vatican II onwards, purging any whiff of anti-Semitism and anti-Judaism from its teaching. Salvation still comes out of the Jews. This means also an end to any proselytizing.

Further to the above, the mainline Christian churches need to disavow the theologically bankrupt Christian Zionism. This has been done in Israel/Palestine by the Christian churches, led by Catholic patriarch Michel Sabbah. Their position reads in part:

"Christian Zionism is a modern theological and political movement that embraces the most extreme ideological positions of Zionism, thereby becoming detrimental to a just peace within Palestine and Israel.

The Christian Zionist program provides a worldview where the Gospel is identified with the ideology of empire, colonialism and militarism. In its extreme form, it laces an emphasis on apocalyptic events leading to the end of history rather than living Christ's love and justice today.

"We categorically reject Christian Zionist doctrines as false teaching that corrupts the biblical message of love, justice and reconciliation."

Amen to this.

A second solidarity is based on the prophetic consciousness of the Gospel identification with the humiliated, in this case, the long-suffering Palestinian people. This gospel imperative, forcefully stated at Vatican II and ratified several times since, was best expressed by the Lutheran martyr of the Nazis, Dietrich Bonhoeffer who said, just before his execution in April, 1945: "We in the resistance have learned to see the great events of world history from below, from the perspective of the excluded, the ill treated, the powerless, the oppressed and despised ... so that personal suffering has become a more useful key for understanding the world than personal happiness."

This solidarity will not shrink in the name of a false ecumenism, from speaking truth to Israeli state power. It will no longer collude with Jewish empowerment and allow the memory of the Holocaust to render Christians mute in honest criticism of the state of Israel. Further, it will, in the name of true brotherhood and sororal relations, use all non-violent means of persuasion, including boycotts, to bring Israel to its senses. Much like South Africa, Israel will be treated as a pariah state until it wakes from its trance to acknowledge the full humanity and legitimate rights and national aspirations of the Palestinian people.

For years now I have cherished the answer Archbishop Michel Sabbah, the Latin patriarch of Jerusalem, the highest Roman Catholic prelate in Israel, gave to a Reform rabbi here in Toronto years ago. When the rabbi told him that his remarks were too one-sided, Sabbah replied, "I'll tell you

what, Rabbi, when your people are treated like mine, I'll change sides."
Sabbah articulated an important dictum of faith: *"Vox victimarum, vox Dei"* ("the voice of the victims is the voice of God").

ACKNOWLEDGEMENTS

To Gerry McCarthy of the Social Edge (www.thesocialedge.com), where several of these essays first saw the light of day. For seven years now Gerry has been producing the best online Catholic and catholic journal around, and it has been a privilege to air these ideas on contemporary theological issues there. Gerry has provided cyberspace for the necessary dialogue in the Church to continue. These essays, of course, have all been updated, changed and added to since that time.

To St. Paul University in Ottawa for the chance to present orally the ideas in Religion and Politics.

To the readers, supporters and colleagues at *Catholic New Times* (1976-2006), a publishing miracle which carried the fresh breezes of Vatican II across Canada when it was springtime in the modern Catholic Church. The dialogue with readers during my years as columnist and editor sharpened my perceptions and forced me to go deeper.

Many thanks to hawk-eyed proofer and editor George Down, whose trained eye has helped reshape these probes.

To Maureen Whyte of Seraphim Editions, who goes "where angels fear to tread" in her attempt to give serious ideas the ventilation they need.